The Virus, Vitamins
and Vegetables

The Virus, Vitamins and Vegetables

The South African HIV/AIDS Mystery

edited by
Kerry Cullinan &
Anso Thom

First published by Jacana Media (Pty) Ltd in 2009

10 Orange Street
Sunnyside
Auckland Park 2092
South Africa
+2711 628 3200
www.jacana.co.za

ISBN 978-1-77009-691-2

Set in Ehrhardt 11/15pt
Printed by CTP Book Printers
Job No. 000928

See a complete list of Jacana titles at www.jacana.co.za

For our children, Nikita, Naledi and Siya –
We are working to free your world from HIV/AIDS

Contents

Introduction

by
Kerry Cullinan and Anso Thom

'How many ways can you splice a history? Price a country?
Dice a people? Slice a heart? Entice – what's been erased –
back into story?'

– Shailja Patel, 'How Ambi Became Paisley',
Migritude I: When Saris Speak

When stand-in President Kgalema Motlanthe gave his first state of the nation address in October 2008, we rejoiced because it was the first time in nine years that we had heard our President say that the fight against HIV/AIDS was a priority. Given that AIDS-related illnesses are by far the biggest killers of South Africans, Motlanthe's comments should have been normal, run-of-the-mill politician-speak. But in the era of President Thabo Mbeki and his Health Minister, Manto Tshabalala-Msimang, nothing progressed as expected. For almost a decade, the field of HIV/AIDS has been a terrain of bitter fighting as Mbeki and Tshabalala-Msimang fell under the influence of a small group of discredited people convinced that HIV does not cause AIDS.

A few days before Motlanthe's address, activists braved an icy Cape Town night and huddled outside Parliament's gates to celebrate the end of the Mbeki and Manto era. It had just been announced that Tshabalala-Msimang had been re-deployed to the Presidency and replaced with Barbara Hogan, a backbencher who had been demoted after attempting to deal with HIV/AIDS treatment while chair of the parliamentary finance committee. Iconic AIDS activist Zackie Achmat called Hogan on his mobile phone to tell her that the group would be serenading outside her flat, which is within walking distance of Parliament. Once at the flat, Hogan waved from her window before joining the activists in the street, where they danced. One young woman was shouting at the top of her voice: 'Denialism is dead. Thank God this denialism is dead!' The unplanned, impulsive moment was another chapter in our country's AIDS horror story, which for the first time had the prospect of a happy ending.

But it has left many casualties in its wake. Thousands of South Africans have no idea that they are living with HIV because it is not easy to get an HIV test. Thousands more, influenced by Mbeki and Tshabalala-Msimang's scepticism about antiretroviral medication and their promotion instead of diet and traditional medicines, have turned their backs on the only medicine known to slow down the progression of the virus. The trust that many citizens once had in their democratically elected government has also been ruptured. How did Mbeki and Tshabalala-Msimang – once heroes of the anti-apartheid revolution – and all their sychophantic supporters stray so far from acting in the best interests of ordinary people? Could they not see the suffering of the millions of their electorate through the bullet-proof, tinted windows of their official vehicles, as they died painful and lonely deaths, made to feel ashamed that they had contracted a virus while having sex?

The speed with which our 'liberation-era politicians' became estranged from their support base has made many South Africans question our current electoral system of proportional representation, which ensures that politicians serve their parties rather than citizens.

This book is an attempt to document some of the madness, sheer weirdness and despair of a decade with Mbeki and Tshabalala-Msimang. We are doing so to safeguard the future. We want to present this book as evidence to citizens of this country and the world and say, 'This is what happened and we need to ensure that it never happens again.'

In many ways, Mbeki's official biographer, Ronald Suresh Roberts, provided the final spur for this book. When he started to promote his thesis of the 'poor misunderstood President', claiming that Mbeki had never been an AIDS dissident, we looked at each other in disbelief. History was being whitewashed before us – spliced, diced and sliced so that Mbeki's actions seemed harmless. It gave us the impetus to document HIV/AIDS in the Mbeki and Manto era, along with some of the key writers and role-players in the field

In many ways, Health-e News Service is ideally placed to do this. We were established as a non-profit agency in 1999 with the aim of improving the coverage of public health issues, particularly HIV/AIDS. The very first HIV/AIDS story that we published related to the death of Gugu Dlamini, an AIDS activist stoned to death in Durban for being open about her HIV status. Since then, we have travelled from Musina in the north to Khayelitsha in the south, documenting the effects of HIV/AIDS on South Africans. Our quest to cover the AIDS epidemic has taken us from San Francisco to Bangkok, via Europe and neighbouring African countries. We often joke that we are 'long-term slow progressors' – a term usually used to refer to people infected with HIV who take a long time to progress to AIDS – although, in our case, it is our reluctance to walk away and find a gentler way to make a living. We are by far the longest-surviving HIV/AIDS reporters in the country. It is not a job that makes you sleep easily at night, because once you see the effects of HIV/AIDS it is impossible to 'unsee' them: the matchstick-bodies; the listless babies; the rasping whispers of those whose throats are raw from thrush; orphaned children, betrayed partners, rejected family members.

But what compounded the everyday tragedies in homes throughout the country was the failure of those in powerful positions to acknowledge that a crisis was unfolding in South Africa. Instead of mounting massive HIV prevention campaigns and fighting for the best possible treatment for South Africans, President Mbeki and his Health Minister denied the problem or underplayed its severity or offered mere trifles – garlic, beetroot, lemons – as solutions.

Weaknesses in South Africa's HIV/AIDS programme resulted in an estimated 330,000 people dying unnecessarily during the Mbeki era, according to recent research published by the Harvard School of Public Health.

Many hospitals and clinics joined the denial, turning AIDS patients away by saying that there was nothing that could be done for them. The burden of care was thus 'privatised' and passed on to families who could least afford it. These desperate families became easy targets for quacks offering 'cures' for a virus that has no cure. Discredited scientists flocked to South Africa, rejuvenated by Mbeki's interest in their theories.

We found ourselves coming back time and time again to several leading figures. On a whiteboard in our Cape Town office we recorded the names of all those operating on the dark and dodgy side of the AIDS world. It became increasingly clear that many were connected: the same names kept popping up. The story was crying out to be told. But where to start? Who to include, who to leave out? The main characters were obvious –Thabo Mbeki, Manto Tshabalala-Msimang, Anthony Brink, Tine van der Maas and Matthias Rath. Then there were those on the other side of the fence – health workers and AIDS activists.

Eventually we decided to start with Virodene. James Myburgh's cracker chapter methodically shows Mbeki's connections with the industrial solvent punted as an AIDS cure and how central it all was to his questioning of the accepted wisdom on HIV and AIDS.

Michael Cherry, the first South African reporter to make the link between Mbeki's scepticism about AZT and the international AIDS dissidents, then steps in and describes the gathering of the 'flat earth society', Mbeki's Presidential Panel on AIDS.

One of the 'casualties' of the government's AIDS denialism was former ANC MP Pregs Govender, who ended up resigning from Parliament in protest against the multi-billion-rand arms deal. She offers insight into the thoughts and feelings of party members and parliamentarians, for whom loyalty to the President was more important than speaking on behalf of those crying out for HIV treatment.

Two doctors, pushed into the limelight for different reasons, share their stories. Ashraf Coovadia sees himself as an 'accidental activist', driven to take a stand after watching helplessly as his young patients died when their deaths could so easily have been prevented. He describes his personal battle for the establishment of a prevention of mother-to-child HIV transmission programme and his inner struggle in coming to terms with his new activist role.

Thys von Mollendorff shunned the big city lights to work in a public hospital in Mpumalanga caring for patients who could not afford private health care. A soft-spoken, gentle man, Von Mollendorff's life was made a hell by the Provincial Health Minister because he allowed an NGO to provide rape survivors with ARVs so as to prevent them from contracting HIV. Eventually, he was tossed out of his position as head of Rob Ferreira Hospital.

Kerry Cullinan describes how Mbeki, Tshabalala-Msimang and their acolytes formed alliances with some very strange people in order to promote their AIDS crusade. One of the key contact points was the lawyer Anthony Brink, who linked up a number of dangerous denialists and quacks. Brink's main motive was to find a platform for his belief that AZT was toxic.

Anso Thom exposes the antics of German vitamin seller Matthias Rath. He arrived on South Africa's shores in 2004 and came in touch with the country's foremost denialists, conducting unethical trials on poor people and promoting his multi-vitamins as an alternative to antiretrovirals. Not only did Rath enjoy the support of Tshabalala-Msimang, but he was given free rein to make outrageous statements that sowed confusion and caused damage that will be felt for years to come.

Liz McGregor shares the tale of how Dutch nurse Tine van der Maas offered fruit, vegetables, olive oil and a concoction called 'Africa's

Solution' as a wonder cure for any ailment under the sun. Van der Maas managed to gain the ear of the Health Minister, who introduced her to patients desperate for a cure, and even allowed her access to hospitals where she was able to try out her 'miracle diet'.

Many journalists would be accused of being 'un-African' or racist for daring to claim that some traditional concoctions may be dangerous. Kanya Ndaki spent time interviewing some so-called healers who sell untested remedies to people willing to believe that their murky liquids and odd practices offer some form of healing for HIV.

No book chronicling any aspect of the history of HIV/AIDS in our country would be complete without the inclusion of the Treatment Action Campaign (TAC), the most powerful civil society organisation to emerge post-1994. The TAC played a vital role in bringing about the recent changes we have witnessed, especially while trying to limit the damage of the pervasive denialism. Many of their members made huge sacrifices along the way. But it was not immune to tensions over gender issues and strategy. Janine Stephen has the impossible task of trying to chronicle this movement's history in her essay, including the resignation of its secretary-general.

Khopotso Bodibe goes behind prison bars to find out why the government was not prepared to give treatment to prisoners with AIDS, and speculates that homophobia might be behind the authorities' resistance to providing condoms to male prisoners to protect themselves while having sex.

Claire Keeton goes behind the scenes to unravel the events that led to the sacking of Deputy Health Minister Nozizwe Madlala-Routledge, considered by many working in the AIDS field as one of their lowest moments. Not known to mince her words, Madlala-Routledge described to Keeton the impossible task she had of trying to do her job against all odds. It's a story of a jealous Health Minister not prepared to share power. A twist of fate – the sudden illness of Tshabalala-Msimang and her extended absence from office – would see her deputy seize the day and become a driving force behind the establishment of one of the world's most ambitious HIV/AIDS plans. However, the minister survived a liver transplant and came back to vent her anger on her deputy, orchestrating her firing.

The TAC leader Zackie Achmat reminds us of the losses, pain and sadness of the past decade when he reflects on his organisation. Finally, Sipho Mthathi in her postscript warns of future perils under the 'chauvinism' of Jacob Zuma and argues that beating HIV/AIDS means beating poverty.

When this book went to print we were still basking in the afterglow of the new Health Minister's appointment. She has unequivocally stated her intention to get more people on ARV treatment and help prevent new infections. However, we remain realistic and slightly tentative as to what the future holds. We have no doubt that Barbara Hogan will do her best to improve our health system. But given the painful lessons of the recent past, we believe that it is important to maintain a healthy scepticism about the future. Our President-in-waiting, Jacob Zuma, while no AIDS denialist, has made a number of dubious statements about AIDS. While on trial for raping an HIV-positive woman, he remarked that he had protected himself against infection by taking a shower afterwards. In addition, his patriarchal practices – numerous wives and girlfriends – and utterances are enough to make us wary: unequal relationships between men and women drive much of the HIV/AIDS epidemic.

Mbeki's legacy is a South Africa filled with AIDS orphans, child-headed households, grandparents forced to parent their dead children's children, poor women having to home-nurse the sick and dying without remuneration, and a phalanx of businesses selling untested remedies to desperately ill people with promises of healing and cure.

Healing our nation from all of this will be one of the biggest jobs of the future government.

* * *

So many people have helped and encouraged us with this book. We should like to thank the authors for their commitment to documenting this painful time. Russell Martin from Jacana did some splicing and slicing himself to make the book far more palatable. Health-e office manager Nina Taaibosch helped enormously to keep everything on track. We would never have been able to do any of this work without the generous support of the Atlantic Philanthropies, which has supplied core funding for Health-e for many years. Thanks also to Sarah Nuttall and Achille Mbembe from the Wits Institute for Social and Economic Research, who were the first to plant the seed of a book in our minds. Thanks to Andrew Brown for casting a legal eye over the manuscript. Finally, we would like to thank our families, particularly Nikita and Naledi Kekana, Gerda and Siya Kruger, who are heartily sick of Mbeki, Dr Beetroot and all their antics.

1

In the beginning there was Virodene

by
James Myburgh

In late March 2000, in the early months of President Thabo Mbeki's challenge to the Western science on HIV/AIDS, the *Mail & Guardian* ran an editorial under the headline 'What's behind Mbeki's crusade?' This was clearly a question on many people's minds at the time, and the editorial noted that his 'behaviour has also led to unhelpful speculation about why he is so strangely exercised by the issue'. But the paper was at a loss when it came to providing a meaningful answer, saying only that 'there are no obvious reasons' for Mbeki embarking on 'this stubborn, silent' campaign.

This was a question that would remain largely unanswered for the next several months. It certainly seemed to stem from Mbeki's deep racial preoccupations. But for a long time, it was generally regarded as inexplicable. The issue was also muddied by the efforts of Mbeki's protectors to deny his denialism. For instance, on 15 September 2000, the newspapers of the Independent group published a government statement which claimed that 'neither the President nor his Cabinet colleagues have ever denied a link between HIV and AIDS'. Such claims had greater purchase than they deserved, partly because of the lack of any obvious motive for Mbeki's behaviour.

The explanation for Mbeki's stance seemed to be answered by the famous speech he gave at Fort Hare University in early October 2001, in which he accused those campaigning for the provision of antiretroviral drugs of seeing black Africans as 'germ carriers, and human beings of a lower order that cannot subject its passions to reason'. This appeared to solve the puzzle. The *New York Times* noted that Mbeki's irresponsibility around AIDS 'seems to be rooted in a defensiveness about race'. Chris McGreal wrote in the British current affairs magazine *Prospect* that 'Mbeki is obsessed by race'. The orthodoxy that proceeded to settle over the matter was that Mbeki's stubborn opposition to the provision of antiretroviral treatment for the prevention of mother-to-child transmission – and also as a post-exposure prophylaxis for rape victims – was a product of his AIDS 'dissidence' or 'denialism'. This in turn was rooted in his belief that Western scientific claims about the origins, causes and spread of HIV/AIDS stemmed from deeply entrenched white racial stereotypes of black Africans. There was much evidence in Mbeki's writings to support this view. And it is one that I certainly bought into, and argued for, for a long time.

It was a number of years later, while piecing together the available evidence for two chapters on Mbeki's views on AIDS for my doctoral dissertation, that I was forced into seriously reconsidering this view. As it became clear to me, the key to understanding Mbeki's crusade lay not in his racial obsessions – important though these may have been – but in the ANC's promotion of, and involvement in, an alternative AIDS cure, Virodene.

Virodene had first exploded into the public consciousness on 22 January 1997 after the promoters of the drug had made a presentation to the Cabinet claiming that they had discovered a possible cure for AIDS. The incredible properties of the substance, N,N. Dimethylformamide (DMF), had been discovered by Olga Visser, a technician at Pretoria's H.F. Verwoerd Hospital, in late 1995. She had saturated a rat heart in the substance, frozen it, and then (it was claimed) made it beat again. The *Sunday Times* reported in October 1995 that this discovery 'arguably matches, or even surpasses, the first heart transplant performed by Chris Barnard in 1967', for it would, potentially, allow donor organs to be stored for long periods. In December that year Olga and her husband, Jacques Siegfried 'Zigi' Visser, established a company, Cryopreservation Technologies (CPT), to patent and develop this compound.

Nothing much would come directly of this discovery, as other scientists were unable to recreate Visser's experiment. But it was while doing a literature search on DMF that Visser first came across its 'anti-viral' properties. The publicity generated by her claims also led to an introduction to the then Minister of Health, Nkosazana Zuma. In July 1996, the Virodene team – then made up of the two Vissers, the head of cardio-thoracic surgery at the University of Pretoria, Professor Dirk du Plessis, and a medical registrar, Carl Landauer – met with Zuma to discuss the possibility of conducting a clinical trial on AIDS patients. DMF could not easily be ingested orally and the researchers had, rather ingeniously, developed a skin patch with which to apply the substance.

In mid-January 1997 the team returned to Zuma with the miraculous results of the trials. Virodene, they claimed, worked quickly, allowed patients to regain weight rapidly, and reversed even terminal cases of AIDS. Zuma – who was going to be away in Cuba – arranged for Deputy President Thabo Mbeki to introduce the researchers to Cabinet. In her presentation, Olga Visser claimed that the drug 'destroyed the virus in a test tube', could reverse full-blown AIDS, and had minimal side-effects. What had most impact, though, was the testimony of two of the participants in the pilot study. As Mbeki commented in a press conference afterwards, 'The Aids victims described what had happened to them as a result of the treatment. They were in the Cabinet room, walking about, perfectly all right. It was a worthy thing to see because the general assumption is that if you get to a particular point with AIDS, it really is a matter of time before you die.' *The Star* reported that at the end of the presentation, the Cabinet 'stood up in spontaneous applause'. 'It was like a church confessional,' Jakes Gerwel, Director-General of the Presidency, would later tell Samantha Power of the *New Yorker*. 'The patients said they were dying, they got this treatment, and then they were saved! The thing I will always remember is the pride in South African scientists.'

The attraction of Virodene was not just financial – alternative antiretroviral combination therapy was still in its infancy and hugely expensive – but also psychological. This 'medicine developed in Africa for Africa', as Olga Visser described it, would racially affirm the new government, and disprove once and for all Western stereotypes of black African incapacity. Salim Abdool Karim, director of HIV prevention and vaccine research for the Medical Research Council (MRC), told the *Washington Post* in 2000 that 'the Cabinet ... believed the discovery would validate South Africa's black majority in much the same way that Christiaan Barnard's first successful heart transplant in 1967 affirmed apartheid South Africa to the world'.

In their testing of the substance on human subjects, the Virodene researchers had failed to get approval from either the Medicines Control Council (MCC), South Africa's drug regulatory authority, or the University of Pretoria's ethics committee. As soon as it heard about the trial from the media, the MCC, chaired by Professor Peter Folb, intervened to put a halt to further testing. The MCC conducted a brief review after which it banned the provision of the drug to patients in early February. If the researchers wanted the drug to be tested any further, they would have to address the MCC's concerns, and gain the necessary approval. It soon became clear to the scientific establishment that the Virodene researchers had had no idea what they were doing. Apart from failing to get permission to conduct their trial, they had jumped straight from discovering the literature on the supposed anti-viral properties of the substance (which they had misread) to testing the drug on human subjects, had had no toxicological experience themselves, and had massively miscalculated the safe dosage of the drug. The trial itself had failed to control for the placebo effect.

During the course of 1997, the MCC would reject one research protocol after another from the Virodene researchers. Behind the scenes, however, Zigi and Olga Visser lobbied Zuma and Mbeki to try and get them to overrule the MCC. They also travelled overseas to commission reports from international experts, which they used to undercut the authority of the MCC with Mbeki and Zuma. By the end of the year, Zuma was publicly expressing her frustration that she lacked the power to overrule the MCC. It was after a third research protocol was rejected by the MCC in September 1997 that the illegal provision of Virodene started up again. When the MCC heard about this, they called in the Narcotics Bureau and, in late November, the Vissers' offices were raided.

It was a falling-out between the Virodene researchers – partly over the illegal distribution of the drug – that would first expose the degree to which Mbeki had become intimately involved in their affairs. In early December 1997, the minority shareholders in Virodene – including Du Plessis and Landauer – were granted an interim High Court interdict against the trade in, dispensing of or research into Virodene by the Vissers. Mbeki intervened to try and secure a resolution of the dispute. He met first with the Vissers and then with Du Plessis and Landauer. Mbeki's initial plan was to appoint a manager from the public sector to take over the company CPT, but in the end a neutral and well-respected administrator, Hugo Snykers, was brought in from the private sector instead. Mbeki would later explain that he was concerned that if the dispute was not resolved, the company owning Virodene 'could be auctioned to the highest bidder'. If this came to pass, 'the intellectual property represented by "Virodene" could fall into the hands of people who could shut down the research effort or sell "Virodene" at unaffordable prices, should it be licensed as efficacious medication'.

In early March 1998, the affair reached crisis point after Democratic Party (DP) MP Mike Ellis publicised a memorandum from the Vissers to the other shareholders in CPT which stated that the ANC had been promised a 6 per cent shareholding in the company. On 2 March, Ellis wrote to the Public Protector, Selby Baqwa, requesting an investigation into whether the ANC had a financial interest in the development of the drug. The ANC flatly denied that its involvement in the promotion of Virodene was motivated by anything other than altruism. Zuma meanwhile lashed out at Ellis saying, 'The DP hates ANC supporters. If they had it their way we would all die of AIDS.'

In an article published in all the Sunday newspapers on 8 March 1998, headed the 'War Against Virodene', Mbeki launched an impassioned defence of the Vissers. 'In our strange world,' he wrote, 'those who seek good for all humanity have become the villains of our time!' He concluded: 'I and many others will not rest until the efficacy or otherwise of Virodene is established scientifically. If nothing else, all those infected by HIV/AIDS need to know as a matter of urgency. The cruel games of those who do not care should not be allowed to set the national agenda.'

Later that month senior officials at the MCC were removed from their positions under opaque and disputed circumstances. Peter Folb was replaced by Helen Rees, an ANC-aligned appointee. In late May 1998, a group of 'mysterious black investors' – as the *Mail & Guardian* described them – bought a majority shareholding in CPT and a new company, Virodene Pharmaceutical Holdings (VPH), was established.

From then on, Virodene would steadily recede from the public consciousness. The promoters of the drug – and their supporters – seemed to lose interest in forcing the MCC to allow the testing of the drug. In December 1998 the MCC rejected Virodene once and for all. In January 1999 Baqwa wrote back to Ellis to say that a preliminary inquiry could find no evidence that Zuma or Mbeki 'have had any financial interest in the development of Virodene P058' and there was no need for further investigation. The last word on the whole affair was seemingly uttered by the head of the Medical Research Council, Malegapuru Makgoba. While presenting the Council's annual report to Parliament, he described Virodene as 'nonsense' and without 'scientific authority'.

By the time of the March 2000 *Mail & Guardian* editorial quoted at the start of this chapter, the Virodene scandal was hardly remembered and even less well understood.

I first took a real interest in the story in mid-2000 after hearing first-hand how Mbeki and Zuma had, through the course of 1997, tried to pressure the MCC into allowing the testing of the substance on human subjects. It was then, too, that I first read the Commission for Conciliation, Mediation and Arbitration (CCMA) ruling that carefully documented the callous way in which Johann Schlebusch, the Registrar of the MCC, and his deputy, Christel Brückner, had been stripped of their positions in late March 1998. Both had been summoned to a meeting with the Director-General of Health, Olive Shisana. There they had been presented with two choices: either to resign and receive a severance package or to be suspended with immediate effect, and charged with misconduct. Schlebusch was then escorted to his office and forced to surrender his office keys and entry card, his computer and cellphone. He was only allowed to take his briefcase. The same happened to Brückner. The locks to their offices were changed, and guards were placed outside Schlebusch's secretary's office. Staff at the MCC were ordered not to make contact with them. The CCMA commissioner found that 'Schlebusch and Brückner had been unceremoniously removed from office, escorted from the premises and treated like criminals. In addition, no convincing operational reasons for this action have been shown.' He further stated that the Health Department 'should have known from the outset that its conduct was wrongful and unfair, especially as far as the manner in which it had acted is concerned. Notwithstanding this, it steadfastly refused to reinstate the applicants in their former positions.'

While this earlier episode was clearly important to understanding Mbeki's later views on AIDS, its exact significance was unclear. The Virodene episode seemed to foreshadow later AIDS 'denialism' in certain ways and contradict it in others. In both cases, Mbeki had taken it upon himself to dispute the authority of the scientific establishment. Outside experts had been brought in to contest the prevailing scientific view and Mbeki had then set himself up as the final arbiter of the views of the two contending camps. At the same time, Mbeki's claims about the toxicity of the antiretroviral drug AZT and his opposition to off-label use of the drug stood in marked contrast to his earlier insistence that AIDS sufferers were 'morally entitled' to take Virodene as 'mercy treatment', despite the MCC's concerns about its toxicity. Virodene was also meant to act as an antiviral agent, and it was implicit in this understanding that HIV caused AIDS.

In 1997, shortly after the Virodene researchers' presentation to Cabinet, Mbeki euphorically declared the dawn of an African renaissance. At that stage the drug held the possibility of a kind of racial vindication for the black African majority. But when the promise of Virodene was dashed, it seems that Mbeki descended into an obsession with AIDS 'denialism' and the 'demon' of white racism. These offered an escape from racial humiliation. Mbeki would argue in his 2002 dissident manifesto, *Castro Hlongwane*, that the Western science of HIV/AIDS was simply an expression of 'deeply entrenched and centuries-old white racist beliefs and concepts about Africans and black people'. This rather elegant theory was soon ambushed and destroyed by a gang of brutish facts. The problem with this thesis, and the orthodox view of Mbeki's AIDS denialism, was that they didn't fit the chronology. Zuma and Mbeki had put a stop to the piloting of AZT for the prevention of mother-to-child transmission in October 1998. As Mbeki acknowledged to Allister Sparks in 2003, he had first been introduced to the 'alternative viewpoint' on AIDS – sometime in mid-to-late 1999 – through the writings of the Pietermaritzburg lawyer Anthony Brink. In other words, Mbeki's introduction to AIDS denialism postdated the initial decision to block AZT by several months at least.

From late 2001 onwards there was also a steady trickle of new information about Virodene. In September 2001 Mark Schoofs of the *Wall Street Journal* broke the story that Phase 2 trials of Virodene were being conducted in Tanzania. In June and July 2002, *Rapport* and the *Mail & Guardian* reported that the ANC had had an ongoing involvement in Virodene until earlier that year. According to the *Mail & Guardian*, 'The ANC secretly arranged millions of rands in funding for Virodene.' The conduit for most of this money had been the businessman Max Maisela, but ANC Treasurer-General Mendi Msimang, husband of Health Minister Manto Tshabalala-Msimang, had played a lesser role. Existing accounts of Mbeki's AIDS 'denialism' failed to accommodate, or satisfactorily explain, this ongoing involvement by the ANC in 'Project V'.

Drawing together the information provided in interviews, court papers, press reports, and the documents reported on in the *Mail & Guardian* and *Rapport*, I was able to construct a different and more compelling narrative. This story of the involvement of Mbeki and the ANC in Virodene needs to be told in some detail. In mid-May 1998, Zigi and Olga Visser had sent a fax to Mbeki warning that patent fees were going to fall due later that month and if these were not paid the patents would be lost. They requested any possible assistance 'in the form of introductions to possible partners/funders for a joint venture which will be beneficial to all'. There is no record of Mbeki's response.

At the end of May a consortium of investors led by the businessman and MK veteran Ngengelezi 'Zach' Mngomezulu and including Joshua Nxumalo and one John Waithaka bought a 60 per cent shareholding in VPH for R4.8 million. The deal was constructed to hide the identity of the ultimate purchasers – and to this day it is not known who they were. The new owners were initially short of money and VPH had to borrow R700,000 from Waithaka to settle a patent bill which had fallen due. This was secured through a loan on a bond on Mngomezulu's house. The repayment, which fell due the following year, was recorded in VPH accounts as 'Mngomezulu Cash from TG' – a reference, according to the *Mail & Guardian*, to ANC Treasurer-General Mendi Msimang.

The Virodene researchers had initially expected a more sympathetic hearing from the new chairperson of the MCC, Helen Rees. But they were soon disappointed. Their efforts to get the substance tested in South Africa were basically checkmated in mid-1998 by an audit of the 1996 pilot study conducted by Professor Antoine van Gelder, the head of the Council's clinical committee. This audit, according to a later MCC statement, had found that 'the clinical data that was presented to council to support the investigators' argument for efficacy contained duplications, incorrect figures and omissions'.

Yet even as space was being closed down in South Africa, it was opening up elsewhere. In September 1998 Phase 1 trials – designed to assess Virodene's safety – were begun at Guy's Drug Research Unit (GDRU) in London. That same month, Olga Visser approached the health ministry in Botswana about the possibility of carrying out a formal clinical trial in that country. On 9 October 1998, Visser wrote two letters addressed to Deputy President Mbeki. The one stated that the Phase 1 trials were nearing completion 'with excellent results and absolutely no toxicity at the proposed levels of doses'. Visser requested 'urgent consideration' to settle a bill of £95,423 from GDRU which had fallen due. This account was paid the following Tuesday. In the VPH accounts, payment was coded as having come from 'No. 2'. In the other letter, Visser claimed that the government of Botswana was close to approving funding for Phase 2 trials in that country. On that same day (9 October) Mbeki launched an R80 million AIDS prevention campaign based, incidentally, on a perfectly standard view of AIDS as a sexually transmitted disease caused by the HI virus. At the launch, Nkosazana Zuma announced that the government had put a stop to the piloting of AZT for the prevention of mother-to-child transmission. The headline of the *Sunday Times* was 'Save our babies, Dr Zuma: Decision against drug treatment puts thousands of infants at risk'. From mid-November 1998, the Vissers' insatiable requests for funding were redirected from Mbeki to Max Maisela, a businessman and confidant of both Mbeki and Zuma. Between January 1999 and March 2000, Maisela would channel millions of rands to the Vissers to pay for patent applications and lawyers' fees. The Vissers also kept in close contact with Zuma, supplying her with patent documents, accounts, the structure of the Virodene holding companies, status reports, and the results of the Phase 1 trials at GDRU.

In early 1999, the Virodene developers suffered a severe setback, when the possibility of conducting the Phase 2 trials in Botswana fell through. At the same time, the government was coming under increasing pressure, not least from the newly formed Treatment Action Campaign, to provide AZT through the public health-care system. On 17 March 1999, the AIDS dissident and lawyer Anthony Brink wrote an article in *The Citizen* entitled 'AZT: a medicine from hell'. The article commended Zuma for refusing to allow the provision of AZT to pregnant mothers, stating that while she had defended her decision on purely financial grounds, one day she would be commended for her 'great prescient wisdom' in keeping this 'toxic' drug from 'pregnant women and their foetuses'. The article also claimed that 'several actions for loss of support have been launched against Glaxo-Wellcome in England and the US, arising out of the deaths of family members killed by their doctors' prescriptions of AZT'. At the end of the article he listed his email address 'for references and elucidation'. He also stated that 'an exhaustive literature review of the pharmacology of AZT is in press for publication in a special supplement to the medical journal *Current Medical Research and Opinion*'.

On 24 March 1999, Zigi Visser wrote to Nkosazana Zuma enclosing Brink's *Citizen* article and alerting her to the pending publication of the journal article. Olga Visser contacted Brink, who wrote back to her to say that the review was in press as a 30,000-word special supplement to *Current Medical Research and Opinion*, April/May issue, and he would send it to her as soon as it was published. On 27 April 1999, Zigi Visser wrote to Mbeki: 'As discussed, herewith enclosed is a very important article from the *Citizen* March 17 1999 page 6 ... Please note that an exhaustive 30,000 word literature review of the pharmacology of AZT is in press for publication in the April/May edition of "Current Medical Research and Opinion", of which I will obtain a copy for the Deputy President. This completely supports the Honourable Minister of Health's stance on AZT.'

On 21 October 1999, Zigi Visser sent two batches of documents to (now) President Mbeki. The one was a copy of the US patent for Virodene, which had been granted on 10 August 1999. Visser stated: 'With great pleasure and pride, I herewith enclose a copy of the granted US patent, which we prosecuted beating all objections raised by the examiners and being granted all claims without exception. This effectively means that we will beat any examining country's objections, since the US is known to be the strictest.'

The other set of documents included the *Current Medical Research and Opinion* journal article and a copy of Brink's updated version of his earlier articles, entitled 'Debating AZT'. Visser noted that Brink 'is running a case in which the scientific merits of AZT will be tried in the High Court in Pietermaritzburg next March/April [2000], which could hopefully assist in banning AZT in SA'.

The following week, in an address to the National Council of Provinces on 28 October, Mbeki drew heavily on this material to justify the continued refusal to allow for the provision of AZT. He stated: 'There also exists a large volume of scientific literature alleging that, among other things, the toxicity of this drug is such that it is in fact a danger to health. These are matters of great concern to the Government as it would be irresponsible for us not to heed the dire warnings which medical researchers have been making.' This speech represented a major shift in rationale from the government's previous position – that providing AZT was simply too expensive.

The speech also represented the beginning of Mbeki's conversion to AIDS 'dissidence'. He would proceed to read up voraciously on the 'dissident' view of AIDS, assisted initially by the journalist Anita Allen and then David Rasnick, the prominent American AIDS 'dissident'. As Mbeki was researching the 'alternative viewpoint' on AIDS in November 1999, there was a real possibility of conducting Phase 2 clinical trials in Tanzania. In March 2000, Zigi Visser informed Maisela that they had received permission to conduct trials in Tanzania. From April 2000 onwards massive sums of money became available to finance Virodene's development. In this regard, one of the last key pieces to the whole Virodene puzzle was provided by Fiona Forde in the *Saturday Star* in September 2007. She reported that, according to her sources, the money used to finance the Phase 2 trials had often been collected in briefcases from 'the Presidency, in the Union Buildings ... always in US dollars, and always $100-bills'. One source said, 'I would safely say we picked up about $5-million throughout 2000, either from the Union Buildings or through [Max Maisela].'

The actual testing of Virodene on human subjects began in September 2000 and ran until March the following year. It was a double-blind, placebo-controlled trial, the purpose of which – a later VPH brochure stated – was to evaluate the 'safety, tolerability, pharmacokinetics and efficacy of multiple doses of Virodene PO58 on 64 HIV/AIDS infected male volunteers'. The trials were conducted by the Tanzanian military under the supervision of a clinical trial manager at two sites in Dar es Salaam: Lugalo General Military Hospital and Chadibwa Medical Clinic.

As the trials were winding down, the (new) Minister of Health, Manto Tshabalala-Msimang, paid the test sites a visit. The details were outlined in a fax sent to the minister's Cape Town office by Olga Visser on 27 February 2001. The fax confirmed 'that the main purpose of the visit will be to inspect the sites where the Phase II Virodene Trials are taking place so that you will be in a position to obtain a clear picture of the progress and furthermore to avail yourself of the success of the Phase II Virodene Trials to date'. In reply to a later parliamentary question, Tshabalala-Msimang acknowledged that she had visited both trial sites along with her adviser, Ray Mabope, and her private secretary, Ms N.

Zigana. She had been accompanied on her inspection by Zigi and Olga Visser. The purpose of the visit, she said, was 'to evaluate the usefulness of Virodene'.

Because the Tanzanian study was double-blinded, neither the patients nor the researchers knew who was receiving Virodene and who was receiving the placebo. Olga Visser nonetheless claimed that it had once again performed wonders. On 6 May 2001 the virologist who had first identified HIV, Luc Montagnier – then in negotiations with the Vissers about performing in vitro testing of Virodene – composed a draft letter to Maisela in which he reported on a meeting with Visser two days previously. She had told him that half the 64 HIV-infected patients in the Tanzanian trial 'showed after a six-week period of weekly applications of Virodene, a ten times drop in viral load in their blood and a significant increase of CD4+ T cells'. 'Such changes', Montagnier commented, 'are generally not observed so quickly with classical antiretroviral therapy.' It is not known whether the other persons in the project shared Visser's optimism.

However, in or around late March 2002 the promoters of Virodene received the report on the unblinded results of the Phase 2 trial in Tanzania, and their statistical analysis. This proved that Virodene was no cure for HIV/AIDS. It had no effect on the HI virus, although some statistically significant improvement in the CD4+ count was apparently recorded. For those invested in Virodene these results were, quite obviously, a massive disappointment. An acrimonious falling-out among the Virodene researchers followed. Olga Visser would end up ceding her stake in the company to the ANC-linked businessman Karim Rawjee. Zigi Visser told the *Mail & Guardian* that Maisela was a 'total cabbage'. Not long after, on 17 April 2002, the Cabinet announced an abrupt reversal of its policy on antiretroviral drugs. It stated that not only would nevirapine be provided to all pregnant women – as it had been instructed to do by the courts – but also that antiretroviral treatment would be made available to rape victims, something Mbeki had vigorously argued against in 2000. *Business Day* reported on the announcement under the headline 'Government stages a dramatic about-turn on its AIDS policy'.

There are obviously many questions around the Virodene affair which have yet to be answered. Who were the real purchasers of the company CPT in 1998? Where did all the millions of US dollars come from to finance the Tanzanian trials? For how long did Mbeki remain a true believer in Virodene's potential? How can one reconcile Mbeki's AIDS 'denialism' with the ANC's continuing involvement in the development of Virodene? As far as this last question is concerned, there is perhaps less of a contradiction than one might assume. The MCC's basic problem with Virodene was that the researchers could neither explain how the drug acted against the HI virus, nor provide any evidence of efficacy beyond the results of the ethically and scientifically flawed pilot study of 1996. As such, there was no possible benefit to counterbalance the danger of exposing AIDS patients to this toxic chemical. In an effort to address such concerns the researchers had commissioned Ana/lysis GmbH, a German company based in Frankfurt, to conduct in vitro tests of the substance. Andreas Immelmann, the researcher on the project, told the *Financial Mail* in April 1998 that they submitted the compound to 'in vitro cell culture and did not find any significant anti-HIV activity. Our conclusion was that this compound has no direct antiviral effect.' Thus, while Virodene's true believers were convinced that the drug worked wonders in the treatment of AIDS, they could never explain how the substance acted against the virus. In these circumstances, the dissident view that AIDS was not caused by a single virus, but by a whole host of factors, exerted an obvious attraction. The path to AIDS 'dissidence' was one followed by a number of the early promoters of Virodene, including Zigi Visser.

James Myburgh is editor of the South African political news website, www. Politicsweb.co.za. He wrote his DPhil at Oxford on the African National Congress under the presidency of Thabo Mbeki (1997–2002). Before that he worked as a researcher for the Democratic Party in Parliament.

2

The President's panel

by
Michael Cherry

It was the last week in October in the last year of the millennium, and I was on the telephone to David Dickson, news editor of the journal *Nature*, for which I had been contributing correspondent in South Africa for the past decade.

'One thing before I go, David,' I said. 'Thabo Mbeki has made an off-the-wall comment in his first address to the National Council of Provinces [South Africa's upper house of Parliament], since he became President in June. He has argued that a large body of scientific literature claims that the antiretroviral drug AZT is so toxic as to be a health hazard, and that he would not take the irresponsible step of supplying it to HIV and AIDS sufferers until its safety has been established. I don't suppose it's worth writing about?'

'Oh, I do,' he replied. 'Why don't you see what more you can find out about it? I'd be surprised if the AIDS dissidents aren't involved in this in some way.' He proceeded to tell me that in the early 1990s a group of 'dissidents' led by Berkeley biochemist Peter Duesberg had caused some consternation by questioning the link between HIV and AIDS.

In the same speech, Mbeki had further claimed that legal cases were pending in South Africa, the United States and Britain against the use of AZT on the grounds that it was harmful. I called Peter Moore, medical director for sub-Saharan Africa for Glaxo Wellcome, the drug's suppliers. Unruffled, he denied this, and told me that he had requested a meeting with Mbeki to clarify the issue. He said that the company had been negotiating with the government for the past three years over the price of supplying the drug to state hospitals.

Mbeki had asked Health Minister Dr Manto Tshabalala-Msimang to investigate the status of AZT but had said that until her investigation was complete, it would be irresponsible for the government to ignore researchers' warnings. His statement had profound implications: in South Africa at the time, 22 per cent of women attending antenatal clinics, and 7 per cent of new babies, were HIV-infected.

At that stage, AZT, which acts by preventing the AIDS virus from replicating itself, was in use in more than a hundred countries, and one of its uses is to prevent mother-to-child transmission (MTCT) of HIV. Like many medical interventions, it has negative side-effects. However, in the case of chronic illness, patients, in consultation with their doctors, have to make choices based on the benefits and risks associated with treatment.

Adults who are HIV-positive, health-care workers who are accidentally exposed to the virus and rape victims have to make a choice about whether to take antiretrovirals if they can afford to do so, or if their medical aid schemes make provision for this. In South Africa at that time, those reliant on the state health-care system were denied access to AZT on the grounds that it was too expensive, and now, it would appear, on misguided grounds of safety.

MTCT, which can happen during pregnancy, during labour and delivery, and during breast-feeding, was admittedly more complicated. Without intervention, only between a quarter and a third of infants whose mothers are HIV-positive become infected with the virus. A programme to prevent MTCT would have been cost-effective, but it raised the question whether state hospitals should treat all pregnant mothers who are HIV-positive and their newborn infants, thereby exposing some infants who are not HIV-positive to the drug – a choice that should ultimately lie with their mothers. But such programmes had reduced MTCT drastically in other countries. In the UK, for example, by 1998, 97 per cent of all infected women who gave birth had received AZT and 62 per cent of infants born to HIV-positive women were delivered by caesarean section, which further reduces the possibility of transmission during delivery. The combination of these two interventions reduced transmission from 32 to 4 per cent between 1995 and 1998.

In November 1999, Tshabalala-Msimang received an interim report from the country's statutory body for drug control, the Medicines Control Council (MCC), compiled by the Council on its own initiative after Mbeki's claims. This report concluded that, although AZT had some negative side-effects, they were outweighed by its potential advantages.

Tshabalala-Msimang replied that the government would not make AZT routinely available at state hospitals until it received the MCC's full report, due in two months. But she added that the drug would not at that stage be withdrawn, and that those receiving it should continue to be treated, pending the final report. Moore immediately met with Tshabalala-Msimang, and reported that she was unable to identify any specific safety concerns or any specific side-effects about which she was concerned.

According to Mbeki's spokesman, the President got his information on the drug from the internet. But I heard that Mbeki may have been influenced by a Pietermaritzburg-based lawyer, Anthony Brink, who had been campaigning against the use of AZT. Brink had participated in a debate earlier in 1999 in *The Citizen*, a Johannesburg newspaper, for which he had written an article entitled 'AZT: a medicine from hell'.

I called Brink, who appeared rather flattered by being approached by *Nature*. He appeared to hold views similar to those of Duesberg, whom he described to me as 'a paragon of scientific integrity in relation to conventional orthodoxy'. Brink claimed proudly that he was indeed the source of Mbeki's information, having provided it to Tshabalala-

Msimang. He also claimed that Mbeki's office had contacted him for more information after Mbeki's speech in Parliament. Brink denied that Duesberg, an outspoken proponent of the view that AZT is unacceptably dangerous, was the progenitor of his ideas. But he confirmed that he and Duesberg had been in contact, and that he shared his view that AIDS is not related to any specific virus.

It seemed clear to me that a senior medical authority should debunk the myth being perpetuated in government circles. So I contacted immunologist Malegapuru Makgoba, president of the South African Medical Research Council (MRC), who appeared as puzzled by Mbeki's stand as I was. Makgoba described the grounds of Brink's argument as 'nonsensical'. 'I've read nothing in the scientific or medical literature that indicates that AZT should not be provided to people,' he added. He stressed the need for government policies to deal with three issues which he felt had become confused in the minds of the South African public: the AIDS epidemic; the high incidence of rape in the country; and the provision of AZT by the state. Mbeki's statement was widely seen in medical circles as an attempt to justify his government's failure to develop such policies.

Meanwhile, the government showed it meant business by laying five charges of misconduct against the flamboyant Dr Costa Gazi, head of public health at Cecilia Makiwane Hospital in East London, for allegedly contravening the Public Service Act. The charges arose from an article in a local newspaper earlier in 1999 in which Gazi, health secretary of the opposition Pan Africanist Congress, was quoted as criticising the government for not providing AZT to pregnant women with HIV.

Next, Tshabalala-Msimang set about proselytising among her Southern African Development Community counterparts. In the first instance, she appeared to enjoy some success. At a meeting in November to discuss a co-ordinated response on HIV/AIDS, a joint statement was issued by the health ministers of South Africa, Botswana, Zambia, Namibia, Mozambique, Swaziland, Lesotho, Zimbabwe,

Malawi, Tanzania, Angola and Rwanda. The ministers acknowledged that administering either AZT or its cheaper alternative, nevirapine, could approximately halve the numbers of HIV-positive children born to mothers who are HIV-positive. But they expressed 'grave concern over possible side effects as a result of their toxicity and the potential development of resistance to these compounds'. They felt it was necessary to research the effects of 'unnecessary exposure of children and mothers to these drugs'.

On 25 November, officials of a US foundation expressed concern at the statement. The California-based Elizabeth Glaser Pediatric Trust had earmarked $1 million for paediatric AIDS prevention in Africa using nevirapine, an antiretroviral which is less expensive than AZT and simpler to administer. A single dose to mothers at the onset of labour, and a single dose to the baby in its first three days of life, cost less than $4 per treatment at the time. Both AZT and the oral form of nevirapine were registered with the MCC, but the suspension form of nevirapine, which is administered to infants, had not yet been submitted to the Council for registration.

South Africa went on holiday for the summer. Having broken the story in *Nature* about the link between Mbeki and the dissidents, I penned an opinion piece for *Business Day* on the need for a policy on MTCT, but it lay unused until mid-January 2000, when it appeared under the title 'Mbeki's claims on AZT are problematic'. The article concluded thus: 'According to Mbeki's spokesman, the president obtained his information on AZT from the internet. The problem with this is that unlike articles in scientific journals, which are subject to peer review, anyone can set up their own website without being responsible for the veracity of the information it contains.'

The day after it appeared, I received a hand-delivered letter in response from President Mbeki. Enclosed, among other dissident literature downloaded from the 'virusmyth' website (www.virusmyth. com), was an article by Eleni Papadopulos-Eleopulos of the Royal

Perth Hospital, Australia, and other dissidents in a supplement to the November 1999 issue of a journal called *Current Medical Research and Opinion*, which Mbeki asked me to evaluate. The article claimed that the drug was unacceptably toxic, and appeared to have been a major influence in Mbeki's refusal to sanction state provision of the drug. Mbeki's letter was filled with sarcastic inferences implying that I was an internet Luddite, and was clearly offended by my criticism that his statements had caused public confusion.

'When I spoke in Parliament and raised the matters you say "caused immense public confusion", all I said was that our Minister of Health should investigate the assertions that have been made by scientists and others, who question almost everything you and I "know" about the issue of HIV–AIDS,' said Mbeki.

'I am amazed that scientists, whatever their specific discipline, take offence at the decision that we should carry out a scientific inquiry to arrive at the truth. I am very concerned that scientists oppose scientific inquiry on the basis that there exists an established, orthodox scientific "truth". This leads to the denunciation of unorthodox scientific views virtually as a religious heresy that must be suppressed and its adherents excommunicated or burnt at the stake. We dare not allow that science in our country should take this dangerous road.

'As you know better than I, scientific knowledge progresses in part through the open contest of competing views. Such progress would be difficult, if not impossible, if any scientific view were prohibited on the basis that it might "cause immense public confusion". Any "new truth" must, by definition, "cause immense public confusion". I am certain that, in its time, the truth about Thalidomide had the same effect!'

This notwithstanding, I was encouraged by his continuing: 'I made no "claims" about AZT. I reported to Parliament and the nation on the existence of the views expressed in the enclosed articles. The challenge you face as a scientist is to contest the assertions made in these articles. In the interest of the furtherance of correct public health decisions by our government, I would be most interested to receive your scientific response to the history and the scientific assertions made in these articles.

'I have no personal stake in the outcome of the ongoing and critically important international discussion on HIV-AIDS. Accordingly, I would have no difficulty whatsoever in publicly stating that I was wrong, if anything I have said is proved wrong.'

Believing that he was well intentioned, I wrote back to Mbeki immediately, saying that I would be honoured to advise him in this matter but would like to do so together with a colleague who was a specialist in the field. On Sunday, 6 February 2000, my father, my then partner Sandy Todd and I were reading the *Sunday Times* in the living room of my flat. The main drawcard on that day was a long interview the paper had secured with Mbeki, the first he had given since becoming President nine months earlier. Sandy was reading this, and suddenly exclaimed loudly that she thought Mbeki was talking about me. He was quoted thus:

'Take this very difficult issue that we raised about HIV/AIDS. It really would be very good if people could read. A university lecturer wrote an article for one of the daily papers and said that he and the president of the Medical Research Council, Professor [Malegapuru] William Makgoba, have not read any article in medical and scientific literature which speaks against the use of a particular drug. The conclusion was: "Therefore we don't know what this President is talking about". I wrote to the lecturer and said: "You know, it's possible that you people haven't read any such articles, please find enclosed an article published in 1999 in a very senior scientific journal. A very lengthy article with millions of references, presenting whatever that particular group of scientists thought about that matter." There you have university people, professors and scientists who haven't read. I was very surprised in that particular incident when [the lecturer] wrote back to me and said, "Mr President, I will respond to you in a fortnight, I'm afraid I don't know very much about this subject, I'm going to consult a friend of mine." Well, why did he write the article? What do you do if professors won't read articles about subjects they write about? What do you do?'

'I think he has got the wrong man,' said Sandy (who thought that I was spending rather too much time reading at that particular juncture). I was distressed both by his dishonesty – the 'I'm afraid I don't know very much about this subject' statement was pure conjecture – and by his complete lack of understanding about how science works. But the latter, at least, was explicable, and I thought that the issue was too important for me to take umbrage.

I had never even heard of the 'very senior scientific journal', *Current Medical Research and Opinion*, to which Mbeki was referring, which was unsurprising as it had a very low impact factor. Natasha Loder from *Nature*'s London office contacted its managing editor, Peter Clarke, who was quoted as saying: 'I felt that what the authors were trying to do – that is, critically appraise existing published material – was legitimate and deserved an opportunity to be made public. At the end of the day I took the value judgement that it needed to go into the public domain to be debated.' But in reading the article, I realised that it did not present original research findings but purported to synthesise and review the findings of workers in the field. The literature, which was already vast, had been highly selectively reviewed. I did a search and found at the time 6472 peer-reviewed articles available on AZT. The authors had ignored almost all of the articles written over the previous five years (in other words, since AZT had been widely used in MTCT) – a quite astonishing omission.

I pointed this out in a letter replying to Mbeki, written together with pharmacologist Dr Gary Maartens and virologist Dr Carolyn Williamson of the University of Cape Town (having decided to consult both a clinician and a virologist). All three of us offered to meet Mbeki in person to discuss the issue with him. Mbeki did not respond to this offer but merely passed our reply on to the authors of the *Current Medical*

Research and Opinion article, who responded to it. We, in turn, wrote a very detailed reply countering their arguments, which Mbeki chose to ignore.

In particular, we pointed out that since the early nineties AZT has been more commonly used in combination therapy with other drugs. The early AZT monotherapy studies were conducted before the development of the techniques currently available to quantify the virus accurately in humans (in vivo). We drew Mbeki's attention to two recent studies (which, needless to say, had been ignored by the review written by the dissidents) that had clearly documented a decrease in HIV-1 RNA in vivo in association with the administration of AZT alone.

But we were not alone in being ignored by Mbeki. Later in February, the government announced that it had rejected two reports commissioned from the MCC on the safety of AZT, both of which endorsed its use. The week after the opening of Parliament, Tshabalala–Msimang said that their contents (which the government was not prepared to release) 'were not to our satisfaction'. She also refused to reveal the findings of a third report compiled by the Council which she said she had just received on 31 January, adding that she had read only its first few pages and was therefore 'not quite ready' to comment on it. Tshabalala–Msimang had also received two further reports, one commissioned by the government from the MRC, and one from the World Health Organisation (WHO). Both recommended the use of AZT in reducing MTCT of HIV.

At this stage, the government started to come under heavy fire from AIDS activists. Mark Heywood, an executive member of the AIDS Consortium, the country's largest coalition of non-governmental AIDS organisations, criticised both the Health Minister and the President for failing to meet their legal and moral responsibilities to improve access to health care in South Africa. 'They are wilfully ignoring the best scientific advice, internationally and locally, on the safety and benefits of providing AZT through the public health sector,' he said.

In the first week of March, Tshabalala–Msimang announced that the Health Department was setting up a panel of experts to tackle the AIDS epidemic, to 'explore all aspects of... developing prevention and treatment strategies that are appropriate to the African reality'. She would not confirm or deny the rumour that Duesberg would be on the panel: 'Those with more extreme views are unlikely to participate because we are looking for a consensus,' she said. The panel's brief was to review both the general prevention and treatment (as well as the causes and diagnosis) of HIV/AIDS and opportunistic infections, and the prevention of infection following rape or needle-stick injuries, and from mother to child.

Tshabalala-Msimang said that the decision not to give antiretroviral drugs to pregnant women could be reconsidered if the panel convincingly showed that such treatment would be effective. But an 'ingenious solution' to the difficulties of financing the treatment would need to be found in such a case, she said. The newly formed Treatment Action Campaign (TAC) responded that the panel was 'a justification for the immoral, unscientific and unlawful decision' not to provide the drugs, and challenged the minister to produce evidence from any scientific study to prove that provision of AZT was not economically feasible in South Africa, or that AZT was toxic to mother or child when given to women in the last trimester of pregnancy.

The following week, leading AIDS dissident David Rasnick claimed that Mbeki had requested his scientific opinion on eight questions related to HIV and AIDS in January. Rasnick and Duesberg had co-authored an article entitled 'The AIDS dilemma: drug diseases blamed on a passenger virus', which was published in the journal *Genetica* in 1998. Rasnick posted the text of Mbeki's alleged questions on the 'virusmyth' website, along with his reply, co-written with another AIDS dissident, the historian Charles Geshekter of California State University. Duesberg confirmed that he had not been asked to sit on the panel but said he had written to Mbeki confirming his stand on HIV/AIDS.

Tshabalala-Msimang, meanwhile, was booed by angry activists

at a dinner in Durban at which she declared, referring to the use of antiretroviral drugs, that she didn't want to 'plunge into something I don't understand'. This followed a stinging attack by Appeal Court Judge Edwin Cameron, who is HIV-positive. Cameron criticised the government's policies on AIDS for causing 'considerable grief and confusion', and also questioned Tshabalala-Msimang's competence as a minister.

In Parliament in April, Jacob Zuma, Deputy President and chairman of the lame-duck South African National AIDS Council, denied that Mbeki had at any stage said that he challenged the view that HIV causes AIDS. Rallying to the President's position, he proclaimed: 'We should not, and we will not, leave any stone unturned, even if this means including the views of the so-called dissidents.' Additional support for Mbeki's stance came from an unusual quarter when the ultra-rightwing Boerestaat Party applauded the President's efforts to 'investigate the biggest hoax in the twentieth century'.

The composition of the 37-member Presidential AIDS Advisory Panel ended up being controversial, as just under half of its members were dissidents. 'The panel has pretty well everyone on it who believes that HIV is not the cause of AIDS, and about 0.0001 per cent of those who oppose this view,' commented AIDS researcher John Moore of Weill Cornell Medical College in the USA. Tshabalala-Msimang had announced the names of 33 panel members only days before its inaugural meeting, including the French discoverer of the AIDS virus, Luc Montagnier. Twelve were US-based, and ten were African, including seven South Africans and representatives from Uganda, Malawi and Senegal. There were also members from Cuba, Mexico and India. Significantly, with the exception of Professor Sam Mhlongo from the Medical University of Southern Africa, none of the African representatives belonged to the dissident camp.

There was speculation that a last-minute deal to add three extra non-dissident members to the panel – thereby creating an overall majority of non-dissidents – was brokered at a high level between the South African and US governments. But several prominent South African AIDS researchers, all of whom had been outspokenly critical of the dissident movement, were excluded. Apart from Carolyn Williamson and Gary Maartens, these included paediatrician Professor Hoosen Coovadia of Natal University (convener of the World AIDS Congress to be held in Durban), Professor James McIntyre of the University of the Witwatersrand, immunologist Dr Johnny Sachs, Dr Barry Schoub and Dr Lynn Morris of the National Institute for Virology, and epidemiologist Dr Brian Williams of the Council for Scientific and Industrial Research. 'Engaging with fringe groups is not the way forward,' said Professor Glenda Gray, of Chris Hani Baragwanath Hospital, who was also excluded from the panel. 'These people should never have been given a platform.'

In the first weekend of May, the inaugural meeting of the panel was held in Pretoria. The meeting was closed to journalists, except for the opening session and closing press conference. In opening the two-day meeting, Mbeki emphasised the high level of heterosexual AIDS transmission in South Africa. He referred to the first South African paper on AIDS, authored by panel member Professor Wally Prozesky and published in 1985, which predicted that the disease would remain largely confined to male homosexuals. The panel's task would be to try to explain why this situation had not changed in the West but had done so in South Africa, he said, adding that the conclusions would have a direct bearing on the government's response to the problem. Mbeki admitted that he was 'embarrassed to say' that he had 'discovered that there had been a controversy about this for some time'. Quoting the Irish poet Patrick Henry Pearse, Mbeki pondered, prophetically, whether his having raised the issue was 'folly or grace'.

At the closing session, it was announced that the MRC would team up with the US Centers for Disease Control (CDC) in Atlanta, together with two prominent AIDS dissidents, to devise a series of surveys to investigate the relationship between the disease and the virus. Professor Makgoba said that the surveys could involve the clinical identification of a sample of AIDS sufferers, who would be tested for HIV. Another possibility was an epidemiological study correlating HIV-positive children with the HIV status of their parents. A task force made up of Makgoba, Dr Helene Gayle of the CDC – which placed its database at the team's disposal – and two prominent dissidents, Duesberg (who did end up participating) and biotechnologist Harvey Bialy, was appointed to conceptualise exactly what research needed to be done. Khotso Mokhele, president of the National Research Foundation and head of the panel's secretariat, said after the meeting that funding would be sought from the South African government and other bodies once the agenda had been clarified. He emphasised that existing knowledge, based on completed studies, should provide the basis for any new work.

Although Tshabalala-Msimang described the meeting as a 'wonderful experience', it was apparently very acrimonious, with the dissidents finding themselves in a minority in each of three groups appointed to discuss the causes, prevention and treatment of AIDS. Instead of a final round-table discussion, the meeting apparently divided into groups representing the mainstream and dissident views. The panel's chief facilitator, lawyer Stephen Owen of the University of Victoria in Canada, said at the press conference following the meeting that reaching consensus had not been the objective. 'Divergent points of view remain, in very stark terms,' he said. The panel entered into a 'closed internet debate' over the next two months, before reconvening for a four-day discussion before the start of the World AIDS Congress on 9 July.

Five days before the start of the 13th World AIDS Congress in Durban, the second meeting of the panel took place in Johannesburg. I was one of two journalists accredited to attend the proceedings. During the two months which had elapsed since the first meeting, the panel had been enlarged from 37 members to 52, with the new members largely consisting of mainstream South African and Ugandan AIDS researchers. This led to hopeful speculation that the government might be about to review its policy. The non-dissident panel members drew up a proposed government policy on the prevention and treatment of AIDS, while the dissident faction had continued to argue for policies based on their claims that AIDS is not contagious and not sexually transmitted. In the intervening two months, it appeared that members of the dissident and mainstream camps on the panel had worked largely independently of each other.

At the meeting, made even more depressing for being held in a soulless Sandton hotel, Makgoba presented statistics on changes in mortality obtained from data compiled by the South African Department of Home Affairs. These showed that in 1990, 48 per cent of deaths among South African men occurred in the 15–49 age group, but a decade later, that age group accounted for 87 per cent of the deaths. For women, the rise had been just as alarming, from 27 to 68 per cent.

Further evidence that HIV causes AIDS came from a study presented by McIntyre and Gray (who were among those appointed to the enlarged panel) on a cohort of babies born to HIV-positive mothers in Soweto who were not treated with antiretroviral drugs. Infant mortality rates after one year were 17/1000 in babies who were HIV-negative after delivery, compared with 326/1000 in those who were HIV-positive.

It was very clear during the two-day meeting that there was no chance of a consensus emerging between the dissident and mainstream panelists. Nothing of any substance was presented by the dissidents, who merely reiterated their views with angry, religious fervour. In a sense this was surprising, as they had been given a golden opportunity to persuade the world that they should be taken seriously – one would have thought that they might at least have attempted to put on a good show. 'The crunch has come for the dissidents, as experimental evidence in support of their view is being demanded of them – something they have never been able to supply,' declared Makgoba.

The meeting hammered out a broad proposal to test the accuracy of

HIV testing in South Africa by comparing the results of Elisa (enzyme-linked immunosorbent assay) tests for HIV with those of other HIV tests, including the isolation of the virus. Makgoba presented evidence to the panel that the percentages of false positives – the concern of the dissidents – and false negatives recorded in South African laboratories were similar to those in Western countries. Despite this, the panel agreed to test the accuracy of Elisa 'in the interests of keeping the peace', according to panelist Professor Salim Abdool Karim, then head of AIDS research at the MRC. I sat next to Tshabalala-Msimang for the duration of the meeting. She took copious notes, and I couldn't help wondering whether this was still her idea of a wonderful experience.

Khotso Mokhele, head of the panel's secretariat, was faced with the unenviable task of compiling a report for Mbeki before his opening address to the Durban congress. Clearly fed up with the process, he said after the meeting that he hoped the testing of screening procedures might persuade one side to 'shut up once and for all'. But of course dissidents and orthodox members were unlikely to agree on what isolation of the virus actually meant. South African HIV statistics are based on antenatal surveys analysed at laboratories across the country, using a standard protocol. Researchers were in favour of centralised testing, eliminating the marginally differing levels of false negatives and positives recorded. So although panel members agreed this was desirable, it was unlikely to alter estimates of HIV prevalence significantly.

Nonetheless, everyone was optimistic that Mbeki would use the opportunity of opening the conference in Durban to announce a major shift in government policy. Instead, Mbeki focused on the well-documented impact of poverty on AIDS but made no reference to an appeal in the form of the 'Durban Declaration', signed by 5000 scientists including about 400 from Africa, stating that the evidence that HIV causes AIDS was overwhelming, and condemning revisionist theories on the cause of the disease. Mbeki referred to the need for accurate statistics rather than 'estimates based on projections' – another of the dissidents' arguments – but ignored the mortality data compiled by his own civil servants. 'I'm disappointed that an opportunity was lost, both to set the record straight on the causation of AIDS, and to present a concrete plan to reduce mother-to-child transmission,' commented Abdool Karim afterwards. Glenda Gray was less diplomatic: 'Mbeki waffles on, while Rome burns,' she remarked. The following day Mbeki's presidential spokesman, Parks Mankahlana, clarified his position, by suggesting that the Durban Declaration belonged 'in the dustbin'.

Delivering the closing address to the same conference a week later, former president Nelson Mandela urged that this debate be 'put on the back-burner, so that we can address the needs of those who are suffering and dying', adding, 'history will judge us harshly unless we do so right now.' 'I do not doubt', said Mandela, 'that President Mbeki will proceed with the resolve for which he is known. The challenge is to move from rhetoric to action on an unprecedented scale.' Mandela went on to describe measures to prevent MTCT as 'essential', following the examples of Uganda, Senegal and Thailand.

Initially, both the local scientific establishment and the local media were reluctant to criticise Mbeki's standpoint. One particular example will suffice. In September a full-page advert appeared in the Johannesburg *Sunday Independent*, which purported to detail the government's AIDS policy. It was noteworthy in one respect. The newspaper's editor, John Battersby, had been abroad when the advert was placed. On his return he took the unusual step of issuing a public apology to the newspaper's readers for having misled them in an editorial in the same issue which stated that the government had bought the advertisement space when, in fact, it had been given. It emerged that it was placed by Mbeki's special adviser on media, Tony Heard, on behalf of Essop Pahad, Minister in the Presidency, through the good offices of Shaun Johnson (then managing director of Independent News and Media in the Western Cape), who, acting for Ivan Fallon and Tony O'Reilly (respectively publisher and chairman of Independent Newspapers PLC), facilitated its publication free of charge.

After a respectable three months' wait, Mbeki told the National Executive Committee (NEC) of the ANC in October that he was withdrawing from the debate on the relation between HIV and AIDS. A party spokesman confirmed that the Cabinet had agreed that Zuma should chair a Cabinet committee on the debate initiated by Mbeki. According to the Johannesburg *Sunday Times*, Mbeki, with uncharacteristic understatement, told the NEC – the party's highest-ranking decision-making body – that his participation in the debate was indeed causing confusion. It had also divided the ANC and its allies, the Congress of South African Trade Unions, and the South African Communist Party. Mbeki apparently told the committee that he would leave his ministers, led by Tshabalala-Msimang, to liaise with the panel, and that the Cabinet committee, not he, would receive and process its report.

At first, Mbeki's disengagement appeared to herald the onset of a less dogmatic approach. In the same week, Tshabalala-Msimang announced that HIV-positive pregnant women would be given nevirapine at seven hospitals in KwaZulu-Natal, the country's worst-affected province, as part of a 'pilot programme'. Dr Ayanda Ntsaluba, Director-General in the Department of Health, declared publicly that HIV causes AIDS (but, clearly disillusioned with the prospect of continuing to work for his minister, he left the Health Department in 2003 to take up the position of Director-General of Foreign Affairs).

Initially due at the end of 2000, the report was handed to Tshabalala-Msimang on 18 January 2001, but she returned it to the panel's secretariat to deal with what she called 'editorial changes of a non-scientific nature'. According to Abdool Karim, 'the process of compiling the report was out of the hands of the panelists' and it was finally authored by Mokhele. The first version had met with disapproval from both its dissident members, who regarded it as unsupportive of their position, and the mainstream members, who felt that it lacked a coherent synthesis of the debate.

In April 2001, the panel's South Africa interim report was released. The report contained several contradictory recommendations, designed to accommodate both sides of the argument. It recommended, for example, that testing for HIV infection be suspended 'until its relevance is proved especially in an African context, given the evidence of false positive results in an African setting'. But it also called for continued 'surveillance of HIV prevalence in antenatal clinics, blood banks and among workers'.

The report outlined a programme of experiments under way to satisfy any doubts about whether HIV causes AIDS, only the first of which, based on the proposal hammered out at the panel's second meeting, had been completed. In it, blood tests for HIV from five laboratories in South Africa were retested at the CDC. The new tests were 99.9 per cent consistent with the originals, indicating that HIV testing in South Africa is highly reliable.

A second experiment was proposed to investigate the claim made by some dissidents that these test results were disrupted by reactions with antibodies raised in response to other diseases, such as malaria and tuberculosis. This was due to be completed within six to nine months. A further experiment suggested using an approach based on the polymerase chain reaction to screen test samples simultaneously for several diseases (or strains thereof) while significantly reducing the risk of contamination. This work was intended to measure the number of multiple infections, and to help identify strains of both tuberculosis and HIV that are resistant to treatment.

Mokhele recommended at the press conference that yet another committee be established to consider the merits of these proposals, and Tshabalala-Msimang dreamily expressed the hope that at least some financial support would be forthcoming from outside South Africa. Mercifully, neither materialised. Later that month, the MCC announced that it had registered nevirapine for use in preventing mother-to-child HIV transmission.

But in November 2001, almost a year after announcing his withdrawal from the AIDS controversy, Mbeki appeared unable to resist revisiting it, by writing to ask Tshabalala-Msimang to reconsider government spending on AIDS because it was not the country's major cause of mortality. In the letter leaked to *Business Day*, Mbeki used out-of-date (1995) figures from the WHO's website to question the view that AIDS had become the major cause of death in the country. 'Needless to say, these figures will provoke a howl of displeasure and a concerted propaganda campaign among those who have convinced themselves that HIV/AIDS is the single biggest cause of death in our country,' he wrote.

Two weeks later, this was followed by the leak of an MRC report showing that AIDS had indeed become the leading cause of mortality in the country, having caused the deaths of 40 per cent of people aged between 15 and 49 in 2000. Makgoba confirmed that the MRC had decided not to release the report publicly until it has been distributed among policy-makers. Despite this, Tshabalala-Msimang threatened the MRC, saying that MRC workers, 'who themselves are government employees, have chosen to act in ways which place themselves in a hostile position vis-à-vis the government, and it will be necessary for this serious situation to be attended to'. (The MRC is a statutory council that relies on state funding for two-thirds of its income, but the government appoints the majority of its board members.) This proved to be no idle threat. When Makgoba's term as president expired at the end of the following year, it was made clear to him that he need not bother to apply for a renewal of his contract.

On reflection, the panel's inconclusive report enabled Mbeki to portray the link between HIV and AIDS as 'deeply contested, and contestable', to use Nicoli Nattrass's words.[1] Certainly, the AIDS dissidents couldn't wait to participate, as this was their moment of glory, but should orthodox scientists have participated in the panel at all? Even in retrospect, this is a difficult question to answer. Once leading South African scientists

– including those like Makgoba who had been courageously outspoken in their criticism of Mbeki – had agreed to do so, others were bound to follow suit in support. In turn, members from outside the country who in good faith believed that their colleagues within South Africa deserved the same, agreed to participate. But ultimately it became clear that these efforts were a waste of time, as there was no possibility of consensus being reached between the panel's two diametrically opposed camps.

Mbeki used this lack of consensus to justify a national policy that refrained from a roll-out of ARVs until late 2003, although some of the country's nine provinces, which enjoy a level of autonomy on matters relating to health, defied this with varying degrees of success. By this stage TAC's activism threatened to make AIDS an issue in the 2004 election, and Cabinet responded by revolting against Mbeki's stand. But the effect of this four-year delay was an estimated 343,000[2] deaths, for which Mbeki and his Cabinet must bear collective responsibility.

* Michael Cherry is a professor of zoology at the University of Stellenbosch. He holds an honours degree in zoology from the University of Cape Town, and a doctorate from Balliol College, Oxford. He is the author of 46 peer-reviewed publications and numerous popular articles on science. Since 1989 he has been contributing South African correspondent for Nature, *the weekly international science journal. Since November 2008 he has been editor-in-chief of the* South African Journal of Science.

1. Nattrass, N. 2008. AIDS and the scientific governance of medicine in post-apartheid South Africa. *African Affairs* 107/427, 157–176.
2. Ibid.

3

Love, courage, insubordination and HIV/AIDS denialism

by

Pregs Govender

In 1998, Thabo Mbeki, then Deputy President, responded with urgency to HIV/AIDS and called for clarity and compassion: 'HIV/ AIDS is among us. It is real. HIV/AIDS is not someone else's problem. It is my problem. It is your problem.'

At the time of his call, as an ANC Member of Parliament, I felt confident that government leaders were taking the right steps. South Africa was leading the fight to ensure that the imperatives of public health superseded commercial interests. The Minister of Health, Nkosazana Dlamini-Zuma, and her Director-General, Olive Shisana, for instance, played a major role in the World Health Organisation (WHO) as the 14 SADC countries joined with others to stop the 'developed' world from blocking our access to affordable and safe generic antiretroviral (ARV) medicine. As a result, the WHO had to adopt a new strategy on drugs, by monitoring the pharmaceutical and public health implications of trade agreements, and considering things like local manufacturing capacity and access to, and prices of, medicines.

At the same time the Treatment Action Campaign (TAC), a non-governmental organisation founded by Zackie Achmat, an ANC member who had contracted HIV, was playing a significant role in the local and international campaign against the greed of the pharmaceutical companies. Such greed motivated the case brought by the United States against Brazil, at the World Trade Organisation, for Brazil's insistence on putting patient rights before the patent rights of pharmaceutical firms. Access to generic equivalents would help ensure affordable treatment for those who were poor and HIV-positive.

In early 1999, Mbeki, now President, stuck to the government's commitment to affordable medicine. In bilateral trade talks with the United States in which US Vice-President Al Gore punted the interests of the US pharmaceutical industry, Mbeki made his commitment clear.

Yet opposing objectives in relation to patents existed within government policy and was reflected in the approach of two key departments. The Department of Health argued for greater flexibility around patents in an attempt to ensure affordable treatment. In February 2001, the Constitutional Court made its decision on the pharmaceutical industry's challenge to the Medicines Act, which enabled government to obtain affordable generic equivalents. The judges ruled in government's favour, arguing that South Africa's Constitution, especially our Bill of Rights, placed a responsibility on government to provide good, safe and affordable health care. This judgment gave government the opportunity to take this victory further by challenging patents to provide affordable medicine. Instead, the position of the Department of Trade and Industry prevailed and as a result South Africa bound itself to protect patents 'as rigidly as the developed world', to use the words of Edwin Cameron, an Appeal Court judge living with HIV.

It would not do to take on the power of international capitalism. The constitutional objective of providing affordable health care was traded in for government's objective of trying to secure foreign direct investment. The poor would again bear the cost.

But by late 1999, things changed for the worse. The country had a new Health Minister, Manto Tshabalala–Msimang, who declared in Parliament that government would not supply antiretroviral AZT 'to people infected with HIV/AIDS, and people who have been infected

through rape or needle-pricks on two grounds: affordability and ...
the absence of proper research on the possible side-effects of AZT, in
particular its toxic profile'.

I sat listening to her after spending hours chairing hearings on violence
against women and access to justice. As a medical doctor herself, the
minister must have known that all serious medications have side-effects
that have to be clinically managed. To crown it all, we had the ludicrous
situation of her distributing copies of a chapter from a book by the AIDS
dissident William Cooper, who claimed that the 'Illuminati' (a group of
Jews, communists and international bankers) had introduced AIDS to
Africa to reduce its population. But HIV/AIDS was not ludicrous.

In early 2000, as I celebrated the birth of my third child, Saien, the
lives of other children were bearing the brunt of a terrible disregard that
was growing at the highest levels of power in the country as the ancient
principle of *ubuntu* – 'my child is your child, your child is mine' – was
discarded in favour of expedience.

The choices I had over my health and during childbirth were still not
available to most women. In fact, the choices for poor women who were
HIV-positive were being diminished, not just by the illness, but by the
state's response. At that time Parks Mankahlana, the spokesperson for
President Mbeki, was interviewed by *Science* magazine about why the
Department of Health refused to provide ARV medicine to mothers.

'That mother is going to die and that HIV-negative child will be an
orphan. That child must be brought up. Who is going to bring that child
up? It's the state, the state. That's resources, you see,' he responded. The
simple logic that we should use treatment to save the babies as well as the
mothers escaped not just Parks but key international donors. Neither the
state nor Parks seemed prepared to acknowledge responsibility for the
children. In his private life, Parks refused to pay maintenance for two of
his children until ordered to do so by the courts.

Parks also announced that President Mbeki had convened an
international panel of experts to resolve 'whether there is this thing

called AIDS, what it is, whether HIV leads to AIDS, whether there is something called HIV'. The panel met and their deliberations began, issuing in a controversial report that did not help the situation on the ground at all. How could we move forward when the Presidential AIDS Advisory Panel was still debating, even if in more sophisticated terms than those Parks used, whether there was a thing called AIDS? Both in Parliament and in the ANC caucus, the reasons for government's refusal to provide ARV medicine shifted from doubting the link between HIV and AIDS to toxicity and affordability, and round and round in circles. Though fruitless in many ways, the debate had dire repercussions, for ARV treatment was premised on the scientific conclusion that a virus, HIV, caused AIDS. Parks himself died a few months later, reportedly from AIDS.

In 2000 I attended Beijing Plus Five – a challenging time for the women's movement. In the preceding years an unholy alliance had been forged between the US government, traditional religious groups including the Catholic Church, and some new fundamentalist Christian and Islamic groups. Women's bodies were once again the battleground, with every authoritarian power attempting to assert control. The ancient equation of sex equals sin equals temptation by women had reasserted itself powerfully around HIV/AIDS as women were cast as both the cause (as whore) and the cure (as virgin).

At the United Nations, this negative bloc, opposed to abortion, and in favour of sexual abstinence and the death penalty, pitted itself against the progressive women's movement. They tried undoing the gains made in Beijing, such as the right to reproductive choice and the right to challenge the adverse impact of globalisation on women. At Beijing Plus Five, however, the global women's movement succeeded in holding back the tide and the final document that came out of the meeting upheld the original position enunciated at Beijing in 1995. An important ideological battle had been won. Women had to use the power we had to benefit the poorest of women. I argued that the policies we fought for 'could not be the policies of division, exclusion or elitism. Unless women draw on each other and support each other, we are going to be co-opted, no matter how large our numbers.' This observation would prove dishearteningly true of the response to HIV/AIDS by many South African women in power.

At home one evening in June 2000 while breastfeeding Saien, I watched the coverage on TV of a march in Durban organised by the TAC during the international AIDS conference. Their poster was painted a vivid red, and contained a child's face imprinted with the words 'One AIDS death every 10 minutes'. It was prophetic of the fate of Nkosi Johnson, a passionate AIDS activist who addressed the conference and who died soon afterwards at the age of 12. While Nkosi was still speaking, President Mbeki left the conference. His departure at that moment was a sign of the blindness which would later lead him to say he did not know anyone who had died of AIDS.

A month later Beryl Samantha Lockman, then 28 years old, died of AIDS. She was the granddaughter of Walter Sisulu's sister Rosabella. The family had to decide whether to disclose that the cause of death was AIDS. Walter himself, whose words, presence and actions embodied the best in the male leadership in the ANC, was an astute and humble man, and his marriage to Albertina was characterised by gentle, romantic caring. Their son Max publicly disclosed the true cause of Beryl's death, noting that the decision to make it known was taken at a family meeting at which everyone was present. It was a reflection of the family's commitment to fight AIDS. It was precisely this open and dignified acknowledgement of the reality of AIDS that was so keenly looked for in the public pronouncements of the government – and was so lacking.

Around this time, Mbeki addressed us in the ANC caucus on HIV/AIDS. There, and later on in both Parliament and the media, what he said directly undermined the commitment and conviction of his 1998 speech. As he spoke in the caucus, I made notes and wanted to ask him why we were not challenging the real issue of the power of pharmaceutical firms and of governments like the US that placed profits from patents above the lives of those with HIV/AIDS. Instead we were being distracted into a debate about whether HIV existed, with Mbeki pronouncing triumphantly that a virus cannot cause a syndrome. When Mbeki sat down, I put up my hand to raise my questions. Comrades seated nearby glanced sideways at me, their eyes urging me to put my hand down. The chairperson looked away, saying that there was to be no discussion, and moved swiftly on to the next item on the agenda. Clearly, others in caucus were as stunned as I was at the President's comments. One of them leaked Mbeki's address to the *Mail & Guardian*, which published an accurate report of what he'd said, because when a sweep of the chamber was done later no bugging devices were found.

Soon afterwards Mbeki addressed Parliament on HIV/AIDS. I sat hoping that he would talk with the clarity we'd respected before. Instead he only deepened the confusion as he asked, no longer in the relative privacy of the ANC caucus but in the glare of the world media, 'How can a virus cause a syndrome?' The fact is that if you deny the existence of the virus, it follows that you will deny the need for treatment to cope with it.

When I tried to understand what I saw as a growing confusion, a friend in the Cabinet said: 'You don't understand the complexity of the issues like we do. It is not as simple as you think. I wish you could hear the information that is presented to us in Cabinet.'

'Then help me understand,' I replied. 'Why should people who are poor die from a disease which we would receive treatment for, from our medical aid? We use medicine all the time. I chose the epidural during childbirth when all the natural options failed to ease the pain. Why can't all women make choices around what is best for our own bodies? What makes this disease different from cancer or any other life-threatening illness? Cancer patients can choose whether or not to have chemotherapy in public hospitals even though the side-effects are horrible.'

My comrade shook her head. 'This HIV/AIDS thing is too complex. Also,' she added decisively, calling for closure, 'we are not allowed to discuss confidential information.'

As I saw it, my intelligent comrade failed to match the 'complex' arguments and information the President provided in Cabinet with what she saw with her own eyes. What did it mean to be a loyal party member when mothers, fathers, daughters, sons, brothers and sisters, husbands and wives, were dying of AIDS? Over and over again the same thing was repeated: 'The President is a very intelligent man. He is extremely well read. He does his homework' – until I wanted to scream out, 'Yes, but he's not infallible. He needs to look at what's actually happening. He doesn't need defenders, we're not out to destroy him – we want him to beat HIV/AIDS and end economic apartheid everywhere.' In the ANC caucus and in Parliament I looked at Thabo Mbeki, son of Govan and Epainette, and wanted him to open his eyes to what was happening to women who have HIV/AIDS, and use his power for their lives.

In October 2000, it was time that the parliamentary committee I chaired, the Joint Monitoring Committee on the Improvement of the Quality of Life and Status of Women, developed its own understanding, not just of the problem but of solutions. I asked two of Parliament's best researchers to investigate and develop research briefs for the committee on several issues: women and HIV/AIDS; generic medicines; multilateral trade agreements; the Brazilian national drug policy; the government's mother-to-child transmission policy and programme; and its policy on the treatment of rape survivors. The research briefs were ready in November and copies were circulated to committee members. We also commissioned Masimanyane, an NGO based in the Eastern Cape, to research the situation of women and HIV/AIDS in five provinces. We asked research organisation CASE to survey HIV/AIDS service organisations to find out what type of programmes and projects existed and in which areas; the funding received; and how government could assist them to provide services to help people, households and communities affected by HIV/AIDS. We had to understand what was going on and how the committee could intervene most effectively to improve the lives of women with HIV/AIDS. That was our mandate – as our very long committee name spelt out.

Later that year an NGO in Mpumalanga called the Greater Nelspruit Rape Intervention Project (Grip) approached us to say that they had been ordered to stop providing ARV treatment to rape survivors who were under threat of contracting HIV/AIDS. Someone in our ANC study group cynically observed, 'They're just a group of conservative white women who don't mind experimenting with our people's lives.' I didn't know the women in Grip and didn't know their politics. But Grip's reports clearly showed that, like many other NGOs, it seemed to be responding to the crisis of gender-based violence. After being asked to stop providing post-exposure prophylaxis to rape survivors, the NGO was evicted from the Rob Ferreira Hospital on the orders of the female MEC for Health in the province, Sibongile Manana. By this stage, they had helped 74 rape survivors, half of whom were under 16 years of age. Grip took the department to the High Court and the department was forced to settle out of court.

The following year, I received a letter from Amnesty International saying that, in the same province, the MEC had issued threats of dismissal to doctors providing ARVs to rape survivors. We discussed Amnesty's letter in the committee and delegated Priscilla Themba, our deputy chair who was from Mpumalanga, to meet with the MEC to try to resolve the situation. Priscilla met with her, but her report-back showed us clearly that there was no possibility of resolution.

At the root of the growing confusion in the state and among its officials about the implementation of the government's HIV/AIDS policy was the President's questioning of its basic premise – that HIV caused AIDS. At the same time there was a glaring contradiction between Mbeki's stated commitment to ending poverty and the government's decisions on the arms deal and HIV/AIDS. We all agreed with him that poverty exacerbated AIDS, but it seemed he was going further and implying that poverty actually *caused* AIDS. Many of Mbeki's trusted foot-soldiers such as the Health Minister and some of the MECs were using their power to refuse to provide treatment for HIV/AIDS in public hospitals and clinics, even in circumstances such as rape, which exacerbated the possibility of contracting HIV. In this way they contributed to the suffering and early death of those who were HIV-positive, poor and dependent on the public health system – and they were being promoted for doing so.

At the same time, all of us MPs, ministers, MECs, government bureaucrats and the President himself belonged to a medical aid with cover for HIV/AIDS, including ARV treatment, which we could draw on if we or our children were raped or contracted HIV/AIDS. We could afford skilled doctors to help manage the side-effects. Our medical aid even covered a host of alternative healing modalities, including traditional medicine. We, who were denying choice to others, had real choices after the February 2001 Constitutional Court ruling that enabled government to obtain affordable generic equivalents.

Later that year, I used my position as committee chair to initiate hearings on HIV/AIDS. I wanted women's voices to be heard by President Mbeki and Minister Manto. I hoped that if the information was presented to the President, he would act on it. Perhaps he was surrounded by too many sycophants, all afraid to 'speak truth to power'. I believed that the public hearings would bring ministers and ordinary MPs far closer to women with HIV/AIDS, and to the scientists, doctors, experts and practitioners who worked daily with the problem. We had to cut through the fear and the authoritarianism we had submitted to when we reneged on the government's own Strategic Plan on HIV/AIDS 2000–2005 to ensure that people had access to treatment as well as prevention.

Our committee announced the holding of public hearings on how South Africa could best address the impact of HIV/AIDS on women and girls. Even though we began at the height of the HIV/AIDS controversy, I was emboldened by the words of former president Nelson Mandela, who was moved to plead at the international AIDS conference: 'If 27 years in prison have done anything to us, it is to use the silence of solitude to make us understand how precious words are and how real speech is in its impact upon the way people live and die ...'

I asked Dr Abe Nkomo, chair of the parliamentary health committee, for a copy of their report on hearings they had held in May 2000. It seemed to have vanished into Parliament's bureaucracy and it took a while before a copy was located. Abe's report argued that the South African government needed to use the scope of the Medicines Act and exemptions from trade-related aspects of intellectual property rights (TRIPS) to access and eventually produce good-quality generics so that affordable treatment could be available for HIV-positive patients who needed it. The recommendations in Abe's report had not been implemented, and no one had even mentioned them.

Our committee's hearings began in September and ended in October 2001. We heard the testimonies and recommendations of many people, some of whom had experienced the effects of HIV/AIDS at first hand and gave moving addresses. There were many submissions which dealt in detail with the social and economic reasons why women and girls bore the worst brunt of HIV/AIDS. These included the powerlessness of poverty; job losses in the formal sector, which pushed women into prostitution; traditional gender roles; definitions of masculinity premised on multiple relationships with no responsibility for contraception; 'skin to skin' sex and violent coercion as the first experience of sex for many girls; and the belief that raping a virgin could cure HIV/AIDS.

Amidst all these problems there were also innovative solutions such as trying to find female-controlled prevention methods; a campaign to mobilise men to educate other men about joint responsibility and respect for the sexual rights of women and girls; and academic research that was not controlled by pharmaceuticals with a narrow profit agenda. However, there was a major stumbling block to developing a unified national response.

On 23 September, the president of the Medical Research Council (MRC), Professor Malegapuru Makgoba, was slated to address us on the MRC report on HIV/AIDS. This revealed that AIDS was the biggest killer in our country. It estimated that 40 per cent of adult deaths in the 15–49 age group in 2000 were due to AIDS and that between 5 to 7 million South Africans would die from it by 2010. Shortly before the hearing Professor Makgoba sent a fax apologising that he couldn't attend, due to 'urgent MRC matters'. There was much speculation as to why he suddenly cancelled, especially when, soon afterwards, President Mbeki disputed the MRC's statistics and quoted outdated 1995 WHO figures for Africa showing that heart disease and malaria were the two biggest killers. That weekend, the ANC health committee secretary, Saadiq Kariem, was quoted in the media as saying, 'My opinion is that we need to make sure that our judgements are scientifically based. We've obviously got to use the latest figures.' We agreed.

At our hearing, the Health Department sent a bureaucrat who re-read the government's 2000–2005 HIV/AIDS plan with which we were already familiar. Their departmental team included a female director, Dr Kammy Chetty, who listened in silence to his presentation. Kammy, whom I had first met when we were student activists, looked embarrassed. She surely knew the truth about HIV/AIDS that her minister seemed to be denying. Their spokesperson was clearly nervous and kept saying he was unable to answer even the simplest questions posed by the committee, as 'only the minister can deal with that'. It was frustrating. 'If you are not empowered to address any questions at all, surely we should hear from the minister herself, who has the power to respond to our questions,' I advised. This was the key department, and they had sent a bureaucrat who had no power.

Shortly after tea, the Health Minister flew in. She wanted to address us immediately. Although the Director-General of Social Development had arrived punctually, she graciously agreed to be rescheduled. Tshabalala-Msimang was furious as she lectured the committee in a rapid-gunfire way, mainly about the MRC report. When she was through, she left without any discussion. Her hostile manner seemed to undermine the good work that many people in her department were doing.

The departments of Education and Trade and Industry gave submissions on the programmes they had instituted. All these government departments were doing commendable work, but there was no coherent, overall leadership to pull the diverse initiatives together. The lack of political will was already clear to us: not a single minister apart from Tshabalala-Msimang, who arrived unexpectedly and in response to our prompting, had accepted our invitation to address the hearings.

Then we heard from Dr Olive Shisana, head of the HIV/AIDS directorate of the Human Sciences Research Council. Olive, the former Director-General of Health, is a formidable scientist. She contradicted Mbeki's insistence that the biggest killers were heart disease and malaria. 'HIV/AIDS is the leading cause of death on the African continent,' she asserted. She also challenged the toxicity argument of the President and the Health Minister as she explained: 'There is not a single medicine that has no side-effect.' Olive explained how government could provide affordable treatment through importing ARVs and other medicines from countries like Brazil and Thailand and learn from these countries to produce generic medicines.

We received the Brazilian national drug policy together with a paper, 'Brazil: people first, profits later', from their health ministry. Brazil had faced similar predictions to South Africa of a looming HIV/AIDS crisis in the early 1990s. In response, it had developed a comprehensive prevention and treatment campaign. The country made a significant policy choice to provide free ARV treatment, which acted as a powerful incentive for Brazilians to get an AIDS test and act to prevent the spread of HIV. In the document, the head of Brazil's AIDS programme explained how prejudiced critics such as senior US government officials had been confounded. 'The main criticism from developed countries was that we did not have the conditions for ARV treatment. They said it would be dangerous for other countries, that we would cause resistance. They also said that uneducated people can't stick to their treatment regime, that it was too expensive, and that our health system was too fragile.' On all these points, the critics were proved wrong.

We noted Brazil's efficiency. In 1994, when we voted in our democracy, Brazil's government began producing generic equivalents of ARVs in state laboratories. By 1996, it had passed intellectual property legislation to enable Brazil to import and produce generic ARVs. The cost-saving from declining hospitalisation and treatment for opportunistic diseases which flourished on AIDS-weakened immune systems offset about 85 per cent of the cost of ARVs.

Then came the eye-opener: Brazil had offered to transfer the technology they had developed for making generic ARVs. It was prepared to train other countries on the practicalities of treatment. It would do all this free of charge as long as the country involved was prepared to provide free treatment to its own citizens with HIV/AIDS. The obvious question was why all our governments had not jumped to accept Brazil's offer. As I've already indicated, the answer has nothing to do with the debate we'd been distracted into about whether HIV causes AIDS but is about how the World Trade Organisation works through its trade-related aspects of intellectual property rights agreement to promote the rights of large companies like the pharmaceuticals as well as the bilateral trade agreements that almost all poor and middle-income countries have signed with the United States, which over-rides their right to produce or import access affordable generic medicine.

In Parliament, while the usual rhetorical speeches droned on, I sat working on the committee's report. The report needed to be written with clarity, avoid red herrings, and propose solutions. I wrote that the committee's hearings started from the same premise as government's in the 2000–2005 plan – that HIV causes AIDS. Our committee's conclusion was that South Africa needed to respond holistically on prevention and treatment, tackling HIV/AIDS, poverty, and gender-based violence; that the key was addressing gender inequalities; and that government's response should be informed and driven by people living with AIDS.

In Parliament, the ANC chief whip finally confirmed that our report on HIV/AIDS would be dealt with in the ANC's special caucus workshop on 10 November. Beforehand, I had presented the report to an ANC chairs of committees meeting. Very few chairs attended but at least there was some support for our recommendations to take to the caucus workshop. I also canvassed support among a few significant ANC members.

I knew that every member of the caucus needed to see this report, even though the chief whip told me it was only necessary to make three copies, one for the chair of each of the workshop's commissions. On the day, an ANC staff member kindly volunteered to get to work at 5 am to make copies for everyone. When the workshop began, every single MP received a copy. President Mbeki did not attend. The Health Minister spoke for a very long time and said nothing we had not heard before. There was very little time left for me to deal with the committee's report.

When Tshabalala-Msimang finally finished, a woman MP moved that 'Since Comrade Manto has already covered the question of HIV/AIDS, there is no need to spend any more time having Comrade Pregs do another presentation on HIV/AIDS.' Many voices interrupted her, insisting that they wanted to hear, and the chair gave me permission to proceed. I kept focused on the report; there was little time to capture the essence. At the end there was a spontaneous burst of applause, and a tangible sense of relief filled the space. The whip announced that the report would be discussed in the commission on HIV/AIDS after lunch. There were many calls of 'Thank you' and 'You said what we have all been thinking', and quiet tears – many had lost close family and friends.

In the caucus commission on HIV/AIDS after lunch, the report came under attack. But several MPs had had enough of equivocating. They knew people were dying in their constituencies, villages and families, and they refused to be silenced. Henry Fazzie, Dr Essop Jassat and Barbara Hogan, among others, spoke clearly and forcefully on the issues. This workshop represented a watershed in that, for the first time, ANC MPs debated and discussed a comprehensive alternative, including treatment, to the denial and fear that had characterised discussion since 1999. Many MPs said that there was no turning back on government's need to provide medicine that would treat HIV/AIDS.

The great problem was that the debate on HIV/AIDS was swiftly becoming highly adversarial. This was the very thing we'd been trying to avoid. We wanted everyone to face the facts together and work harmoniously. Shortly after our report was discussed by the ANC caucus workshop, President Mbeki delivered a public lecture in which he smeared those in the ANC who were demanding treatment, as people who believed in and perpetuated racist colonial stereotypes: 'Some who call themselves our leaders join a cacophony of voices ... Convinced that we are but natural-born promiscuous carriers of germs, unique in the world, they proclaim that our continent is doomed to an inevitable end because of our unconquerable devotion to the sin of lust.'

Mbeki's speech raged at, but did not engage with, the substance of what we were demanding in the committee's report. His speech reinforced the deep prejudices and secrecy surrounding sex as he invoked the old stereotype of sex as 'the sin of lust'. HIV/AIDS had thrown us way past the simple black and white dichotomies that he was reasserting. The pandemic could have impelled us to think in new ways of solutions that would be far-reaching, but this would have entailed a fundamental paradigm shift. In the face of this tragedy, South Africa and our President could have led the world by challenging and beginning to transform the old patriarchal paradigm binding us to stereotyped roles and relationships that were literally killing men and women. Instead of reinforcing the medieval notion of 'sex as lust', what would have happened if Mbeki moved sex beyond the inequality, the violence, the virgin–whore dichotomies in which it was trapped, in which we remained trapped?

In the ANC caucus the following week, the President was there. I came under attack, especially from two powerful men. I kept my response brief and to the point. I explained the political process that the committee's

ANC study group had followed. The study group had supported the draft report unanimously, yet weeks had passed without any ANC bodies responding to our request for discussion. By default, then, our multi-party committee on women had met and unanimously adopted it.

Afterwards, as I was about to start my car in the parking basement, Jeremy Cronin of the South African Communist Party (SACP) walked up to me. 'I thought you should know,' he said, 'that when they were attacking you, I watched the President. I was sitting closely behind him and his face clearly reflected that he did not like his supporters' behaviour.'

Blind followers seldom understand the nuances of their leaders' arguments. On the other hand, leaders should discourage this blind loyalty and clarify their positions. Mbeki didn't do so. All that happened was that at the weekend the caucus meetings made front-page news, one headline reading, 'Mbeki faces revolt from women'. I was not the source of their story, but those exposed in the article as opposing the report believed I was. Their attitude hardened, making positive discussion still more difficult.

In January 2002, while some comrades in the study group went on trying to derail the tabling of the report, I instructed the committee clerk to follow the normal bureaucratic procedure. Committee reports that have been formally adopted by the committee have to be tabled by Parliament's bureaucrats, who usually don't keep track of what it all means. Our committee had unanimously adopted its report, so of course it had to be tabled. On the morning before the President took the podium to open Parliament in February 2002, while some comrades were still arguing the status of the report, the tabled list landed on all politicians' desks, announcing the arrival of our report on HIV/AIDS.

In March 2002, Parliament held its customary debate to mark International Women's Day. That year, the theme was 'Women's rights as human rights'. The day before, the ANC whip in charge of the debate, Mbulelo Goniwe, summoned me to his office and instructed me not to speak about HIV/AIDS.

Our committee's HIV/AIDS hearings and report had exposed the connections between gender inequalities, gender-based violence, misogynous beliefs, and poverty. It questioned the priorities of macroeconomic policy, the arms deal and war. In debating 'women's rights as human rights', I had been instructed not to address HIV/AIDS. How and why did we get to a point of such confusion?

I could not understand why or how we had moved from clarity to such confusion on HIV/AIDS in the ANC. When we were fighting apartheid we were absolutely clear that the new state would have to undo the damage apartheid had caused to the health of its citizens. Yet in 2002 we seemed to have forgotten those who had placed their trust in us to use our power to help change our country and enable them to change their lives.

After one ANC caucus, we were asked to gather outside the Assembly to listen to then Deputy President Jacob Zuma, who headed the National AIDS Council and the Moral Regeneration Campaign. Zuma is a popular speaker, with a reputation for making people feel included – he has what is called the 'common touch'. We were asked to join him in an HIV/AIDS candle-lighting ceremony. People passed candles around our large semicircle. The Deputy President pointed to two young people on either side of him. 'Look at them,' he announced jovially. 'Don't they look beautiful? He is so handsome he could be Mr Universe, and she could be Miss World. Don't you agree? They are so healthy and they are HIV-positive. But they are not taking any medication – no ARVs. They are looking after themselves naturally. They are government employees who work well and are both productive. I want you to hear them for yourselves.' He turned laughing to the young man. 'Come on, Mr Universe, let these MPs hear you.' The two young people explained that they were HIV-positive and not taking ARV treatment, and yet were very healthy. It was a crude propaganda exercise against ARVs.

'Oh, God, this is sick,' Barbara Hogan, who was standing next to me, muttered. The Deputy President of our country was parading young people who were government employees before us as proof that you don't need to take ARVs if you have HIV/AIDS. He was standing outside the National Assembly, joking about an issue that was claiming an average of 600 people every day. MPs lit their candles and sang the national anthem. I felt sick to the stomach as I wondered what the young people at his side would do when they were at an advanced stage of AIDS and wanted to change their minds about taking medication.

Meanwhile, in Parliament and outside it, MPs and other friends in the ANC quietly told me about their ill daughter, son, sister, wife, themselves. A provincial ANC leader confided that 'those young TAC women were my sister's support before she died. Then at her funeral they were singing anti-Mbeki songs. I had to ask them to leave even though I knew what they had done for her. I mean, this is my organisation and he is my President.' He didn't have to describe how painful it was to ask his sister's friends to leave her funeral. The pain was knotted in his fingers and in his eyes that tried to look calm.

'I need to talk to you, Pregs. I am ill.' My friend, whom I had not seen in a while, hugged me warmly. I refused to believe her. 'Don't talk shit. You look as healthy as ever,' I laughed, 'and as beautiful.' Her brown eyes pierced through me – direct, excruciatingly honest. She wanted to trust me with her secret. Ours was a friendship born in the days of struggle, over our escapades and laughter. We did not see each other regularly. We did not write or phone each other but when we saw each other, our hearts reconnected. We knew little of the details of each other's everyday lives, yet she knew I would not judge her in a time of moral-regeneration crusaders. But just then I could not bear to hear what she was telling me. I could not listen to what she wanted to tell me. I refused to talk about illness and death. 'Listen, we are going to party together until we are 80, OK?' Today she is dead. I'm a coward. I did not want to hear the truth my friend wanted to share. I did not want those I loved to die.

In March 2002, on the eve of International Women's Day, I prepared myself to speak in the debate on 'Women's rights are human rights'.

Early that morning, before the sun rose, I got up, lit a candle, and sat in silence. I needed to feel a sense of calm. I wanted to reach the hearts of my comrades, to touch the love that inspired the courage they had expressed in the struggle against apartheid. I wanted them to remember who we were and why we were in Parliament. When I took the podium, I began with my poem 'Fragments'. 'We no longer see our own faces, we no longer hear our own voices ...'

I reminded MPs of how apartheid had institutionalised violence, including misogyny, the hatred of women, and had contributed to widespread poverty and gender inequality. Now, individually and together, we had to ensure that young women were not crushed by poverty, rape and HIV/AIDS in a country where a third of young men believed that 'forced sex with someone you know is not sexual violence' and one in four young South Africans believed the lie that 'sex with virgins cures AIDS'. Above all, I wanted to ensure that the commitment I had secured from the chief whip for a debate on our HIV/AIDS report would not be left as a discussion between two individuals behind closed doors. Contrary to his instruction, I concluded my speech by talking about HIV/AIDS and the committee hearings on the horrific impact of AIDS on women and girls, and confirmed that our request for a debate on the report had finally been agreed to.

At the end of 2001, a baby who was given the pseudonym Tshepang was raped in the Northern Cape. The horror of this echoed across the country and filled our hearts with shame. Tragically, it was not the first or the last rape of a child. The year before, the Minister of Safety and Security reported to Parliament that child rape had doubled from the previous year. To add to the horror of Baby Tshepang's story, the media revealed that a doctor at the hospital had been reprimanded for providing her with medicine to prevent her getting infected with HIV. Pressure from the Health Department led to a hospital circular that doctors were barred by the department's policy from administering ARVs to rape survivors.

In March 2002, Parliament appointed a task team on child rape. Several ANC chairs were appointed to it, myself included. Its brief was to hold hearings on child rape and make clear recommendations about what could be done. The task team was potentially powerful. Parliament had power, at the very least, to ensure that children who were raped were not doubly traumatised by HIV/AIDS. We could insist that state hospitals provide survivors with the option of ARV medicine.

After the legal, medical, religious and social welfare experts had presented their evidence, we finally heard from the children themselves. A child rights organisation had arranged for two children from each province to testify. They spoke of being raped by fathers, uncles and strangers. During a harrowing testimony from a young girl, an ANC MP interrupted: 'No, this is not what we were supposed to be hearing from these children. They were supposed to present what was happening in provinces, not their individual experience.'

The DP MP supported him and MPs from other parties joined in, expressing anger with the children's organiser for 'misleading us'. I looked at the child who had been so rudely interrupted, and the children around her. The response was completely disrespectful towards them. This should have been an empowering process for the children. Instead, they looked confused and intimidated. I put up my hand and insisted on being heard immediately: 'Point of order, Chair! It is unacceptable that we discuss this here. I move that we immediately adjourn for a caucus of all MPs and sort out our problems there.'

In the caucus, I was aware of the pained confusion in the eyes of the ANC MP who had raised the objection. A courageous opponent of apartheid, he seemed unable to comprehend the brutality of those who rape their children. Though I was sympathetic, I felt he had to understand the impact of his intervention on the children. The experiences the children shared were too close to the bone and required clear focus for us to listen properly. Whatever our own experiences and expectations, we had no right to subject the children to our own confusion.

Before returning to the room, we agreed that our team chair would apologise to the children on behalf of us all and ask them to carry on presenting what they had prepared. The children, noticeably subdued, listened to him before continuing hesitantly. The last young boy ended his presentation with a plea to us: 'My child is your child, your child is my child. We believe in *ubuntu*.' I excused myself and left the room. Alone in the cloakroom, I put my face in my hands and wept.

In the ANC caucus at that time, few openly argued for ARV treatment and no one else publicly supported it. In fact, there were several who openly argued against it. The task team hung back from taking a stand on the question of children and HIV/AIDS, and its draft report made no recommendations on HIV/AIDS. Instead of tackling child rape, it seemed stuck in a political quagmire. In the ANC study group, 'crisis management' of the public uproar around HIV/AIDS and child rape seemed to have replaced the problem of child rape itself.

The Cabinet was scheduled to meet in May 2002 to discuss government's response to HIV/AIDS. In the run-up to it, I met with several ANC members to try to influence the outcome. The TAC and other organisations were demonstrating in the streets, and Parliament needed to use its leverage. I was chairperson of a successful committee that had held hearings and made clear recommendations: I decided to use all I could to shift the Cabinet's mind.

For this, contacts made during our hearings across South Africa proved valuable. One of Gauteng's most capable MECs, Mary Metcalfe, provided important support for the issues, backing the Premier of Gauteng, Mbhazima Shilowa, who took a public stand in favour of treatment for HIV/AIDS. Cabinet would not be able to ignore the premier of South Africa's most powerful province. Cheryl Carolus had old friends and comrades in high places. I met with her and shared the report's recommendations, and she agreed to speak to Cabinet members with whom she had worked in the UDF in the 1980s. I even made contact with the wife of a Cabinet minister. She was passionate as she promised to draw up a memo for her husband: 'If he does not stand up in Cabinet,' she laughed, 'I will divorce him!'

Together, we must have all made a difference. In the month in which I resigned from Parliament, Cabinet committed the government to the committee's key recommendations on treatment; to prevent mother-to-child HIV transmission, for post-exposure prophylaxis after rape, and to pursue affordable medicine. However, between Cabinet's statement and its implementation lay a vast swamp of confusion. That confusion continued to drag government away from its responsibility to challenge the international patents regime so that it can provide affordable health care for its poorest citizens.

On the brink of Jacob Zuma's elevation to the position of President of South Africa, the questions raised in this chapter remain on the table, especially after Zuma and his supporters espoused opinions about women, HIV/AIDS and homosexuality during his rape trial that reflect the very patriarchal, authoritarian values that perpetuate HIV/AIDS. The challenge is to ensure that civil society and Parliament remain vigilant in defence of these rights.

*Pregs Govender is the author of Love *and* Courage: A Story of Insubordination. *She is a former Cosatu unionist and served as an ANC MP from 1994 to 2002, when she resigned after being the only MP to register opposition to the arms deal in the Defence budget vote, arguing that the money should be used to address HIV/AIDS, poverty and violence. A feminist activist, she currently chairs the Independent Panel reviewing Parliament and is a member of the Human Rights Panel of Eminent Persons tasked with developing a global Human Rights Agenda by December 2008. This chapter is an amended version of passages from her book.*

4

Courting mortality: The fight to prevent mother-to-child HIV transmission

by
Ashraf Coovadia

My name is Ashraf Coovadia. I guess if I had to try and describe myself I should say I am a husband, a father, a South African and a doctor – not necessarily in that order. Becoming a doctor always felt right; it was the natural choice for me. I wanted to help, use my medical skills to relieve pain, heal and, hopefully, in the process make the world a better place. Never in my wildest dreams did I think that being a doctor in South Africa's state sector would turn me into an activist, mediator, negotiator and protester.

Standing at the side of a cot, witnessing life drain slowly and painfully from a little body, while down the hall you know there is a drug that could have prevented this situation in the first place – it goes against everything I believe in as a human being and as a doctor. Such situations have the potential to breed anger and resentment against those arrogant people that decide who lives and who dies; the people that keep these simple lifesaving remedies out of touch.

There is a frame hanging in my cluttered office at Rahima Moosa Mother and Child Hospital (formerly Coronation Hospital) in the west of Johannesburg. It holds a piece of paper called 'The Oath of a Muslim

Physician' and I hope I will be forgiven for quoting sections of it here, but it really encapsulates what I and, I believe, many of my colleagues stand for, no matter what our religions, cultural backgrounds or race. It also serves as a daily reminder why it is important to stand up for what I believe is right, why we had to stand up for our patients.

'Give us the strength to be truthful, honest, modest, merciful and objective. Give us the fortitude to admit our mistakes, to amend our ways and to forgive the wrongs of others. Give us the wisdom to comfort and counsel all towards peace and harmony. Give us the understanding that ours is a sacred profession that deals with your most precious gifts of life and intellect. Therefore, make us worthy of this favored station with honor, dignity and piety so that we may devote our lives in serving mankind, poor or rich, wise or illiterate, Muslim or non-Muslim, black or white, with patience and tolerance with virtue and reverence, with knowledge and vigilance, with thy love in our hearts and compassion for thy servants, thy most precious creation.'

I hope that I have stayed true to this oath, and even though I have sometimes been forced to step outside my comfort zone, in the end I wanted to remain true to my calling – that of a doctor who wants to create a better life for all, more specifically for our children.

I had the good fortune to have a happy childhood. I have incredibly happy memories of growing up in Ndola, a busy but peaceful city in the Zambian Copperbelt, about 320 kilometres north of the capital, Lusaka. My overriding memories of my birth country are of a peaceful country with friendly people where we all lived in racial harmony. My parents had met in Ndola. Mom had moved there ten years before Dad, having grown up in Mafikeng and Northern Rhodesia (my grandfather could not obtain citizenship in South Africa, so they settled there). Dad had been born and bred in Johannesburg but moved to Ndola in the early 1960s on his return from England, shortly after completing his law degree. There were many expatriates in Zambia at the time, and Dad's friends encouraged him to join them as they found the country peaceful and prosperous, with good racial harmony – an important consideration in the sixties. Listening to their stories at the all too frequent social gatherings at dinner time, I got to feel that I had two homes – Zambia and this other place I had yet to see.

After completing my schooling in Ndola, I went to study medicine at the University of Zambia in Lusaka. I worked incredibly hard, not wanting to disappoint my parents who had sacrificed so much for us. Fresh from my university studies I travelled to Johannesburg in 1991, to commence my year of internship as I wanted to be close to my parents, who had left Zambia two years earlier. South Africa was at the time a wonderful place to be. Nelson Mandela had been free for almost a year and the rainbow nation was presenting itself in its full glory. I was excited by the significant role medicine could play in improving the lives of the millions of South Africans who had been oppressed for so long under apartheid, most of them unable to obtain quality health care.

I completed my internship at Natalspruit Hospital, a battle-racked hospital on the East Rand which for years found itself at the centre of a full-blown war between African National Congress and Inkatha Freedom Party supporters in the volatile townships of Thokoza and Katlehong. Not sure what I wanted to specialise in, I found myself joining the Paediatric Department at Natalspruit Hospital. I had discovered my calling. It was a pleasure to see children responding to treatment. Being able to make a difference to a helpless and vulnerable set of patients was not only challenging, but also enormously rewarding. I applied to join the paediatrics specialist training section at the University of the Witwatersrand in July 1994 and, four years later, I qualified as a paediatrician at Coronation Hospital, where I still work. I now head the Paediatric HIV services, which is part of the 'Enhancing Children's HIV Outcomes (ECHO)' group of clinics of which I am a founding member.

Shortly after qualifying in 1998, I realised there was a desperate need to focus on paediatric AIDS, which was devastating the children's wards. At the time children could not obtain ARVs in the public sector, so it was a case of trying to relieve their suffering as much as possible. It was horrible. You grow attached to your patients; you get to know them. The feeling doesn't leave you when a patient dies. Then you are confronted with the thought of what you could have done differently. What happened? Why did this happen to this patient? Why should a young child have to die so early?

It's tough for all the staff, not just the doctors, especially when you feel the death was preventable in the first place. When a person has an incurable disease and dies from something that you could not prevent, you come to accept their death almost as a natural thing. But when a child dies from HIV, you feel frustration and enormous anger because you know the country has failed him or her. It was frustrating to know there was a way to stop children from being infected in the first place, but we weren't putting it in place. Estimates are that HIV-positive pregnant women carry a 30 per cent risk of infecting their baby – mostly during birth and breastfeeding – but there are simple drugs that can remove the risk almost entirely.

As long ago as 1994 one of the biggest discoveries was made in the science of HIV. Researchers in the USA announced that they had found in a landmark study called ACTG 076 that mono-therapy with AZT dramatically reduced the risk of mother-to-child HIV transmission. At the same time, it was realised that a long time would pass before we could see the effective use of AZT in South Africa. Not only did it have to be given to the mother early in her pregnancy, but the cost of AZT at that time and the resistance of the government to its use were great impediments. So the critical search continued for a simpler regimen that could be given in poorer countries.

Despite the realisation that there was no ideal drug, the AIDS Law Project, the Centre for Applied Legal Studies, the Perinatal HIV Research Unit at Chris Hani Baragwanath Hospital and the AIDS Consortium were already lobbying the then Health Minister, Dr Nkosazana Dlamini-Zuma, and her department in 1997 to develop a programme and policy for the prevention of mother-to-child transmission (PMTCT). This made sense as the ruling ANC government had already stated its intention to do exactly this in its 1994 AIDS plan.

In the year that I started practising as a paediatrician, the much-awaited breakthrough came. A clinical trial in Thailand showed that a short course of AZT given to mother and child at 36 weeks still brought significant reductions in mother-to-child transmission. This I felt was surely a good indication that we could do likewise in South Africa and make a difference to the increasing numbers of HIV-infected children being born. It was great news, and my colleagues and I were excited by the prospect of being able to stem the tide of fatally ill children arriving at our institutions.

My province's Health Department was quick to respond and announced the establishment of five pilot sites where programmes using this short course of AZT would be introduced. It was a step in the right direction. At that time it was estimated that about 70,000 children were being born each year with HIV in South Africa. We could see the impact of this on the rising infant mortality statistics. At Coronation Hospital the authorities decided to push ahead with a PMTCT strategy. They said: 'Look, we've got women, they're HIV infected. There's research that shows AZT works. AZT is a registered drug in South Africa. It's been shown to be effective. There's no official policy to use it. However, there is also no official policy not to use it, either.'

So we decided to use AZT, a drug that was available in the hospital, if women had the right indications. I guess we were, in a way, bending the non-existent rules. In 1999, however, we received a message from the powers-that-be in the province telling us that we couldn't use AZT, that it was not national government policy, and that we must stop.

These incidents made us aware that we needed to put more pressure on the government to make AZT widely available. It was unacceptable that, five years after the landmark study in Thailand showing significant reduction in risks to babies born to HIV women, South Africa still did not have a PMTCT programme. The growing need for activism around the issue of accessing ARVs led to the foundation of the Treatment Action Campaign (TAC) in December 1998: one of the primary demands was that government implement a PMTCT programme.

Initially our demands and those of a growing band of activists were met by a sympathetic ear from government. In April 1999, a meeting between the TAC and Health Minister Dlamini-Zuma led to a joint statement that the price of AZT was a major barrier to a PMTCT programme and that the government would seek urgently to establish how much it could afford to pay. This never happened. At the time we believed our battle would be with the pharmaceutical companies and not the government. How wrong we were!

In June, South Africa welcomed Thabo Mbeki as Nelson Mandela's successor to the country's presidency. When Mbeki announced he had appointed Dr Manto Tshabalala-Msimang as the new Health Minister, there was a great sense of optimism. We were really excited that Zuma was no longer in charge and thought we could not do much worse. Her term of office had turned into a disaster with the *Sarafina 2* scandal and her stubborn refusal to make AZT available. We felt that with Tshabalala-Msimang we now had someone who offered a ray of hope. From the little information we could find, Tshabalala-Msimang's past spoke of her commitment to the health care of South Africans. Already while in exile she was central in establishing the ANC's health department and she had warned that something needed to be done to address AIDS. So when she was appointed Minister of Health, she sent the right signals – she had prioritised rebuilding relationships with civil society and was keen on fashioning a more purposeful partnership against AIDS.

On the research front things were moving fast. In July 1999 it was announced that a joint Uganda–US study had found a highly effective and safe drug regimen for PMTCT that was more affordable and practical than any other examined to date. Interim results demonstrated that a single oral dose of the ARV nevirapine given to an HIV-infected woman in labour and another to her baby within three days of birth reduced the transmission rate by half, compared to a similar short course of AZT. Researchers calculated that if implemented widely in developing countries, this intervention could prevent some 300,000 to 400,000 newborns each year from beginning life infected with HIV. Finally, a response was within our grasp – it was affordable and could be given during labour!

Within days the BBC reported that South Africa planned to draw on the experience of Uganda. The new Health Minister hastily boarded a plane and led a high-level delegation to find out more about Uganda's successful HIV prevention strategy. We all thought: 'Great! Go to a smaller country. It shows that South Africans were not arrogant; that we didn't know everything.' She went and came back and we were encouraged that she was so excited, but it was short-lived.

On 28 October 1999 our world was turned upside down when Mbeki stood up in the National Council of Provinces and uttered the following words: 'Many in our country have called on the Government to make the drug AZT available in our public health system. Two matters in this regard have been brought to our attention. One of these is that there are legal cases pending in this country, the United Kingdom and the United States against AZT on the basis that this drug is harmful to health.

'There also exists a large volume of scientific literature alleging that, among other things, the toxicity of this drug is such that it is in fact a danger to health. These are matters of great concern to the Government as it would be irresponsible for us not to heed the dire warnings which medical researchers have been making.

'I have therefore asked the Minister of Health, as a matter of urgency, to go into all these matters so that, to the extent that is possible, we ourselves, including our country's medical authorities, are certain of where the truth lies.

'To understand this matter better, I would urge the Honourable Members of the National Council to access the huge volume of literature on this matter available on the Internet so that all of us can approach this issue from the same base of information.'

I couldn't believe what I was hearing. And to make matters worse, it wasn't long before the Health Minister made it clear that she was prepared to toe the President's line. Two weeks later, she told Parliament that although she was aware of the positive results of AZT, there were 'other scientists' who said that not enough was yet known about the effects of the toxic profile of the drug, that the risks might well outweigh the benefits and that the drug should not be used. She instructed our drug regulatory authority, the Medicines Control Council (MCC), to review the use of AZT.

Within months the MCC released a report of its careful review of AZT, which concluded that the benefits far outweighed risks. The report was first rejected and sent back to the MCC for further work, and later ignored. All these actions and beliefs flew in the face of the opinions of the World Health Organisation and a multitude of international scientists who believed that AZT and nevirapine were the answer to PMTCT.

Amid all of this we held on to our one lifeline – nevirapine. At least the President didn't seem to have a problem with this drug. It wasn't long, however, before we realised that nevirapine was also under attack when the minister made a speech in Parliament where she confused drug trials involving nevirapine (as one drug among a combination of many) that had resulted in several deaths with its use as a PMTCT drug. This was despite the fact that there were no reports of adverse reactions to using nevirapine as a single-dose drug.

We and the activists started turning up the heat on the new Health Minister, demanding to know when the government was planning to roll out a PMTCT programme. The TAC then took a decision to back off a bit and focus its efforts on drug companies after the government asked to be given time to evaluate results from the SAINT trials – a new study being conducted by my colleagues Dr Glenda Gray and Professor James McIntyre of the Perinatal HIV Research Unit (PHRU) at Chris Hani Baragwanath Hospital. The study, which also included Coronation Hospital and King Edward Hospital in Durban, specifically looked at the safety and efficacy of nevirapine when used for PMTCT. As Coronation also formed part of the SAINT trial, we again bent the rules, by offering nevirapine to all women who came to our hospital – not only those who were part of the trial. We felt it was unethical not to do so – we knew nevirapine worked and was effective. I think the Gauteng Health Department chose to turn a blind eye.

The preliminary results of the SAINT trial were soon shared with government – it supported the use of nevirapine, but again there was no action. Hopes were high in July 2000 that President Mbeki would use the 13th International AIDS Conference in Durban to announce a PMTCT programme and endorse the use of antiretrovirals generally.

I couldn't believe my ears when Mbeki didn't even mention HIV in his speech, though he spoke passionately about poverty. This was a huge disappointment for many, if not most, conference delegates. Mbeki didn't even afford one of my patients, the child AIDS activist Nkosi Johnson, the courtesy of listening to his pleas for a PMTCT programme, as he left the stadium before Nkosi spoke. Nkosi had been infected during birth and he understood more than anyone else the difference such a programme could make.

Nkosi's eventual death in June 2001 was certainly a low point for me. There were times when he was under my care at Coronation, and seeing him slowly die was quite traumatic for many people. Ironically, Nkosi's message delivered to the thousands in Durban and the millions watching television is still very relevant today: 'I hate having AIDS because I get very sick and I get very sad when I think of all the other children and babies that are sick with AIDS. I just wish that the government can start giving AZT to pregnant HIV mothers to help stop the virus being passed on to their babies.' If this message couldn't move our decision-makers, nothing would. Nkosi got a standing ovation from the thousands of delegates from all over the world.

While nevirapine was affordable, the government went a step further during the Durban conference and declined an offer by Boehringer Ingelheim to provide a free supply of the drug for five years. Government reaction to the preliminary results of the SAINT study presented in Durban was also lukewarm, to say the least. It started to dawn on me that, no matter what we did or presented, the government was not interested in finding ways to introduce a PMTCT programme soon. The feet-dragging and procrastination were astounding.

The following month the Health Department met with scientists to assess the 'new knowledge' from the Durban conference. MINMEC (now the National Health Council), a monthly meeting of the national Health Minister and her provincial counterparts, decided that the current policy of not using AZT would continue and that the use of nevirapine, once registered, would first be tested for two years at two pilot sites per province, starting in March 2001. This was unacceptable to us. Two years would equate to many, many lives being lost and we couldn't waste any more time. While politicians had the luxury of sitting in their offices making such declarations, we on the ground had to live the reality of telling parents their children were going to die or having to fight the odds and try to relieve the suffering.

I think this was the turning point for many of us. This was when we decided we had to become vocal and that we would have to become activists. That is when we said: 'This is where we draw the line.' Towards the end of the year, a few paediatricians including Haroon Saloojee and myself formed the 'Save Our Babies' campaign. We marked its formation on World AIDS Day by issuing a petition to a representative of the Health Minister at Chris Hani Baragwanath Hospital. Within two weeks, we had managed to collect the signatures of about 273 paediatricians and child health-care practitioners including professors and heads of departments, doctors and nurses, from across the country, demanding action on the part of government to begin a PMTCT programme without further delay. No response from government to this petition was ever received.

This was also the first time I met the TAC's leaders Mark Heywood and Zackie Achmat. Zackie, Mark, Haroon and I got together at Coronation Hospital. We realised that we could work well together. The activists at the time needed accurate medical information as to what was scientifically needed and we medical people needed to know how to deal with HIV from a human rights and legal point of view. We simply didn't have those skills. At the first meeting we didn't really talk about the possibility of a court case. We may have mentioned it, but we agreed that the way to go would be to try and meet with the minister and her department.

Not prepared to continue toeing the government's line, the Western Cape started using nevirapine in January 2001 amid the threat of legal action from the Health Department. Nationally, the pilot sites agreed by MINMEC were due to begin their work by March, but this was continually delayed as nevirapine had still not been registered by the MCC for PMTCT. Not surprisingly, the media started accusing the government of interfering with the registration process. Even more mindboggling was the revelation that the PMTCT protocol would have to be submitted to Cabinet for approval. On 18 April, nevirapine was finally formally registered for PMTCT. MCC minutes given to the TAC revealed that it had already been registered in November 2000, but that there had been a six month delay over the wording of the package insert – something that could have taken far less time if there was the will to press ahead.

In June, Haroon Saloojee and I, the TAC and giant trade union Cosatu, finally met with the Health Minister in her Pretoria office. We were hoping we could convince her to take the PMTCT programme beyond the pilot sites. The disastrous meeting started with the minister aiming her trademark personal insults at the TAC. She then berated a number of people about a range of issues including the donation of the anti-fungal medication Diflucan, which had been negotiated by the TAC. The minister left after an hour and discussions continued with the Director-General, Dr Ayanda Ntsaluba, and the head of the HIV/AIDS directorate, Dr Nono Simelela. They were at pains to respond to our concern as to what to offer mothers who rightfully requested some form of PMTCT intervention like nevirapine. They said they had no answer to this ethical dilemma. Leaving Pretoria that day, I think we realised we would have to consider other measures to force government to act.

In a final attempt to try to get things moving, the TAC followed up with a first letter of demand to the Health Minister and nine provincial MECs. The minister ordered the provinces not to respond individually. Her own response contained a list of barriers to the rolling out of the PMTCT programme including viral resistance, breastfeeding and sustainability. We realised that we would have to turn to the courts. Although we really didn't want to go this route, as we considered it a waste of money, resources and time, the government was simply not prepared to engage with us. How could we have confidence in the process if the attitude was simply: sorry, the door is closed. It produced a real feeling of powerlessness – no matter what you said or what argument you presented, no matter if a thousand experts wrote a letter to the minister, no matter that the WHO made a statement, the door was closed. The government showed complete arrogance in not responding to this clarion call from every quarter for a PMTCT programme. It forced the TAC and its allies to take the next step, and many people offered us encouragement to do so.

Left with no option, the TAC, Save Our Babies and the Children's Rights Centre filed a case on 21 August 2001. We sought a declaration that the current policy was unconstitutional and asked that the government be ordered to make nevirapine available to pregnant women who gave birth in the public health sector, and to their babies. Not surprisingly, the government opposed the application and attempted to persuade the court that its nevirapine pilot programme was reasonable, rational and not a violation of constitutional rights. We had ten days to respond to the voluminous papers from government, which our legal team said were aimed to confuse and deceive. We managed to draw on international contacts who supplied affidavits countering a number of distortions, but the final roll of the dice was an expert affidavit to refute the claim of lack of capacity in the state – Mark Heywood believes that this proved to be decisive in turning the judgment in our favour. At short notice, my University of Witwatersrand colleague Professor Helen Schneider, drawing largely from the government's own published reports, showed how there was in fact significant latent capacity to support the provision of nevirapine in eight of the nine provinces and concluded that 'the complexity of a PMTCT programme is no greater than tackling malnutrition, tuberculosis and other chronic diseases – aspects that the South African health system has committed itself to dealing with'.

What we had feared all along was slowly starting to become clear: the PMTCT policy was based upon a political decision taken at the highest level of government.

Within four months of the court action being launched, Judge Chris Botha handed down his judgment to a tense and expectant court. He found in favour of TAC, Save Our Babies and the Children's Rights Centre. He commented that in government's arguments there was 'no unqualified commitment to reach the rest of the population in any given time or at any given rate … A programme that is open-ended and that leaves everything to the future cannot be said to be coherent, progressive and purposeful.' Botha declared that a countrywide PMTCT programme was an ineluctable obligation of the state. In a blow to government, he instructed them to allow nevirapine to be prescribed where it was 'medically indicated' and where, in the opinion of the doctors acting in consultation with the hospital medical superintendent, there was capacity to do so. Botha also ordered the government to develop 'an effective comprehensive national programme to prevent or reduce MTCT and return to the Court with this programme for future scrutiny before 21 March 2002'.

Our celebrations were short-lived when within days the Health Minister announced the government would seek leave to appeal directly to the Constitutional Court. There was a lot of unhappiness within the

Health Department over this decision and we were told that Director-General Ntsaluba told MINMEC that he could no longer defend the indefensible. TAC used this time to prepare a new application to the Pretoria High Court to seek an order to execute part of the Botha judgment. Two other provinces, Gauteng and KwaZulu-Natal, joined their Western Cape counterparts, and their premiers publicly announced their decision to expand their PMTCT programmes.

Shortly after the provincial announcements, Mbeki opened Parliament and for the first time appeared to signal a shift in government policy by promising that 'continuing work will be done to monitor the efficacy of ARV interventions against MTCT in the sites already operational and any new ones that may be decided on'. In a television interview a few days later, he explicitly stated that provinces with the capacity and resources to do so must be allowed to expand their programmes. Gauteng Premier Mbhazima Shilowa wasted no time in announcing his province's rollout. He promised that in the next financial year he would ensure that all public hospitals and large community health centres would provide nevirapine. The Health Minister was clearly not on the same page as the President and publicly rebuked Shilowa, earning herself the 'Dr No' tag from *The Star* newspaper. She made a statement dissociating herself from Gauteng, claiming it was in breach of the resolution taken by MINMEC.

TAC returned to the Pretoria High Court and, ten days later, the judge granted an execution order. Government still opted to seek leave to appeal against the judgment directly to the Constitutional Court.The appeal was heard in March. The judge again said that he had to balance the loss of lives against prejudice that could never amount to more than inconvenience. He thought it was unlikely that another court would find his decision wrong.

During this time, the WHO and UNAIDS also released a statement supporting the use of nevirapine to prevent HIV transmission. However, it was still not the end of the nightmare. The Health Minister was soon occupying the headlines again when responding to the court ruling during an interview on SABC television. Transcripts reveal that, when asked whether she would be prepared to 'follow what the court says, given these new concerns around the drug', she replied: 'My own view is that the judiciary cannot prescribe from the bench – and that we have a regulatory authority in this country that is interacting with the regulatory authority [Food and Drug Administration] of the USA and I think we must allow them to assist us in reaching conclusions.'

The interviewer then tried to clarify the minister's statement, asking whether she would stand by whatever the court decided. The minister responded: 'No, I think the court and the judiciary must also listen to the regulatory authority, both in this country and the regulatory authority of the US.'

Interviewer: 'So you're saying no?'

Minister: 'I say no. I am saying no.'

She later retracted these statements.

Still not ready to raise the white flag, the government launched a further and final application for leave to appeal – directly to the Constitutional Court. The application was heard in April and a day later the court refused leave to appeal. *The Star*'s headline the following day offered some light relief in what was a very serious matter: 'YES, you will, Dr No'.

While we waited for our day in the Constitutional Court to arrive, Cabinet released a surprising statement promising a universal roll-out plan as soon as possible. For the first time, the government had acknowledged that ARVs could help improve the condition of people living with AIDS. Until then ARV was a taboo word and there was almost a conspiracy of silence around the effectiveness of ARVs. Nowadays everyone says we're running the best programme, but nobody wants to look back and say there was a time when ARVs could not be talked about.

On the first day of the Constitutional Court case, 2 May, activists across the country marched under the banner 'Stand up for your rights'.

For two days, the legal teams presented their cases and then the waiting game started. I didn't attend the court case. I was happy to leave this part to the legal experts and rather use my time to support the use of nevirapine at Coronation Hospital. Almost two months later, the Constitutional Court gave judgment in the challenge to the government's policy of limiting the provision of nevirapine to a few pilot sites. The Health Minister and her nine provincial ministers were ordered 'without delay' to lift restrictions on the availability of nevirapine. Thus ended the legal contest – one year and about 100,000 infant HIV infections after the start of the case, as the *Sowetan* put it.

In the days that followed, the Health ministry offered no apology and no admission that it had been wrong. On the contrary, a defiant Health Minister told a journalist at the 14th International AIDS Conference in Barcelona that nevirapine was 'poison' and that she was unhappy with the Constitutional Court ruling. Unperturbed by the minister's earlier attempts to discipline him, Gauteng Premier Shilowa announced that nevirapine was now available at 70 per cent of the province's health facilities. There are not many occasions when politicians make one feel proud to be associated with them, but this brave premier certainly got my support, especially since his job was on the line.

Such announcements must have been a source of great embarrassment to the national government, which had been trying to create the impression that the hurdles to making PMTCT widely available were just too big. But here was a province showing that it could be done, and in fact had already done so for more than a year in places like Coronation Hospital.

Four years later, the Health Minister would again use an international AIDS conference, this time in Toronto, to embarrass her country when she opened the South African stand in the exhibition centre, surrounded by lemons, garlic and African potato – clearly showing what she thought the priorities should be. This for me was one of the lowest points. I was not in Toronto, but many colleagues were. There was so much frustration as we had become the laughing stock of the world.

Another low point for me was the firing of the popular Deputy Health Minister, Nozizwe Madlala-Routledge. In her we saw a champion: she was prepared to speak out for the rights of patients and for the good of the HIV programme. Truly speaking 'truth to power,' as she put it. She was someone who was not prepared to toe the line and for that reason she was sacked. Many of us felt angered by her dismissal: we believed President Mbeki had sacked the wrong minister. We all had enormous respect for her because of her integrity and outspoken nature, whether about HIV or babies dying. It was tough for us as we were making such good progress with the National Strategic Plan (NSP) and the South African National AIDS Council was taking shape. The NSP is a plan that sets very clear targets on reducing the rate of prevention and making sure people who need treatment can get it by 2011. The plan was the culmination of many, many hours of negotiation and sharing of ideas between government, civil society and all those affected by the epidemic. There was a very real danger that this newfound partnership between civil society and government could be destroyed as a result of her being fired. But we hung on and things continued moving forward.

It was difficult to remain in the field and not become frustrated, angry and resentful all the time – especially when Tshabalala-Msimang made controversial statements. One learnt to take her with a pinch of salt.

We couldn't get away from the fact that HIV had become politicised when we were expected to follow ministerial orders rather than the best international recommendations. It was hampering our efforts to save lives – having to wait for a ministerial letter to arrive and say 'you may start' or 'you may not start'. It went against what we believed in. But it doesn't help to dwell on the negatives.

There have been further victories along the way. Government has agreed to introduce dual therapy – AZT and nevirapine – for use in PMTCT, years after the WHO had recommended it and much poorer countries have implemented it. I think that our programme, had it not been for the unfortunate politics that we've suffered, would have put us years ahead. We've lost ground because of failed politics and I think the officials of President Thabo Mbeki's government failed by not being forthright in coming out and saying, 'Sorry, we've messed up. We've followed a failed policy.'

The national Department of Health is very quick to take the credit for programmes that are running today with large numbers and claim that we are winning the fight, but it's on the back of a lot of activism and struggle, the hard work of HIV clinicians and activists alike who have swum against the tide. They are the unsung heroes.

This kind of obstructionist attitude on the part of government spurred many of us into action. I didn't come into medicine wanting to be an activist. I wanted to be a simple doctor, treating children. But the HIV/AIDS epidemic, for all its politics and controversies, has forced me to be militant; it has forced me to be an activist. I didn't know the first thing about advocacy before HIV. But with HIV you could not move ahead without being outspoken and being an advocate, and for that I owe my thanks to the two previous Ministers of Health.

Sadly, the battle is still far from over. If you go to any of our paediatric wards right now, we are still admitting very ill children who die in their droves. South Africa today has one of the worst infant and under-five mortality rates and currently it does not look like we're on track to meet the Millennium Development Goals on child and maternal survival. This is despite the fact that we have had PMTCT and ARV treatment programmes for several years now. We haven't by any stretch of the imagination won the war against HIV. We're still battling it in a big way. At the end of the framed oath hanging on my wall there is a quote from the Qur'an: 'Whoever killeth a human being . . . it is as if he hath killed all mankind. And if he saveth a human life, he hath saved the life of all mankind.' The time will come when history will judge severely the senseless waste of time and life because of the poor HIV/AIDS policies and lack of progress of our past. But for now we cannot afford to look back. We need to look ahead and try not to repeat the inexcusable mistakes of the past.

(I want to acknowledge and thank my friend and colleague Mark Heywood, head of the AIDS Law Project, for allowing me to use his thorough writings so liberally in formulating my timeline and putting dates to events. More specifically I would like to acknowledge the information I gleaned from his paper 'Preventing Mother to Child HIV Transmission in South Africa', which was published in the *South African Journal on Human Rights*.)

*Dr Ashraf Hassen Coovadia is the head of Paediatric HIV services at Rahima Moosa Mother and Child Hospital (formerly Coronation Hospital), Johannesburg, where he has been for the last ten years working within the Department of Paediatrics and Child Health of the University of the Witwatersrand. He is married and has two children aged 14 and 12 years. Dr Coovadia currently plays an active role in advocacy and treatment support in the areas of paediatric HIV and PMTCT, within both civil society and government structures.

5

Daring to care: A doctor's persecution in Mpumalanga

by
Thys von Mollendorff

In 1999 I became the senior medical superintendent of Rob Ferreira Hospital in Nelspruit, where I had worked for nine years. At first I did not want to be a superintendent because it entails a lot of administrative duties and my passion lies with clinical work. But I was the most senior doctor at the hospital and best equipped for the position. After some encouragement from my staff, I accepted the post. At the time, health services were rapidly declining at all provincial hospitals and my dream was to restore our hospital to being the flagship of medical care by providing the best possible care to our patients.

When I took up duties, the statistics for Mpumalanga province were increasingly gloomy. From the antenatal survey, we saw an increase in HIV infection from 26 to 30 per cent in the space of three years, which meant that by 2000 more than a million people were infected with the virus. At the same time, cases of rape were also increasing every year. Alarmingly, the women who were being raped were getting younger and younger.

In June 1999 the local Victim Empowerment Committee (a government-driven initiative involving collaboration between all state departments, NGOs and community-based organisations) visited Rob Ferreira Hospital and reminded management that, according to the

National Policy Guidelines for Victims of Sexual Offences, we were supposed to establish a care room for rape survivors. I was very keen to start the care room and seized the opportunity to improve the plight of rape survivors. Towards the end of 1999, we identified an unused office in the Outpatients' Department. Apart from being quiet, private and adjacent to the Casualty Department, it also had a private waiting area. With assistance from the Department of Public Works and funding from the Police Service, the room was refurbished and equipped for its new purpose.

As a result of the Nelspruit community's concern about the soaring rape statistics and the high prevalence of HIV, a Rape Indaba was held on 16 February 2000. Everybody interested in the plight of rape survivors was invited to attend the meeting in the Civic Centre. Representatives from government departments, the Victim Empowerment Committee and some NGOs and interested parties were all present. At the meeting, a list was drawn up of volunteers willing to help in the areas closest to them. From these volunteers, a co-ordinating committee was elected. They decided to call themselves the Greater Nelspruit Rape Intervention Project (Grip), with a focus mainly on the provision of trauma counselling and assistance to rape survivors. Barbara Kenyon was elected as the chairperson and CEO of Grip, and the organisation was set up as an NGO with a constitution and a fund-raising programme. The local Victim Empowerment Committee invited Grip to combine efforts by joining them in the fight against AIDS. With the help of LifeLine, Grip trained 15 counsellors in emergency defusing counselling and debriefing. The local newspapers kept the community informed on Grip's progress and soon everyone applauded them for their invaluable services.

When the Victim Empowerment Committee visited the hospital for the second time on 23 February 2000, they enquired about the progress we had made in implementing a care room and brought along Barbara Kenyon to introduce her to us. During our conversation about the care room, Grip offered their expertise in emergency counselling to rape survivors and their assistance in many other ways. Grip started to provide counselling services during March 2000, becoming part of a multi-disciplinary team that provided emergency treatment in the care room. They were afforded access to the hospital, in the same manner as all the other 49 NGOs, including the Cancer Association of South Africa, LifeLine and FAMSA, which assisted patients at the hospital.

The care room was officially opened on 17 April 2000. This was announced on the front page of the local newspaper a few days later. At a time when rape survivors were shamefully neglected in state institutions, we dared to care. It was a proud moment for us. We were providing a unique one-stop treatment facility for rape survivors. When a rape survivor arrived at the hospital, she was immediately taken to the care room. The police were then called to take statements and to open a sexual assault file. The doctor then carried out the medico-legal examination in private, with the assistance of a sister. The doctor also completed a form in which he documented his findings. After the examination, Grip was called to do counselling for patients who agreed to it. Although the Department of Health provided prophylactic medicines to prevent the transmission of sexually transmitted diseases and supplied emergency contraception, no provision was made for antiretrovirals to prevent the transmission of HIV for rape survivors.

Rape survivors also received a courtesy pack, collected and assembled by Grip from donations by local businesses, containing a facecloth, soap, toothbrush and toothpaste, sanitary towel and a pair of panties. After the examination, the victim was offered a bath and clean clothes. Apart from the initial emergency counselling, the victim was then referred to other counselling services like LifeLine, for in-depth counselling. Grip also provided assistance up to and during the court proceedings, which included pre-court training for rape survivors.

Statistics that were kept revealed a shocking trend: The number of children who were raped had escalated dramatically. Of the 477 rape survivors treated at Rob Ferreira Hospital during 2001, 219 (almost 50 per cent) were under the age of 15. At first Barbara and the counsellors of Grip were content to do only counselling and caring, but they soon felt it was morally indefensible to see to only psychological needs. Most of the children had been exposed to HIV: if they were not given antiretrovirals within 72 hours, they could contract the virus and eventually die from it.

The National Policy Guidelines stated that rape survivors should be referred for voluntary counselling and testing (VCT). For those who agreed, blood was taken for a rapid HIV test to determine their HIV status. The guidelines also enjoined healthcare institutions to provide any medical treatment that might be required. For everyone at Rob Ferreira Hospital working with rape survivors, Grip included, the same question arose: what was the use of determining the person's HIV status if there was no intention of acting on the information? After sharing our thoughts and realising that AZT and 3TC were the best medicines to use as post-exposure prophylaxis (PEP), we decided to keep PEP starter packs in the care room.

A starter pack contained enough antiretroviral tablets for three days. Grip funded the packs with money they had raised. If the rapid HIV test was negative, Grip would advise the rape survivor about the advantages of PEP with antiretrovirals and provide her with a starter pack if requested. An Elisa test was also done to confirm the HIV result. As the test results were available only after 24 hours, the starter pack would carry the patients until then. If the Elisa test turned out to be negative as well, the doctor issued a prescription as a preventive measure. The patient could then collect the rest of the 28-day antiretroviral at a private dispensary, also funded by Grip at no cost to either patient or the Department of Health.

At the time, only two pharmacies in Nelspruit were open at night until 10 pm. Sometimes, by the time that rape survivors had reached one, the chance for the optimal effect of AZT and 3TC was lost forever. The starter packs helped to initiate PEP in time.

Rape survivors now received the best possible care, and we were proud of our achievement. For the first time it actually felt as if we were making a difference in their lives. It filled me with hope and joy when I saw how just a little care and planning could help rape survivors. In the beautiful Mpumalanga, place of the rising sun, a new day was born for rape survivors.

Grip's field workers also did follow-up visits to rape survivors in the community to repeat the HIV tests at different intervals and to assist patients who suffered from minor adverse effects from antiretrovirals, such as nausea or diarrhoea. The Department of Health did not have any counsellors or field workers to fill this role nor did they have the financial means or human resources to implement and maintain the National Policy Guidelines. Without the help of NGOs it was doubtful if the Department could sustain the assistance to rape survivors.

Although a much better service was now being delivered to rape survivors, forces were building up against our efforts. When an official from the national Department of Health in Pretoria phoned the provincial Health MEC, Sibongile Manana, around September 2000 to enquire about the care room and the provision of antiretrovirals, all hell broke loose. Manana immediately banned the provision of antiretrovirals and tried to evict Grip from Rob Ferreira and Themba hospitals. She also charged the senior management (myself, as the senior medical superintendent, as well as the nursing service manager, the secretary and the senior social worker) of Rob Ferreira Hospital with misconduct. The charges were withdrawn on 1 March 2001 and Grip was allowed back into the hospital on condition that they refrain from supplying AZT and 3TC.

But shortly after the charges against the 'big five' were dropped, they were reinstated again. One moment Grip was allowed back into the hospital, and the next they received an eviction order. This happened four times! It seemed Manana was never going to stop her harassment and that we were being victimised because of her embarrassment at learning from Pretoria that she was completely unaware of what was happening in the hospitals under her jurisdiction.

At the time, the guidelines in the national policy on sexual offences made provision for emergency medical treatment to prevent transmission of HIV. But the Department of Health in Mpumalanga took no notice of these guidelines and never replied to the letter from the Victim Empowerment Committee requesting post-exposure prophylaxis. As management, we asked for directives about antiretrovirals but never received any. For six months, we tried to arrange an urgent meeting between Manana and the hospital superintendents in Mpumalanga but failed. There was no guidance or assistance from the provincial office. I had to act on my own conscience to protect my patients from contracting HIV and my staff from taking the blame for the Department's ignorance. In the end I was accused of bringing the Department into disrepute for applying my own mind.

It became really difficult to manage and control the hospital because there was no transparency and the policies constantly changed without prior notice. The Department seldom put anything in writing and we lived in constant fear of getting into trouble for enforcing existing rules, not knowing if they had been changed in the meantime. I acted according to the best of my knowledge but feared that because the Department didn't share information, there could be grave consequences for the patients, the staff and the Department as well.

We were torn between dual loyalties: should we obey the political head of the Department of Health or put our patients first? For me as a physician, patients always come first and, as a public officer, I was required to act according to the Public Service Regulations (4.1.3): 'An employee shall put the public's interest first in the execution of his or her duties.' Doctors also follow the ethical rules of the Health Professional Council of South Africa, which state that doctors have an ethical obligation to act in the best interest of their patients.

The withdrawal of the charges on 1 March 2001 against the

management of Rob Ferreira Hospital was mere window-dressing. Manana was miserable with the way things had gone and it was now time for her to change her tactics. The National Education, Health and Allied Workers' Union (Nehawu) tried to get rid of some of the staff, by encouraging patients to report them for alleged neglect or not doing proper voluntary counselling and testing. They also tried to dig up dirt on staff members by getting access to personnel files from our human resources office. They even tried to re-open a case against a radiologist three years after the case had been settled. The provincial Labour Relations office dismissed this, however, saying: 'Common sense tells you that you cannot charge a person twice for the same offence ... The previous Superintendent handled the matter correctly.'

Suddenly, Nehawu started to challenge every decision I made. The leadership of the hospital branch of Nehawu would frequently storm into my office, taking up much of my valuable time by questioning my every move and trying their utmost to frustrate me. One of the women always burst out in laughter whenever I said something, shaking her head as if whatever I said was ridiculous. They threatened me with mass action on numerous occasions because, in their view, transformation at the hospital was too slow. To them, transformation had a different meaning, and retaining skills and experience was not of any importance. During one of the numerous mass actions of Nehawu, angry protesters ran through the hospital screaming and shouting, overturning dustbins, whilst terrified patients tried to hide from them. Nurses who tried to clean up the mess were met by angry Nehawu members. I also suspected that my phone was tapped because Nehawu brought up confidential information that I shared only with close friends. Everyone became too scared to inform head office of what was happening and did not dare to say how he or she really felt, because Nehawu reported everything to Manana. Was Nehawu the 'sources of information' that she referred to?

There was also a 'witch-hunt' conducted at the hospital, which impaired trust even further. On 2 August 2001, I was attending a departmental 'Leadership, visioning and alignment' workshop at Philadelphia Hospital when Lucky Molobela, personal assistant of the MEC (who was later promoted to Director of Strategic Planning), conveniently visited Rob Ferreira Hospital in my absence. He informed the hospital of his visit only 15 minutes prior to his arrival. On my return, the staff were upset and immediately informed me of his visit. Molobela had told the senior management that he was part of a task team from the provincial head office that was looking into management systems. He said that head office wanted to assist all the departments in their efforts to reform and encouraged them to share their experiences. Molobela warned the management not to think he was ignorant, because he could assure them that he was well informed. The secretary told him that we had nothing to hide and asked everybody to give his or her full co-operation.

One of the matrons, whom Molobela interrogated, reported that he had intimidated her by saying that he had heard things about her: 'You interfere with your comrades . . . if I was a woman, I would have cried!' He wanted her to report on any incidents of racism that she had witnessed over the past few years. He added that the report had to be at least three pages long. She replied that there might have been a few minor incidents, but that these had been promptly dealt with internally. He then accused her of going against the Department's wishes by calling Grip to attend to rape survivors (this was after Grip's rights were fully restored) and warned her that she should not be surprised if they phoned her for another talk.

I was upset that the visit of the 'task team' had been conveniently scheduled in my absence, and it turned out to be nothing less than a witch-hunt using unethical tactics. I reported my dissatisfaction to the new district manager and made it clear that it was unacceptable that we were not informed of the visit ahead of time. As Molobela indicated that he was coming back, I requested that the new district manager, Gladness Mathebula, should give us a schedule of the departments he wanted to visit and the people he wanted to interrogate, so that the whole hospital wouldn't be disrupted and urgent services delayed because of his visit. I also wanted to check to see whether Molobela was indeed sent by head office. The workshop I attended on the day of his visit had been arranged to build team spirit between middle and senior management. Molobela's conduct contributed to just the opposite.

Nevertheless, conditions at the hospital soon took a turn for the worse. Nehawu launched a campaign of terror. On 1 September 2001, the hospital branch of Nehawu took the senior management of Rob Ferreira Hospital hostage in their offices. They demanded that we bring one of the senior medical officers to them so they could 'deal with him'. They were referring to one of our senior doctors, whom they had been targeting for a long time because he supported Grip and antiretrovirals. Leading the protesting crowd was a male staff nurse, who was head of the hospital branch of Nehawu. The crowd repeated after him as he shouted: 'Bring the doctor, we want to kill him! Bring the doctor, we want to assault him!' The crowd grew bigger and was in a state of mass hysteria. The doctor's life was in real danger, so I phoned him on his cellphone and warned him to leave the premises by the back door, but before he could reach his car in safety, they spotted him and chased him from the hospital grounds with sticks, like a dog, while continually threatening to kill him.

This doctor was also the chair of the hospital's HIV committee. Shortly before he was targeted and chased from the hospital and humiliated in front of his colleagues, he had written a letter to the MEC to ask her for clarity on the unwritten policy of the province on the non-provision of antiretrovirals. He wanted to know what had to be done in the light of the Department of Health's policy documents 'Batho Pele' and the 'Patients' Rights Charter', if patients demanded antiretroviral medication. He said that many patients were making such demands: pregnant women, HIV-positive mothers, rape victims, HIV patients and the families of those infected. The patients argued that if people in the province of the Western Cape had the privilege of receiving antiretroviral medication, why couldn't they? The doctor also pointed out that owing to the medico-legal implications of HIV/AIDS issues, it was important that head office indicate if they would be willing to endorse an indemnity document for the non-issuing of HIV antiretroviral drugs. He asked for a prompt reply. The only reply he received was to be humiliated in front of all his colleagues and patients. I immediately reported the incident to the provincial head of the Department of Health. The doctor was back at work the following week.

Just as matters at Rob Ferreira Hospital seemed to calm down, large crowds of Nehawu members would march through the hospital, as if the place belonged to them. They shouted slogans as far as they went. They were mostly up in arms about issues that could only be resolved by the head office.

Many other doctors were victimised. One of the doctors at the provincial head office was also charged with misconduct because he, together with another NGO, had started a home-based care project as an alternative to hospitalisation for AIDS patients in the rural areas of Mpumalanga (Lowveld area). This enlightened vision could have alleviated the workload of the hospital's personnel, giving AIDS patients the choice of recovering in friendly, familiar surroundings and having their families involved.

Another doctor, Dr Malcolm Naudé, was refused a medical officer's post after he completed his community service year because he openly supported Grip and the provision of antiretrovirals. Initially, he had been told verbally of his appointment in a junior medical officer post, but when Manana tried to evict Grip the second time from the hospital, he had written a supportive affidavit to make the court aware of their good work. Thereafter his application forms were mysteriously 'lost' several times after we resubmitted them. In the end, I was told that he could forget about ever obtaining a post at the hospital. Naudé took his case to the Labour Court, and after a seven-year battle he was finally vindicated in 2007. Judge C.J. Musi ruled that Naudé's dismissal was unfair and ordered the Mpumalanga Health Department to pay his legal costs and R100,000 in compensation. The judge described Manana's rule as 'tyrannical' and 'dictatorial' and some of the Health Department officials, who had appeared as witnesses in the case, as liars.

Nehawu was now openly harassing staff when they called Grip to assist rape survivors. The union intimidated them by saying that it would not defend them if the Department charged them for collaborating with Grip. To avoid confusion and to protect them, I put up a notice in the Casualty Department to inform staff of the procedures in handling rape victims. It was based on the agreement reached in October 2000: 'The status quo remains. When a rape survivor arrives in Casualty, the Casualty sister will contact the South African Police, to take a statement; the doctor on first call, to perform the medical-legal examination; a sister, to assist the doctor; and the NGO, Grip, for emergency counselling and support.'

Manana announced in a press release as well as in her speech to the local legislature on 13 October 2000 that she would not tolerate any 'outside initiative'. She accused Grip of 'sneaking into the institutions as illegal squatters, blackmailing and undermining the government'. She also alleged that 'The lives of poor black people were placed under serious threat by these organisations, which claimed to have the patient's interest at heart, but ignored Government policy on antiretrovirals.'

Manana was relentless in getting rid of everyone who was involved in the provision of antiretrovirals, and finally found a scapegoat. The district manager of the Ehlanzeni district was suspended, disciplined and demoted. But sacrificing her was not enough, for soon afterwards the Department and Manana turned their wrath on me. I was suspended on 6 November 2001 and had to face a government tribunal. For more than two and a half years, I was involved in legal action. I paid a heavy price for caring. I was locked out of my place of work; accused of 'gross misconduct' and 'gross insubordination' and was even called a liar on national TV. The reign of terror continued in the Department and left everybody too afraid to open their mouths. Many became discouraged and left because they just could not take the stress anymore. They chose not to challenge the 'mighty' state.

I tried my best to put an end to the violation of rape survivors' human rights, as it seemed that our outstanding Bill of Rights held no guarantees for them. When I was summoned to the Premier's building for my disciplinary hearing, I realised that the struggle to clear my name had only just begun. I endured five gruelling days in front of a government tribunal, being unfairly charged under an act (the Public Finance Management Act) that was not yet implemented at the time, on grounds that I did not have the authority to give an NGO access to the hospital. The Department of Health was ignorant, however, of its own policies; for example, they did not even know that the National Policy Guidelines gave clear instructions to prepare a care room and to provide counselling services, preferably on the hospital premises, by making use of NGOs. The provision of antiretrovirals did not form part of the formal charges against me, but the questioning revolved solely around that subject, even though the National Policy Guidelines made provision for emergency medical treatment to prevent transmission of sexually transmitted diseases.

I was not considered worthy of receiving the outcome of the disciplinary hearing in a dignified manner and was handed a letter at a busy traffic intersection at the turnoff to the airport, pronouncing me guilty of gross misconduct relating to gross insubordination because I gave an NGO access to the hospital premises to do counselling. All the letters I had written to inform the provincial Department of Health of the declining health services at the hospital were now used as 'proof ' of my insubordination.

Although I immediately appealed, I was not allowed to attend my own appeal hearing. The Labour Court seemed my only chance to get a fair hearing, but the Department of Health did everything in its power to prevent this from happening and my application failed because the Labour Court judge ruled that there was no urgency in the matter and that I had to follow the long route of arbitration and conciliation.

I had to live with continual stress to clear my name and prove that I had acted correctly. On 10 March 2003 the Department of Health suddenly settled out of court. Part of the reason for this sudden turn-around was that the Mpumalanga Department of Health could ill afford to point fingers at anybody else. The media had revealed that the Department had squandered R6 million, which had been earmarked for HIV/AIDS. In a damning report, the Attorney-General found that the money had been spent on the development of a cultural village, youth prayer days and youth bashes, and soccer tournaments. In addition, payments for catering and transport were made to non-existent companies. At the same time it came to light that tenders had been rigged to benefit family members of departmental officials. The report concluded that fraud and corruption reigned in the Department of Health in Mpumalanga.

Nevertheless, while all this money was being wasted, Manana victimised and harassed everybody who cared for rape survivors and provided post-exposure prophylaxis. The small care room was an example of excellent use of government property, as was prescribed in the new Public Finance Management Act. Whilst we were trying to do our best for the public with very few resources, the Department squandered millions of rands on trivia. Manana banned antiretrovirals although they had been scientifically proven to be the best treatment to prevent HIV transmission, because she said that the government first wanted to do its own research to make sure that the patients were not 'poisoned'. Felicitously, the Deputy Director-General of the province advised Ms Manana not to spend taxpayers' money on personal feuds but to direct her attention to her duties in the Health Department.

After this debacle, trust was irreparably damaged and I could not stay on in the public sector. I left to work for a community clinic and hospice that relies entirely on donor funds. In the past, terminally ill

AIDS patients came to the hospice to die in dignity, but this all changed after the NGO 'Right to Care' sponsored antiretrovirals for people in this area. The role of the hospice has now changed to that of a high-care ward and patients who came in on trolleys and wheelchairs – a few gasps away from death – often walk out again after starting antiretroviral treatment.

It warms my heart whenever I see a patient who has been on the brink of death return to life again. I know there is hope for HIV/AIDS patients and that these 'poisonous drugs' really work. Early diagnosis and effective management allow people with HIV/AIDS to lead a relatively normal and productive life. With continuing research, new medicines are being developed which will make it easier to manage HIV and AIDS. If we can stop the spread of the HIV virus by preventing mother-to-child transmission, provide PEP for rape survivors and treat occupational injuries effectively, there is hope for the future. Together with the practice of safe sex and faithfulness, it might just be possible one day to eradicate HIV from the world.

*Dr Thys von Mollendorff, author of the book Dare to Care, *is currently employed by 'Right to Care' at the Aids Care and Training Centre (ACTS), a community clinic and hospice near White River in Mpumalanga.*

6

Government's strange bedfellows

by
Kerry Cullinan

In June 2005, Anthony Brink and a group of young Europeans set up a stall in the exhibition centre at the national AIDS conference in Durban. From it they dished out oranges and pamphlets that condemned antiretroviral medication as poison.

Brink, the country's foremost AIDS dissident, clearly enjoyed the opportunity to throw ideological stones at the conference, which was attended by the country's top HIV/AIDS specialists and activists. Repeatedly insinuating that he had the ear of President Thabo Mbeki, Brink had often launched highly personal attacks on those who questioned Mbeki's AIDS dissident stance, candidly admitting that it is of 'vital importance' to 'always play the man as hard as the ball'. Many of those on the receiving end of his vitriol were at the conference, including Olive Shisana, François Venter, Salim Abdool Karim, Jerry Coovadia, Glenda Gray and James McIntyre. These internationally renowned HIV/AIDS experts had been spurned by the Mbeki government, yet it had embraced a man like Brink.

Whippet-thin with a sharp face and piercing blue eyes, Brink seems to delight in swimming against convention. At university in the 1980s, he wore his hair short when his friends had theirs long. He opted to become a prosecutor in Pietermaritzburg when most of his peers shunned the

apartheid state. By the end of 2003 and in his late forties Brink was, by
his own admission, 'at a loose end'. He quit his job as a magistrate in
a small Eastern Cape town and moved to Cape Town. There he grew
his hair long and reinvented himself as an activist, fighting against
antiretroviral medication and the 'myth' of HIV.

Brink is part of a faction of dissidents called the 'Perth Group'. In a
nutshell, they argue that HIV has never been isolated as an externally
acquired retrovirus; that there is no evidence that HIV causes acquired
immune deficiency syndrome (AIDS) or that HIV can be sexually
transmitted or transmitted from mothers to babies. They also believe
that HIV tests are unreliable as they do not specifically identify HIV
antibodies. Aside from questioning the existence of HIV, Brink
is renowned for his hatred of antiretroviral medicine, particularly
zidovudine (AZT), which he has repeatedly described as being
poisonous. He has campaigned relentlessly against AZT – a standard
drug in South Africa's antiretroviral treatment programme. Like many
dissidents, Brink argues that some ARVs cause immune deficiency and
are the real cause of 'AIDS'.

Brink claims to have been the first person to have alerted Mbeki to
the dangers of AZT, in July 1999. According to Brink, Mbeki 'became
turned on to the trouble about AZT', when he read Brink's manuscript
'Debating AZT'. Brink had sent the manuscript to Health Minister
Manto Tshabalala-Msimang, who then passed it on to the President.
Ian Roberts, adviser to the Health Minister at the time, admitted to
receiving the manuscript and passing it on to her.

In October 1999, Mbeki famously warned in an address to the
National Council of Provinces that AZT was toxic. Interestingly, he also
mentioned legal cases 'pending in this country, the United Kingdom
and the United States against AZT on the basis that this drug is harmful
to health'. The South African case he was referring to was the claim
made by Annet Hayman against the manufacturers of AZT, which she
believed killed her husband James Hayman. At the time, the case was

being spearheaded by Brink, but it collapsed without getting out of the starting blocks.

It is unclear how Mbeki made the jump from questioning the safety of AZT to questioning the entire thesis that HIV causes AIDS. What is known is that Mbeki made contact with US AIDS dissident David Rasnick in January 2000 via fax. According to Rasnick, Mbeki then phoned him to ask for help in answering questions relating to HIV, AIDS and AZT. Rasnick is one of Brink's allies, and started to work with the Rath Foundation soon after Brink did.

Clearly, the dissidents' ideas had a strong impact on Mbeki. By September 2000, while answering questions in Parliament, Mbeki famously questioned the link between HIV and AIDS, asking: 'Does HIV cause AIDS? Can a virus cause a syndrome? How? It can't, because a syndrome is a group of diseases resulting from acquired immune deficiency.' According to Brink, Mbeki reached his AIDS dissident position by reading the Perth Group's work: 'Mbeki understands every jot and tittle of the Perth group critique, concerning the [HIV] isolation and antibody problems [relating to HIV tests],' Brink told me.

Some commentators have condemned Mbeki's AIDS dissident stance as a knee-jerk reaction against 'Western' science, but I think there is merit in Brink's claim that Mbeki was persuaded by science. It appears to be precisely the scientific arguments put forward by the AIDS dissidents – rather than a blanket rejection of Western science – that persuaded Mbeki of the merits of the dissident cause. Mbeki only assumes an Africanist, nationalist, anti-Western approach when dealing with those who criticise his view on AIDS. His critics had bought into the 'so-called orthodox view' of AIDS because they were racists who believed that Africans were 'promiscuous germ-carriers' and that rape was 'endemic' on our continent, according to Mbeki.

While Brink has been happy to hint furiously at the role he has played to encourage the President's dissident position, when I asked him directly about the nature and extent of his engagement with Mbeki, he coyly replied: 'My lips are sealed.' It is thus hard to tell how much of what he claims is self-promotional fiction and how much is fact. However, Brink was invited to attend meetings of Mbeki's Presidential AIDS Advisory Panel in 2002. This brought together so-called orthodox and dissident scientists to discuss what was essentially a dissident agenda – a key question being whether AIDS tests can really identify HIV.

But Brink's brazen tendency to speak as if anointed by Mbeki ensured that he became an important contact person for a disparate crew of people attracted to Mbeki's anti-AIDS orthodoxy for a wide range of reasons. The glue that bound them appeared largely to be the desire to unite against common 'enemies': antiretroviral (ARV) drugs, an 'international conspiracy' led by the pharmaceutical companies that manufacture ARVs, and the Treatment Action Campaign, the highly successful activist organisation formed to campaign for the right of ordinary South Africans to have access to decent, affordable HIV/AIDS treatment.

Brink used these common enemies as rallying points to build a cleverly crafted alliance against the TAC that sought both to win the hearts and minds of South Africans over to the view that ARVs are 'toxic' and to publicly support the President and his Health Minister's dissident stance on HIV and AIDS.

Brink claimed the charismatic former youth leader Peter Mokaba as an ally, saying that they worked closely together before Mokaba's death. Mokaba died in June 2002, aged 43, from pneumonia and respiratory problems that so often prey on those with AIDS. It is likely that Brink and Mokaba worked together on the seminal South African AIDS dissident work, the bizarrely titled *Castro Hlongwane, Caravans, Cats, Geese, Foot-and-Mouth and Statistics: AIDS and the Struggle for the Humanisation of the African*. There is a large section devoted to the toxicity of AZT and some of the phraseology is similar to that used by Brink. Although the *Castro Hlongwane* authors are not named, Mokaba admitted to being part of the 'collective' that wrote it. The *Mail & Guardian* newspaper also traced the embedded signature of the electronic version of the document to Mbeki's own computer. Brink attributes the document directly to the President, describing it as 'Mbeki's radical scientific and ideological analysis and debunk of the American AIDS–HIV paradigm, which he released for discussion at an ANC NEC meeting in March [2002] and continued updating and expanding'.

The *Castro Hlongwane* document was distributed to members of the ANC's National Executive Committee in March 2002. It was also given to Nelson Mandela when he met Mbeki later in 2002 to discuss HIV/ AIDS. It was thus given extraordinary promotion for an 'unofficial' party document, and it is important as it remains the only official record of the views of South African AIDS dissidents. It argues that it is 'illogical' that AIDS is 'a single disease caused by a singular virus, HIV'; that 'the collection of diseases generally described as belonging to the AIDS syndrome have known causes'; and that 'there are many conditions that cause acquired immune deficiency, including malnutrition and disease. HIV may be one of the causes of this immune deficiency, but cannot be the only cause.' In mid-2007, Mbeki was still promoting *Castro Hlongwane* and had a copy sent to Mark Gevisser, who was writing Mbeki's unofficial biography at the time.

Professor Sam Mhlongo, head of family medicine at the Medical University of Southern Africa (Medunsa) and Mbeki's friend and doctor in London, became one of Brink's closest and most important allies. Linking up with Mhlongo was like striking gold for Brink, as Mhlongo provided him with a much desired hotline to the President and Health Minister Manto Tshabalala-Msimang, according to Brink. Mhlongo died in a car crash in October 2006.

In a 'highly confidential' letter written to German vitamin-seller Dr Matthias Rath on 5 March 2004, Brink says that he and Mhlongo 'have been collaborating since we met at the first meeting of President Mbeki's international Presidential AIDS Advisory Panel in Pretoria in May 2000, at which he conveyed President Mbeki's gratitude to me for the trouble I had taken in researching the literature on AZT and drawing it to his attention'.

Brink also claims he was consulted by the ANC and the government about the TAC's court case aimed at getting the government to supply the ARV nevirapine to pregnant women with HIV to prevent them from passing on the virus to their babies. 'Acting covertly, I was closely involved in the nevirapine case brought by the TAC against the department, having been approached and consulted by the ruling party, the ANC, behind the scenes at the highest level,' he says. Brink also credits Mhlongo with delivering a crucial message to him from the President. 'On hearing from the late Professor Sam Mhlongo in 2002 that Mbeki desired an organised effort to get the facts of ARV toxicity publicised, I formed the Treatment Information Group (TIG),' says Brink in his online book *Lying and Thieving: The Fraudulent Scholarship of Ronald Suresh Roberts*.

Brink is more forthright about his mission in his confidential letter to Rath, in which he claims that the TIG was formed because Mhlongo had told him that Mbeki 'desired the establishment of a dissident AIDS activist organisation to serve as a counterweight to the TAC'. The TIG's aim was to 'act as a clearing house for the dissemination of information about the toxicity of ARVs and alternatives to the chemotherapeutic approach to AIDS advocated by the TAC'.

This claim has been denied by the Presidency thus: 'The claims in Advocate Brink's document of secretive counter-mobilisation, intimate friendships and his special influence on the thinking of government leaders do not, we believe, deserve a response' (*Mail & Guardian*, 25 March 2005). However, Brink says that this response was ghost-written by his one-time ally turned enemy, Ronald Suresh Roberts.

Brink's big break came when Rath agreed to support his cause financially. Until then, Brink was largely a lone campaigner and the TIG a one-man band. While the common point between Rath and Brink appears to be their hatred of the pharmaceutical industry, there was also an economic rationale to their collaboration. Rath was trying to establish his vitamin business in South Africa and was looking for political allies and government access while Brink needed financial support for his campaign against ARVs.

In early 2004, Brink was unemployed. An associate of his, Anthony Rees, had just started to work for the Dr Rath Health Foundation and encouraged Brink to apply for financial support. Brink wrote a proposal to Rath and subsequently had a meeting with him and Rees in March 2004. Rath agreed to help support TIG. Brink then moved to Cape Town, found a flat in the same block as Rees, and was soon employed by the Rath Foundation.

However, the relationship between Brink and Rees soured rapidly. Rees claims that he wasn't prepared to follow Brink's dissident line completely while Brink alleges 'a complete collapse of trust'. It appears clear, however, that both men were vying to be Rath's main man in South Africa. By June 2004, Rees had lost the contest and was fired from the Rath Foundation. Rees later leaked Brink's initial proposal to Rath and minutes from the meeting between Brink and Rath. According to these minutes, Brink told the meeting that their collaboration would be mutually beneficial as Brink's goal of undermining ARVs would have the spin-off benefit of creating a market for alternative remedies for immune deficiency, namely Rath's products.

The vindictiveness with which Brink treats his enemies is evident in a 2005 letter to Mbeki, publicly released by Ronald Suresh Roberts, Mbeki's biographer, in November 2007 after his fallout with Brink. In the letter, Brink claimed that Rees had a 'disturbed personality'. He even suggests to Mbeki that 'an NIS [National Intelligence Service] tail on him to track his movements, and an investigation of the source of his current income, is likely to confirm his partnership with the TAC'. He seems to have quite forgotten that Rees helped him to link up with Rath when he was down and out.

Besides Mhlongo and the range of largely US and Australian dissidents who had linked up with Brink for ideological reasons, Brink's circle also included those who were not necessarily dissidents but who wanted to show their support for Mbeki and his Health Minister.

Dutch garlic-and-olive-oil advocate Tine van der Maas was one such person. Van der Maas was drawn to Brink by her own personal hatred for ARVs, but she prefers not to commit herself publicly on whether HIV causes AIDS. She was useful to Brink because of her close relationship to Health Minister Manto Tshabalala-Msimang. In addition, unlike most other AIDS dissidents who only had theories to offer, Van der Maas was prepared to get her hands dirty and actually nurse people with weak immune systems – albeit with her own diet and a concoction called 'Africa's Solution' produced by the company Bermins.

Having failed in their campaign to stop government from introducing ARVs in the public sector, Brink and other key AIDS dissidents regrouped around Van der Maas's programme, using it as an entry point to persuade communities to reject 'toxic' ARV drugs. Brink introduced her to Kim Cools, a radical Belgian AIDS dissident who was running an environmental programme in KwaNgcolosi outside Durban. In late 2004, Cools and Van der Maas produced a documentary called *Power to the People*, which claimed to document the positive effects of Van der Maas's diet on people in that area. The Rath Foundation helped to fund the documentary.

Aside from the AIDS dissidents and those who hate ARVs, others seem to have formed links with Brink because they were – or wanted to be – aligned with Mbeki politically. Chief among these were Christine Qunta and Roberts. Africanist attorney Qunta, formerly Christine Douts from Bonteheuwel in Cape Town, rapidly became part of Mbeki's inner circle of advisers. Mbeki appointed her to the SABC board in 2003. A prolific and controversial newspaper columnist, Qunta often used her space to sing the praises of Mbeki and Tshabalala-Msimang and lash out at their critics, including the media. In 2007, Mbeki reappointed

Qunta to the SABC board against the recommendation of Parliament's portfolio committee on broadcasting.

Qunta's law firm was appointed to represent Rath, and she also defended her client in her columns. Writing in *Business Day* in May 2005, Qunta condemned the 'prevailing orthodoxy in the popular media that stifles the exploration of complementary strategies to combat [HIV/AIDS]. It is an orthodoxy that stifles any view that does not conform to the "official" or "sanctioned" one. Like the issue of Zimbabwe, no dissent is tolerated. The few people brave enough to advance a different perspective are attacked in ways that are often quite vicious.'

She also attacked the TAC, claiming that the organisation's 'messianic' message was 'antiretrovirals or death'. Rath, on the other hand, 'makes a perfectly valid point regarding the value of vitamins and the role they can play in improving the health of AIDS patients. Whether vitamins can cure AIDS is, of course, something that must be proved scientifically,' she wrote.

Interestingly, it emerged in 2007 that Qunta had linked up with one Pastor Freddie Isaacs – the man who once planned his own funeral as he said he had been called to heaven to be an apostle. Isaacs sold a product called Comforter's Healing Gift, which he claimed could cure AIDS. Qunta was a director of the Comforter's Healing Gift company, but when this was exposed, she claimed that the company was 'dormant' and that, until tested, the product was only sold as a nutritional supplement. Qunta was later appointed to serve on a task team to examine the role of African traditional medicine by Tshabalala-Msimang.

Qunta's friend the Trinidadian Roberts also became part of Brink's circle. Clues to Roberts's personality are contained in a 2007 judgment against the bald and bespectacled Roberts by Judge Leslie Weinkove, who dismissed with costs a defamation claim he brought against the *Sunday Times*. Roberts was 'venomous', 'vindictive', 'haughty and arrogant', showed a 'grandiose sense of self-importance', and had been 'unbalanced, paranoid and obsessed' and shown 'excessive emotionality, inappropriate and provocative behaviour' in pursuing a previous complaint against the SABC, said the judge. Rounding off, Weinkove described Roberts as a name-dropper who 'purported to enjoy the patronage of people who occupy high positions in the corridors of power' and an 'evasive, argumentative and opportunistic' witness.

For a time – Brink claims between April 2005 and the end of 2006 – Roberts and Brink were seen together regularly in Cape Town cafés and restaurants in animated discussion and often shared hilarity. Brink says they 'hit it off' right away when they first met in a bookshop and that he had regarded Roberts as a 'good friend', but Roberts has downplayed their association.

In 2007, however, they had a bitter fallout that resulted in Brink calling Roberts 'a liar and a thief of stunning depravity' who 'cannot be trusted by anyone with anything, on anything, ever'. His grievance was that Roberts had plagiarised large parts of his own work on HIV for his book on Mbeki, *Fit to Govern: The Native Intelligence of Thabo Mbeki,* and had then also gone on to insult him in the book, describing him as being in 'a twilight zone where a tiny coven of furious anti-treatment propagandists and amateur statisticians make him their unlikely prophet'.

So great was his sense of betrayal that Brink documented his association with Roberts in a minutely detailed, 443-page online book which he called *Lying and Thieving: The Fraudulent Scholarship of Ronald Suresh Roberts.* In it, Brink claims that Roberts has 'no concern for his fellow man, absolutely none' and that he is 'entirely devoid of conscience or compassion' and is a bully. 'An awful aspect of going out with Roberts anywhere was the regular prospect that he'd start abusing the waiter – in Cape Town, usually a young white male. It was the strangest thing, this compulsion to degrade and humiliate for his evening to be complete. The order would take too long or the wine wasn't cold enough or some other petty thing; and whereas normal people could sort things out, Roberts had to make an unpleasant scene. The endpoint had to be total humiliation,' says Brink.

Roberts counterattacked in the *Mail & Guardian* online in November 2007 by calling Brink 'an extremely peculiar fish', 'a very loony guy' and an 'abject liar'. He also released a letter Brink had asked Roberts to pass on to Mbeki, which 'proved' that Brink was 'not personally known to Mbeki'.

Like the fallout with Rees, Brink's spat with Roberts revolved around who had better access to a powerful man, in this case Mbeki, and who could thus interpret him best. Roberts strongly asserts in his book and elsewhere that Mbeki is not an AIDS dissident and never has been. Instead, insists Roberts, Mbeki had merely asked questions about HIV and AIDS. 'In the end, because of Mbeki's courageous flak-taking, black South Africans, who have their way in general elections, but not yet in the apartheid media, received a far more cautious and sensible antiretroviral roll-out, compared with the frenzied drugs campaign that had been advocated by [Zackie] Achmat and [Edwin] Cameron at their most enraptured,' writes Roberts.

He also disputes that Brink was ever in the confidence of Mbeki. Obviously, if Brink had been in Mbeki's confidence, this would undermine Roberts's central thesis about Mbeki being a questioner of HIV/AIDS 'dogma' rather than a believer in AIDS dissidence. But Roberts also disputes that he and Brink had ever been friends despite the fact that, for a time, they socialised a lot more often than mere acquaintances or work colleagues normally would.

It is often hard to establish the truth when dealing with Brink and Roberts. Brink is notoriously selective with scientific evidence, bending the 'facts' to suit his anti-ARV cause. Although there is overwhelming evidence of the life-saving benefits of a range of ARVs, Brink and his followers – the vast majority of whom have never actually treated anyone with HIV or AIDS – present only the reports that document the negative side-effects that usually afflict a minority. Brink's involvement in the James Hayman case, detailed later, is a clear example of how selective he can be with scientific evidence.

Meanwhile, Roberts has been happy to label his erstwhile friend a liar, but he once had an altercation with me which, when confronted by others about it, he denied ever happening. Interestingly, Brink exposes Roberts in *Lying and Thieving*.

On 15 September 2005, Roberts – a man I have never met – phoned me in my Durban office. He said he was with the Presidency, and would be covering the AIDS debate in a book he was writing about the intellectual traditions of the President. He then said he had been struck by the personalised, 'medieval' level of attacks in the 'AIDS debate' and intended to include me in a chapter on 'vendetta journalism', as I appeared to have a vendetta against Anthony Brink. Then he asked me if I had 'made up' certain things about Brink in an article I had written in the *Financial Mail*. I didn't remember the article he was referring to – at the time, I had mentioned Brink in passing in four articles over five years' worth of writing about HIV/AIDS – so I asked Roberts to fax me the article and any questions he might have about it. I also asked him whether Brink had put him up to phoning me, to which he responded, 'That is preposterous!' He then proceeded to question me about how my news agency, Health-e News Service, functioned and to whom I reported.

A friend took up Roberts's call with Joel Netshitenzhe, a high-ranking official in the Presidency, while I reported on both Brink's and Roberts's attempts to intimidate Health-e staff and other journalists (based on a range of incidents and a defamatory draft of Brink's book, *Just Say Yes, Mr President*) to the South African National Editors' Forum (Sanef). On the basis of my complaint to Sanef, the *Mail & Guardian* decided to investigate what it later reported as Brink's 'loony' attacks on journalists and also contacted Roberts about his call to me.

But when the *Mail & Guardian* reporter contacted Roberts, he denied that he had ever phoned me, claiming that I had made the call up as a 'hoax' and a 'fraudulent' attempt to 'intimidate' him so that I could get an early look at his Mbeki manuscript. He did, however, admit to being quizzed by 'government officials' about his manuscript, but claimed this was all part of my campaign of intimidation! Roberts then threatened to sue the *Mail & Guardian* if they published anything about the phone call.

However, in *Lying and Thieving*, Brink says that Roberts phoned him 'immediately after the call' he had made to me to tell him about it. About a month later, says Brink, Roberts also sent him an email about the incident – almost as if he was constructing a paper trail in retrospect in the event of a legal case. 'In his email Roberts also glibly lied about having threatened Cullinan with writing about her in his book … as if she'd fabricated this,' says Brink.

Although Brink tried to dissociate himself from Roberts's call to me in his online book, it is possible that he and Roberts had decided to organise a 'hit' on Health-e News Service, to borrow a famous Brink phrase. At the time of Roberts's call, Health-e had published and broadcast a number of stories that exposed how the Rath Foundation in Khayelitsha was trying to get people to stop taking their ARVs and take Rath's products instead. At that stage, Health-e was part of a non-governmental organisation that tendered for work from the Health Department. Shortly before Roberts's call, the head of the NGO had been asked by Health Director-General Thami Mseleku about the organisation's association with Health-e. Mseleku had said that 'the President' wanted to know who we were.

The very day that Roberts called me, Brink also phoned my employer three times to demand a response to a letter in which he threatened legal action against me for investigating his role in the Hayman case.

Also that same day, Health Department communication officer Charity Bhengu – who enjoyed a very close relationship with Mseleku and Tshabalala-Msimang – sent an email to Health-e print editor Anso Thom asking her about the source of a story she had written about the Health Department's collaboration with Rath. Later that day, Bhengu phoned Health-e radio editor Khopotso Bodibe and implied that the department was considering legal action against Anso for her article. It seems too strange a coincidence that Roberts's, Brink's and Bhengu's calls happened all on the same day.

When Brink became employed by the Rath Foundation he finally had resources to mobilise support against ARVs, pharmaceutical companies and the TAC. Clearly short of local popular credibility – what with a German doctor, Dutch nurse and one South African doctor who had spent 36 years in exile, on his team – Brink started to court local organisations. Three organisations were drawn in to Brink's strange web: the Traditional Healers' Organisation (THO), the South African National Civic Organisation (Sanco) and the National Association of People Living with AIDS (Napwa).

The THO led by Nhlavana Maseko was a natural ally for Rath. The THO despised Western pharmaceutical companies for threatening their members' livelihoods and supported all the Health Minister's attempts to exercise control over how the pharmaceutical companies operated in this country. In December 2004, the THO's Maseko signed a 'private memorandum of understanding' with the Rath Foundation, represented by Brink. The organisations pledged a 'strategic alliance to join forces against the pharmaceutical business with disease and to support the South African government to realise the vision of a new primary health care system based on side-effect free traditional medicine and natural therapies'. One of the slogans of the alliance was 'Break the chains of pharmaceutical colonialism' and one of its goals was to 'discuss joint legal strategies against the pharmaceutical cartel and its front organisations [read TAC]'.

Sanco was led by Mbeki loyalist Mlungisi Hlongwane. While local civic organisations had played a vital role in fighting apartheid in many areas, Sanco never really got off the ground. It tried to impose a centralised structure on the fiery, independent local civic organisations, insisting that there should be no local negotiations with municipalities or local fundraising. But Sanco was eclipsed by the ANC branches in most areas in post-apartheid South Africa and existed as a faction-ridden organisation floundering around for a cause, a political niche and funding. Brink helped to draw Sanco into an alliance with Rath's Foundation, particularly targeting Khayelitsha in Cape Town as well as the Eastern Cape and KwaZulu-Natal. The choice of Khayelitsha was symbolic as it was the site of the country's longest and most successful ARV programme.

Sanco's deputy president, Ruth Bhengu, already had longstanding ties with Brink's ally Tine van der Maas. Bhengu, an ANC MP who resigned from Parliament in 2005 after being implicated in the Travelgate scam, is thus far the only ANC MP to have announced in Parliament in 2001 that her child was living with HIV. When her daughter Nozipho fell ill in 2003, the Health Minister sent Van Der Maas to her. Nozipho stopped her ARVs because of the side-effects she suffered and went on to Van der Maas's diet but she was dead by 2006.

Probably the most cynical alliance that Brink set up was between the Rath Foundation and Napwa. Although Napwa – with its mission to represent people with HIV – is not an AIDS dissident organisation, like Sanco it was facing a crisis of legitimacy. The TAC had broken away from Napwa and proved to be far more popular, powerful and organised than Napwa was, and it was able to attract serious donor dollars. In contrast, Napwa's fortunes were dwindling and it was in desperate need of income following years of poor and corrupt management. The Department of Health became Napwa's major donor – and the Department got a qualified audit for a number of successive years, in part because of the chaotic state of Napwa's finances.

AIDS activist Lucky Mazibuko, writing in the *Sowetan* in October 2004, described Napwa as being 'strategically turned and manipulated into becoming an unofficial spin-doctoring cover, and to lick the backsides of public servants and to polish the dented image of the Department of Health, who flatly refused to act decisively [against HIV/AIDS]. The taxpayers' money, yours and mine, is being wasted on an unaccountable, ineffective structure that does not seem to have the interests of people living with HIV at heart. Since December 2001 there have been ever-increasing volumes of dissatisfied Napwa office bearers, intended beneficiaries and even board members.'

Short of funds and legitimacy, Napwa needed to prove its loyalty to its biggest cash cow, the Department of Health. Not only did Napwa form an alliance with the Rath Foundation to assist with the distribution of Rath products, but it also joined together with the foundation, Sanco and the THO to bash its rival, the TAC.

'The TAC's credibility has collapsed with the exposure of its financial ties to pharmaceutical front organisations by the South African Traditional Healers Organization (THO), the Khayelitsha branch of Sanco and the Dr. Rath Health Foundation. As a pharmaceutical industry lobby, the TAC has its back to the wall now,' Napwa's director, Nkululeko Nxesi, told the *Mail & Guardian*. Nxesi also admitted to getting a R16,000 donation from the Rath Foundation for a conference.

Napwa continued to receive grants from the Health Department despite being unable to account for money spent and allegations from staff themselves that Nxesi is corrupt and ineffectual (see *Financial Mail*, 30 March 2007).

While no birds of a feather, these disparate organisations and individuals chose to close ranks around Mbeki and Tshabalala–Msimang, and unite against the TAC, which does not receive money from pharmaceutical companies. Brink has led the public campaign against the TAC leaders and those he believed supported them – mounting vicious, defamatory, personalised attacks on all those who dared to disagree with Mbeki.

Brink reserves his most vicious attack for Zackie Achmat, founder and leader of the TAC. Strangely, Brink holds Achmat entirely responsible for South Africa's HIV/AIDS treatment programme – refusing to acknowledge that the Cabinet itself gave the go-ahead for an HIV/AIDS treatment plan that included antiretroviral medication on 19 November 2003. To acknowledge this would be to implicate Mbeki and Tshabalala-

Msimang and admit that their dissident and anti-ARV views had been defeated within the ANC. It was far easier to make Achmat the scapegoat than to accept this reality.

So while others were enjoying New Year's Day in 2007, Brink emerged from the public holiday with a 'criminal complaint of genocide' against Achmat which he then laid on 4 January 2007 with the International Criminal Court in The Hague. Although it is supposed to be a legal document, the 'indictment' is so vicious that it almost trips over itself with excess.

'The ARV drugs that Achmat has personally engineered into the South African public health system and which he continues to promote reckless of the President and Health Minister's warnings that they are dangerously toxic, are killing thousands of South Africans, mostly black,' claimed Brink. He then asked that the court impose the 'highest sentence' on Achmat, namely: 'Permanent confinement in a small white steel and concrete cage, bright fluorescent light on at all time to keep an eye on him … with the ARVs he claims to take administered daily under close medical watch at the full prescribed dose morning, noon and night, without interruption, to prevent him from faking that he's being treatment compliant, pushed if necessary down his forced-open gullet with a finger or, if he bites, kicks and screams too much, dripped into his arm after he's been restrained on a gurney with cable ties around his ankles, wrists and neck, until he gives up the ghost on them, so to eradicate this foulest, most loathsome, unscrupulous and malevolent blight on the human race, who has plagued and poisoned the people of South Africa, mostly black, mostly poor, for nearly a decade now.'

Brink also plays on what he describes as Achmat's 'mental illness' (Achmat has suffered from episodes of clinical depression since childhood), saying that Achmat might try to plead insanity instead of taking responsibility for the damage caused by ARVs. 'Achmat is on record repeatedly claiming to be mentally ill, in that he says he's suffered from severe depression from childhood, for which tragic medical condition he is being chronically doctored with mind-dulling psychiatric drugs that alter normal brain chemistry,' claims Brink. He recommends that, should Achmat try to avoid prosecution on the grounds of mental illness, he should be subjected to a 'full, extended medico-forensic investigation conducted in a suitable lock-up mental hospital'.

Meanwhile, Achmat chose not to respond to Brink, saying that 'any sane, never mind reasonable, person would ignore this complaint and statement as the behaviour of an obsessed and disturbed personality'.

According to Brink, writing in his online booklet *Just Say Yes, Mr President*, the TAC is 'nothing but the lackey of the multinational pharmaceutical industry – moving the merchandise being their common purpose'. He goes on: 'As a potent corporate agency, tricked out in radical chic, the TAC has become a pernicious force in the life of our new democracy, and it needs taking down. Best by deflation, I reckon. So I mean to puncture it. With sharp facts garnished with ample lashings of scorn. If feelings get bruised, too bad. This is a serious matter, for many life and death. Death being a real possibility for anyone who accepts the TAC's claims and proceeds to ingest the drugs it commends – as a legal colleague of mine discovered, killed by a single month's course of AZT and 3TC, reduced like "Nkosi Johnson" to a skeleton in nappies.'

The colleague in question was James Hayman, who died in 1997. Brink planned to use his death as an international test case against GlaxoSmithKline (GSK), the manufacturer of AZT, with the assistance of an 'expert witness', the Perth Group's Eleni Papadopulos-Eleopulos, a medical engineer at Royal Perth Hospital whose job it is to test people for sensitivity to ultraviolet radiation – rather than anything to do with HIV.

In 2001, Brink assisted Hayman's widow, Annet, to file a claim for almost R1.4 million in damages against the pharmaceutical firm for 'fatally poisoning' her husband after he took a month's supply of AZT and 3TC. However, the case floundered as Hayman's legal team failed to meet court deadlines, and it was eventually dismissed by Judge McCall in September 2002. By that stage, both Annet Hayman's senior counsel and her attorney had withdrawn, leaving only Brink as junior counsel.

Brink had written in his book *Debating AZT* that Hayman was killed by AZT and that the case would argue that 'AZT is an unreasonably dangerous drug with no therapeutic or palliative value as an "antiretroviral" whatsoever'. According to papers filed by Hayman's legal team, when Hayman started AZT treatment in July 1997 he 'weighed 68 kgs, was not sick and presented with no symptoms of illness'. A month's supply of the drug made him 'very ill' with symptoms including 'intractable diarrhoea and vomiting' and 'progressive weight loss', according to the papers. He died eleven months later.

But in its replying affidavit, GSK includes an affidavit by Hayman's doctor, Dr Eugene Campher, who notes that before his patient started taking AZT, he had oral thrush, persistent diarrhoea, a chronic cough, tiredness, and a fungal infection, and had reported losing 20 kg over six months. He had also been hospitalised for a chronic cough a month before starting AZT and his CD4 count (measure of immunity in the blood) was 73 when his doctor prescribed AZT and another antiretroviral drug, 3TC. He took one month's supply of ARVs over two months, and then stopped taking them altogether. Despite not following the prescribed dosage, five weeks after starting the ARVs Hayman had gained four kilograms and Dr Campher noted that he 'feels much better ... no cough, diarrhoea has stopped'. However, Hayman then simply stopped taking the drugs without explanation. He died a few months afterwards.

Brink claims that the Hayman case never got to court for logistical and financial reasons. One hold-up was that Papadopulos-Eleopulos could not travel to South Africa to testify as her mother was ill. However, in early 2007, Papadopulos-Eleopulos did testify in a Western Australian court case. She had been called as an expert witness in the appeal of one Andre Parensee, who had been found guilty of endangering the lives of three women by having unprotected sex with them without disclosing that he had HIV. In her evidence, Papadopulos-Eleopulos told the court that HIV did not exist, so it could not be sexually transmitted. Eight HIV/AIDS experts testified against Papadopulos-Eleopulos, including US virologist Professor Robert Gallo, a co-discoverer of HIV, who described the Perth Group as 'delusional'.

In his judgment, Judge John Sulan dismissed the testimony of Papadopulos-Eleopulos and another dissident, Valendar Turner, saying that they 'lacked credibility and were advocates for a cause rather than independent experts'. 'I am satisfied that no jury would conclude that there is any doubt that the virus HIV exists,' said Sulan. 'I consider no jury would be left in any doubt that HIV is the cause of AIDS or that it is sexually transmissible.'

But a 'jury' of South African public officials seemed far less certain. Brink's AIDS dissident belief that HIV/AIDS is a bogus epidemic promoted as part of an international conspiracy by pharmaceutical manufacturers to make profits, struck a chord with a number of highly placed government officials. Brink and his cronies were welcomed into the upper echelons of government. They have at times had the ear of the country's President. Rath's men, Mhlongo and US dissident David Rasnick, were invited to address a meeting of the National Health Council (made up of the Health Minister and her provincial counterparts) in September 2005 at which they condemned ARVs as ineffective and toxic. None of the country's foremost HIV/AIDS experts were invited to address the Council. In mid-2008, KwaZulu-Natal's Health MEC Peggy Nkonyeni hosted a small private meeting in Durban addressed by Tshabalala-Msimang and Brink's allies in the THO at which Rath–THO literature decrying 'pharmaceutical colonialism' was distributed. Nkonyeni's spokesperson described the meeting as an educational meeting for traditional healers, yet the leadership of the Durban traditional healers' association was not invited to the meeting.

Despite having nothing to offer other than ideology in place of ARVs for people with weak immune systems, Brink and his allies managed to ingratiate themselves into South Africa's body politic by exploiting divisions etched by apartheid. They used South Africans' deep – and, given the country's apartheid history, understandable – distrust of Western powers and medicine, as well as the new democratic government's immense sensitivity to criticism, to sow seeds of doubt about an epidemic that is largely sexually transmitted and incurable.

The President and the Health Minister and the key officials that supported them embraced these strange bedfellows at great cost to the country and to people living with HIV. In doing so, they showed themselves to be more interested in gathering support for their dissident stance on AIDS and undermining those who opposed them than in helping South Africans with HIV, who were mostly poor and thus had very little political 'currency' other than as occasional voting 'fodder'. This was a tragic betrayal for South Africans who had waited so long for a democratic government to represent them and treat them with the respect and dignity lacking in our country ever since a white minority took power so long ago.

As Sipho Mthathi said while general secretary of the TAC: 'For many black people living in poverty, either as a result of HIV/AIDS or whom poverty has made vulnerable to HIV infection and premature death, it is tragic that the people who should fight with us to defend our rights are the ones who spit in our faces.'

* Kerry Cullinan is the award-winning managing editor of Health-e News Service. She has been a journalist since the late 1980s, working on anti-apartheid publications such as New Nation and Work in Progress as well as for the Independent Newspapers' parliamentary bureau. She was also active in the South African Youth Congress and the ANC prior to 1994. She has a Master's degree in culture, communication and media from the University of KwaZulu-Natal.

7

The curious tale of the vitamin seller

by
Anso Thom

The short, stocky man shooed the children from the neat makeshift bedroom and ordered them outside. He slowly walked to the front section of his single-room brick house in Khayelitsha, a vast and sprawling township on the outskirts of Cape Town, and lowered himself on to a rickety wooden bench. Zondani Magwebu let out a long sigh and momentarily stared into space, trying to order his thoughts and find a way to reconcile himself with the story he was about to share with me. Unbeknown to him, the story Zondani told me in September 2005 would become part of a string of incidents involving poor people living with HIV who were offered hope of a cure while the South African Health Minister and her allies turned a deaf ear to recurring pleas to intervene.

This is the story of Dr Matthias Wilfried Rath, a German vitamin seller rejected in many parts of the world, who arrived on South African shores in 2004 and departed almost two years later, but not before leaving a trail of confusion, anger and suffering.

A diverse group of people – including AIDS dissidents, scientists, community workers and politicians – would rally behind Rath's multi-vitamin crusade. The upshot was that poor people were persuaded to take high doses of Rath's VitaCell multi-vitamins by being promised that it could boost their immune system and rid them of the raging

HIV infection so prevalent in their communities. Even more devastating would be the less explicit consequences of Rath's actions and those of his collaborators, which would for years manifest in the confusion sown in the minds of vulnerable communities.

The former Health Minister, Dr Manto Tshabalala-Msimang, and her head of department, Thami Mseleku, would eventually fail to protect the most vulnerable. Ultimately it would be left to desperate health professionals and the Treatment Action Campaign (TAC), particularly its resolute policy and research director, Nathan Geffen, to build a legal case against Rath, his supporters and the Health Minister in an effort to stop him. Health-e News Service, a small non-profit news organisation, would further strengthen the groundswell against Rath and the minister, by publishing and broadcasting a series of award-winning reports exposing the dubious operations of Rath and his collaborators and the stories of those who died while taking his pills. The tenacity of health workers, TAC's commitment and the consistent media reports would finally culminate in the Cape High Court four years later, when on 13 June 2008 a judgment sounded the death knell to Rath's South African operations.

Before all this happened, Rath's path crossed that of Zondani and his family. Noluthando, Zondani's young wife and mother of their three little children, died. The memory of her painful and undignified death was hard for Zondani to bear, but he knew that by sharing her horror story he could possibly stop the nightmare for others.

He remembers Noluthando meeting two women at a prayer meeting and being instructed by them to take 20 of Rath's VitaCell tablets every day if she wanted to rid herself of HIV. The young woman, still trying to come to terms with her diagnosis, took the 20 tablets and reported feeling dizzy and nauseous the next morning. Zondani recalled how his wife would vomit every time she tried to eat. He was convinced that his wife had ignored his pleas and those of her clinic doctor to stop taking the vitamins. 'She was never the same after she started taking those tablets. She could do nothing, she was always in bed, I am convinced she overdosed. They finished her.'

A month after being introduced to the vitamins, Noluthando died in a nearby hospital. Asked if he knew who the doctor was who provided the pills his wife took, Zondani didn't waver: '*NguRatha, nguRetha – Kuyinto ezilapho* [Rath, or Reth – something like that].' Zondani was not sure whether Noluthando escaped the humiliation of having to stand semi-naked while being photographed and having a blood sample taken, as other Rath patients reported. The families that I and Health-e colleagues Khopotso Bodibe and Siwiwe Minyi interviewed recalled symptoms of dizziness and nausea similar to those that Noluthando had suffered. One of Zondani's neighbours, Nandipha Sigebenga, spoke of how she had to watch her sister Ntombekaya die an agonising death, as she was too afraid to defy the women who had ordered her not to contact any government health worker if she became ill, but rather to alert them. Within hours of her death the two women entered the house and removed all traces of the Rath products, including the empty pill containers. They didn't even bother to offer their condolences before leaving.

Many similar stories of people being photographed semi-naked and having their blood taken started to surface in 2005. Everyone was hopeful that the government would act swiftly to stop these practices. How wrong we were.

When he first came to prominence, Rath's public campaigns, which focused mostly on Europe and the United States, presented the burly doctor with short-cropped grey hair as a maverick figure prepared to take on mainstream pharmaceutical companies selling drugs for lifestyle diseases. He targeted mainly those with cancer and heart disease. Unable to find mainstream journalists willing to publish his claims, Rath resorted to placing full-page advertisements in the *New York Times* and other international newspapers. Images of him in various poses, including that of a Messiah with arms outstretched, also appeared on several websites he maintained.

On several occasions Rath had been repudiated by scientists and research bodies either for quoting their work out of context or for making false scientific claims to back his products. Setbacks, sanctions and repudiations from highly regarded scientific journals, research foundations and courts were mostly met with disdain and long, rambling epistles to his followers. Seemingly convinced that the pharmaceutical industry and others were out to get him, Rath never went anywhere without a bodyguard and told staff he was convinced that the pharmaceutical companies were following him. While living in Cape Town he holed himself up in a multi-million-rand Hout Bay mansion with the latest security devices, high walls and electrified fencing.

His campaign in South Africa turned out to be similar to his modus operandi in Europe and the United States. By the time he arrived in South Africa, he was a multi-millionaire who had for years been selling his concoctions to mostly elderly Europeans and Americans desperate to find remedies for incurable lifestyle diseases. He managed to establish his products in South Africa despite the fact that several countries were opposed to their distribution for not being classifiable as nutritional supplements, medicines or foods. Yet Rath would be given almost free rein to promote his products in South Africa.

Rath's entry into South Africa was well timed. He arrived in the country at the beginning of 2004 when AIDS was already a highly politicised issue, with the South African government questioning the safety of antiretroviral (ARV) medication on the one hand and the TAC, a highly organised grassroots activist movement, advocating access to ARV treatment on the other. Despite overwhelming scientific evidence and the plummeting costs of ARV treatment, the government would only start making ARVs available in certain public health facilities in the course of 2004.

President Thabo Mbeki had already set a dissident tone in October 1999 when he questioned making available AZT – at the time a widely used ARV to prevent pregnant HIV women from infecting their babies

– stating that the 'toxicity of this drug is such that it is in fact a danger to health'. He urged parliamentarians to read more on this topic on the internet, long used by AIDS dissidents who were unable to get their ramblings published in the mainstream media and scientific journals. Mbeki went a step further and ordered his Health Minister, Tshabalala-Msimang, herself a medical doctor and at the time a supporter of Western medicine, to investigate his concerns. His former comrade-in-arms exhibited blind loyalty to her President, turning into Mbeki's eager messenger and a source of inspiration for dissidents the world over.

At the time the Health Department was also rudderless. The competent Director-General, Dr Ayanda Ntsaluba, had left at the end of 2003. It would take 16 months before the former Education Director-General, Thami Mseleku, would step in to fill Ntsaluba's shoes at the beginning of 2005. From Rath's perspective, this was perfect. Although Mseleku knew very little about health, he readily described the mentality of the pharmaceutical industry and conventional medicine as 'colonialist' and consistently refused to be critical of dissidents and their quack remedies. Mseleku told journalists in 2007 that he was using traditional medicine to treat his own diabetes, but he would not reveal what the treatment involved as he said its intellectual property rights were not protected.

Rath used his tried and tested tactics in South Africa. His massively funded campaign centred around unsettling desperately ill people's beliefs in one system, in this case ARVs and Western medicine, while offering an alternative, his VitaCell multi-vitamins, coupled with what he described as good nutrition. This message found favour with Tshabalala-Msimang, who had taken it upon herself to promote a mix of beetroot, African potato, garlic, lemon and olive oil as alternatives to ARVs with gospel-like fervour, despite international derision.

In hindsight, Rath probably made his biggest mistake by choosing to focus his campaign on Khayelitsha, a township where ARVs were fairly well established and the community was considered to be fairly well educated around HIV. Residents had already had access to ARVs as far back as 1999 when in the absence of government policy a group of renegade health workers, mostly members of the ruling African National Congress (ANC), began dispensing AZT to pregnant mothers to prevent them from infecting their babies. Shortly afterwards a number of Médecins Sans Frontières (MSF) doctors arrived in Khayelitsha and two years later were at the forefront of providing ARVs in an area with one of the highest HIV-prevalence rates in South Africa. The TAC was also active in the community and set up support groups for people with HIV. Rath had opted to hit at the heart of one of South Africa's flagship HIV treatment projects.

Instrumental in setting up the Rath Foundation's office in the city was the Cape Town homeopath Anthony Rees. Rees later became a key informant for the TAC when they took on Rath and the Health Department in the Cape High Court. Rath would later also turn to the court to try to silence a disillusioned Rees who after being fired by Rath had created a website where he questioned Rath's motives for being in South Africa. Interviewed in 2004, Rees related how he had formally met Rath in Germany the year before. Rees had been sponsored by Rath to address a meeting of his supporters. At the meeting, the German doctor asked the homeopath if there was any possibility of promoting his book *Why Animals Don't Get Heart Attacks, but People Do* in South Africa. Rees readily agreed and started the process of opening an office in the Cape Town city centre. At the time, HIV was not on Rath's agenda: his focus was on cancer and heart disease.

Rath's interest in South Africa had been sparked by another South African two years previously. Professor Anthony Mbewu, an Oxford- and Harvard-trained cardiologist, Mbeki associate and South Africa's Medical Research Council (MRC) president, reportedly met Rath at the World Summit on Sustainable Development in Johannesburg in 2002. Rath informed Rees that he had been approached by Mbewu, who enquired whether he was *the* Dr Rath. 'Mbewu told Rath that he had read many of his papers on Vitamin C and that he had subsequently published follow-up papers. He urged Rath to contact him if he returned to South Africa,' Rees recalled. Two years later, Rath was ready to take up the professor's invitation and ordered Rees to set up a meeting. In April 2004, Rath and his longtime employee, the Polish chemist Dr Aleksandra Niedzwicki, made a presentation at the MRC's head office in Parow, north of Cape Town. Rath footed the bill for the two-day meeting, which was attended by scientists and researchers hand-picked by Mbewu.

Rath was keen to investigate the feasibility of conducting clinical trials in collaboration with the MRC, using his 'cellular medicine' to address cardiovascular disease, cancer and diabetes. The *Sunday Times* and *Cape Times* reported on Mbewu's association with Rath and published photographs of a dinner in Kalk Bay on the Cape Town seaboard attended by Rath, Rees, Niedzwicki, Mbewu and his wife, an MRC researcher, Priscilla Reddy. Mbewu never explained his dalliance with Rath, but the growing partnership came to an abrupt end when news broke that the European Union had made a substantial grant to the MRC for research. A furious Rath rounded up his Cape Town staff and told them that the pharmaceutical 'cartel' had learnt of his plans and that this was their way of stopping him.

However, the MRC did provide a link between Rath and the late Professor Sam Mhlongo – academic, former Mbeki physician, member of the Presidential Aids Advisory Panel and dissident, and the only invitee to the MRC presentation who showed keen interest in further collaboration with Rath. Rath was excited by the fact that Mhlongo had links with Mbeki. Until his death in a car accident in 2006, Mhlongo became one of the main driving forces behind the Rath Foundation's unlawful and unauthorised clinical trials.

It wasn't long before Rath and Mhlongo were joined by other dissidents in the persons of Anthony Brink and David Rasnick, another member of Mbeki's Advisory Panel and a dissident American academic.

Buoyed by his rapidly growing alliance with dissidents, Rath settled in South Africa but continued to commute between Cape Town and his head office in Almelo in the Netherlands, a small town on the German border.

Returning from one of his trips to the Netherlands, Rath promptly informed staff (according to Rees) that he intended to change his focus in South Africa to HIV and AIDS, as heart disease and cancer were not as pressing illnesses as in Europe. Having spent a few months in South Africa, Rath was acutely aware that HIV was a highly emotive issue and that the Health Minister had a tendency to support alternatives. Rath sent Rees and one of his senior managers, Chris Fairhurst, to Pretoria where they hand-delivered a parcel containing a selection of his publications to Mbeki and Tshabalala-Msimang. Disappointed with their failure to respond, Rath decided to use community structures to implement his strategy. He wasted no further time.

Once he was set on his path, no hitch or legal system would stop him. Even when a shipment of VitaCell, the multi-vitamin Rath had earmarked for distribution, was impounded by port authorities in Cape Town on the grounds that it was not classified or registered, he managed to find a loophole. In the opinion of the port authorities, Rath required a letter from the Medicines Control Council (MCC), South Africa's drug regulatory authority, to confirm the product's status as either a medicine or foodstuff. Rees made contact with the deputy director of the Food Control Directorate in the Health Department, Antoinette Booyzen, claiming that Rath was intending to bring a multi-vitamin preparation into the country with no associated claims and without any medical endorsement by a doctor. Booyzen ruled that because the levels of nutrients contained in the product were low and no associated claims were made, VitaCell was a foodstuff and did not fall within the ambit of the MCC. She then released a letter signed by herself on behalf of Mseleku confirming this. This letter paved the way for VitaCell to enter South Africa.

When Health-e later contacted Booyzen, she was shocked to learn that the dosages initially indicated to her by Rees and those claimed on the bottle were different. In fact, the dosages on the bottles being distributed were mostly double those given to her. The bottles had clearly been relabelled at some stage, with the original label indicating lower levels than the later one. Rath had also failed to share with Booyzen his true intentions – that he would be marketing VitaCell as an alternative to ARVs. Later it would be revealed that his foot soldiers were advising patients to take very high dosages.

While all this was happening, Rees introduced Anthony Brink to Rath. Brink had sent a proposal to Rath, introducing himself as 'South Africa's leading dissident' and detailing his intense dislike for the mainstream pharmaceutical industry. He proposed that Rath employ him and utilise his Treatment Information Group (TIG), a one-man show set up with the intention of opposing the TAC, to spread his message. It wasn't long before Brink became a spokesman for Rath and the source of many of Rath's venomous attacks on ARVs, journalists, activists and health professionals.

Rath fired his first public salvo on World Aids Day, 1 December 2004, when he placed a full-page advertisement in the *Mail & Guardian*, a respected weekly national newspaper. The advertisement sounded very much as if Brink had written it. It slammed ARVs as toxic and subsequent adverts accused the TAC and MCC of being 'Trojan horses' for the 'drug cartel'. It was the first of many similar attacks.

The TAC later laid a complaint with the Advertising Standards Authority (ASA). In essence, the ASA concurred with the TAC's complaints that the advertisements exaggerated the efficacy of multi-vitamins in 'treating' AIDS, and deliberately misled consumers about AZT. The ASA ordered Rath to desist from publishing similar claims, but the TAC would later have to turn to the Cape High Court and seek an interdict to get him to stop. For the first time, Rath found himself on a direct collision course with one of the world's best-organised activist

HIV movements, a battle that would eventually play itself out in the high courts of South Africa.

Notwithstanding the ASA ruling, the battle intensified when, a week later, Rath blitzed the Cape townships of Khayelitsha, Philippi, Nyanga and Gugulethu with pamphlets and posters attacking the TAC as a 'spreader of disease and death among our people' and accusing the ASA of 'helping to protect drug industry monopolies'.

But Rath was no longer acting alone. A waning Khayelitsha branch of the South African National Civic Organisation (Sanco) and the Traditional Healers' Organisation (THO), an almost defunct body claiming to represent the interests of traditional healers, added their signatures to the Rath posters and pamphlets. A memorandum of understanding emerged later confirming that the Rath Foundation and the THO had signed a formal agreement in December 2004, in essence committing themselves to join forces and support the government.

During this time, Sanco's Khayelitsha chairperson, Ndzanywa Ndibongo, stepped forward as Rath's latest praise-singer. When asked for his view on ARVs, Ndibongo gave a chilling response: 'It's simple. As you see written on that bottle [pointing to a poster] – ARVs are toxic. That's the only thing I can say. These vitamins are not toxic …' Health-e investigations revealed that Sanco members were acting as agents for the Rath Foundation and had set up 'clinics' where they prescribed up to 20 tablets a day for desperately ill people. These Rath agents would target people in their streets known to be HIV-positive or sick and encouraged them to attend one of the Rath 'clinics'. The mostly unemployed agents were keen to spread the gospel and, despite many denials, were reportedly reimbursed around R100 for every patient they recruited.

The Sanco partnership attracted another character, Ndithini Thyido, who was always lurking in the background, whether at Sanco/ Rath meetings or in court. Thyido was often seen trying to intimidate Rath detractors, including my colleagues and me, by filming us with a handheld camera. Further investigation into his background revealed that in 1997 the Truth and Reconciliation Commission (TRC) had refused amnesty to Thyido and fellow Western Cape self-defence unit (SDU) member Zwelitsha Mkuhlwa, following the shooting of another SDU member Bongani Mpisane and a child caught in the crossfire. Thyido was sentenced to nine years' and Mkuhlwa to thirteen years' imprisonment. According to TRC records, Thyido was at the time (1992) an executive member of the ANC Youth League in Khayelitsha and a leader of an SDU but had been suspended by the ANC Youth League because of alleged criminal misconduct. The TRC rejected the men's claims that they attacked Mpisane because they suspected him of misappropriating funds and refused amnesty, stating that none of their actions could be associated with a political objective.

Another Rath ally to emerge was the National Association of People Living with HIV/AIDS (Napwa), a pet organisation of Tshabalala-Msimang. Napwa had been set up in 1994 but when the TAC split from it, Napwa membership plummeted, and it continued to exist mainly with money from the Health Department. Rath's arrival bearing a generous cheque book offered the perfect lifeline to this waning organisation. Napwa chairperson Nkululeko Nxesi, who has been accused by his own staff of corruption, openly sided with Rath, attending the TAC court case (in which the TAC sought to interdict Rath from making defamatory statements) and sitting with the Rath camp. Nxesi was also quoted as stating: 'The TAC's credibility has collapsed with the exposure of its financial ties to pharmaceutical front organizations by the South African Traditional Healers Organization (THO), the Khayelitsha branch of Sanco and the Dr Rath Health Foundation. As a pharmaceutical industry lobby, the TAC has its back to the wall now.'

A few months after the World AIDS Day advertisement, the TAC turned to the courts requesting an urgent interdict to stop Rath from claiming that it was a front for the pharmaceutical industry and was forcing the government to spend millions of rands on toxic drugs. Eight long months later the Cape High Court ruled in the TAC's favour, prohibiting Rath, his South African foundation and the THO from making various statements alleging an improper connection between the TAC and the pharmaceutical industry – in particular, that the TAC received funds from pharmaceutical front organisations in return for promoting antiretroviral medicines and targeted poor communities as a market for the drug industry.

Emotions were running high inside the courtroom where Rath, Rasnick, Nxesi and Brink came face to face with Zackie Achmat and Nathan Geffen of the TAC, among others. Police had to intervene outside the court when Rath supporters and TAC activists almost came to blows after Phephsile Maseko of the THO taunted opposition protesters. Unable to remain on the sidelines, local branches of the South African Communist Party (SACP) and the Congress of South African Trade Unions (Cosatu) issued a strongly worded statement condemning Rath's activities and urging the Health Minister to act.

A distressed Luthando Nogcinisa, district secretary for the SACP, accused Sanco of approaching Khayelitsha families, often with a pack of groceries, encouraging the person with HIV not to take ARVs but to rather use Rath's vitamins, and accused Rath of 'conducting human experiments'. These claims were later backed up by several victims, who said they were also offered money to take the VitaCell.

TAC leader in Khayelitsha, Mandla Majola, also told us at the time that he was concerned that Rath's operations were creating 'huge confusion' within the township. Majola was troubled that Rath's operations were driving a wedge into the community: 'The sad part about the Rath issue is the hatred and animosity that it has given birth to, and it's not between us and Rath, it's between us and our brothers who are Sanco leaders. Both of us are facing or confronting these serious issues of unemployment, homelessness, shacks, people who are really sick from AIDS, crime and abuse.'

Unperturbed by the court ruling, Rath placed a double-page advertisement in a Durban newspaper, boldly sharing details of 'clinical trials' that he had conducted in Khayelitsha, claiming that results were so significant that they had to be published without delay. In the advertisement, he alluded to blood tests and clinical examinations, yet no ethics committee had sanctioned the human trial of Rath's products, as required by this country's scientific protocols. Although there were records of Mhlongo trying unsuccessfully to get his university to agree to trials, Rath did not make any formal application to conduct trials in South Africa.

A month later, a brash Rath published the 'findings' of the Khayelitsha 'trials' in the *New York Times* and *International Herald Tribune*. Two weeks thereafter, South African MPs found an information pack from the Dr Rath Health Foundation Africa in their pigeonholes. The pack included a five-page letter promoting the use of vitamins and micronutrients as an 'effective, safe and natural health solution readily available anywhere in the world to fight the HIV/AIDS epidemic'. Rath shared the results of the 'Khayelitsha Nutrient Programme after only two months involving 18 patients', claiming that in the light of these, the AIDS epidemic was no longer a death verdict for millions of people. Millions of lives in South Africa and billions in health-care costs could now be saved, and the 'drug cartel' which produced 'toxic ARVs' could no longer hold governments hostage. 'Mankind can be overjoyed about the fact that it can rid itself of the AIDS scourge,' he continued.

Not satisfied that his 'scientific breakthrough' was receiving the necessary media coverage, Rath called a press conference at his office in Cape Town. Flanked by Ndibongo and more than 15 Gugulethu and Khayelitsha patients, a beaming Rath called it a 'historic day for the people of South Africa, Africa and the entire world', stating unequivocally that 'the course of AIDS can be reversed naturally'. He insisted that the patients' health improved after a nutritional health programme without concurrent ARV drugs, and their AIDS symptoms decreased or disappeared completely. 'With micronutrients alone, the AIDS patients could reverse the symptoms of AIDS and lead almost normal lives again,' he said, claiming that the solution for AIDS had been around for decades but had been deliberately withheld from the world by the drug companies.

In a later twist to the Rath story, a group photograph taken at the press conference showed Marietta Ndziba, leader of the Rath support group in Gugulethu, smiling broadly. She was known for speaking passionately at community meetings and funerals about the healing powers of the Rath vitamins and her rejection of ARVs. However, four months later Ndziba, who was HIV-positive, was dead – as the result of what the family described as an 'undisclosed illness'. Years later, her story and photograph still appeared on some of Rath's websites as one of his proven successes. But two other patients who attended the press conference later admitted to Health-e that they were on ARVs all along and had been bribed to speak at the meeting with promises of food and money.

To intimidate his detractors, Rath served court papers in November 2005 on various newspapers, journalists, the opposition Democratic Alliance, academics and the head of MSF's mission in Khayelitsha, Dr Eric Goemaere, suing them for millions for defamation. Rath also gave notice that he intended to sue Health-e and its journalists following the series of stories written and broadcast about the activities of his foundation. Four months later he withdrew his defamation case. He also sued the senior ANC leader Professor Kader Asmal, who had lambasted Rath, describing him as an 'AIDS denialist', saying his 'kind of quackery deserves the old Afrikaans response: Voetsek' (an offensive term used to chase a dog).

During all of this, the silence from Health Minister Tshabalala-Msimang was deafening. The MCC, which falls under the Health Department, did announce in April 2005 (three months after being told) that it was investigating Rath's claims. MCC registrar Humphrey Zokufa announced that the Council would act with 'a sense of urgency' in response to a complaint laid by the TAC. Although Zokufa and Director-General Mseleku stated on more than one occasion that an investigation was ongoing, court papers later revealed that, by Mseleku's own admission, the so-called investigation entailed two telephone calls, one to Brink (at the time a Rath employee) and another to Rees (who was at the time no longer employed by Rath). Rees denies ever receiving such a phone call.

In fact, in a clear sign that the Health Department did not want the investigation to lead to anything, its chief investigator, Lionel Snyman, who was making moves to arrest Rath, was hurriedly pulled off the case. No report into the so-called investigation has ever been released.

The Health Minister was presented with several opportunities to sanction Rath and put an end to the controversy. Activists and lawyers had sent her a myriad of letters with information on Rath's unlawful activities. In April 2005 Rath attended a public meeting staged in Khayelitsha by the Health Minister. Hopes were high at the time that Tshabalala-Msimang would use the platform to state her opposition to Rath's activities. Instead she made an unfathomable statement: 'I am not for TAC and I am not for Rath, I am for the ANC.' When Tshabalala-Msimang insisted that she was supporting the constitutional right of people to choose the treatment they wanted, a mass walkout by TAC supporters and health workers followed.

Many thought this was the first time that Rath and the Health Minister had met. However, it later emerged that they had held private talks earlier in the year. Tshabalala-Msimang admitted in Parliament that they had been alone and, according to her, they discussed Rath's 'concern' for people infected with HIV and suffering from the impact of AIDS. Defiantly she said she would only distance herself from Rath if it could be demonstrated that his vitamins were poisonous.

A few days later Tshabalala-Msimang took her support of Rath a step further when she told journalists at the Union Buildings in Pretoria that the work Rath was doing did not contradict government health policies. 'Dr Rath's work complies with and complements our programmes,' she said. She repeatedly commented that the side-effects of ARVs were under-reported. 'I can't stand on a pedestal and say it is all good. It is obviously critical to educate people on the side-effects of anti-retrovirals, and if by doing so I endorse Dr Rath, then I don't know,' she added.

While Tshabalala-Msimang faced increasing criticism for not denouncing Rath, another salvo in support of Rath came from one of the minister's allies, the lawyer Christine Qunta. Qunta's law firm would later step forward as Rath's lawyers when he sued his detractors for daring to criticise his actions. She would also defend him against the TAC court action. Qunta used her privilege as a newspaper columnist to attack respected TAC leaders Mark Heywood and Nathan Geffen for being 'self-righteous' and 'arrogant'. She went on to say that the arrival of Rath had sent the TAC 'into a frenzy which is quite frightening'.

She did not try to hide her admiration for the German. 'Rath is loud, forceful and uses quite intemperate language in his advertisements ... In the midst of all this noise, Rath makes a perfectly valid point regarding the value of vitamins and the role they can play in improving the health of AIDS patients.' Three years later Qunta would be exposed as the director of a company which sold 'natural remedies' that one of her co-directors claimed was a cure for AIDS.

Increasingly, doctors in Khayelitsha were growing worried that Rath's VitaCell bore an uncanny resemblance to efavirenz, one of the main ARVs in the drug combination offered to HIV-positive patients. Disillusioned by the government's inaction, 199 of the Western Cape's top doctors, nurses and academics sent a strongly worded letter to the provincial Health Minister, Pierre Uys, urging him to take action. Describing Rath's activities as 'one of the largest challenges our health services have ever been confronted with', the health workers voiced their outrage at government's failure to protect patients. However, Uys was not prepared to tackle Rath and referred all matters relating to Rath to the national Health Department.

Of equal concern was the fact that Rath and his allies were planning to expand to the Eastern Cape and KwaZulu-Natal, both provinces with high levels of HIV infection and buckling public health services.

Those concerned realised that Rath needed to be stopped at all costs and it was clear that the politicians were not going to take the lead. On 25 November 2005 the TAC and the South African Medical Association, a body representing most of South Africa's doctors, finally lodged legal papers with the Cape High Court. They cited twelve respondents, including Rath and his helpers Mhlongo, Rasnick, Niedzwicki and Brink as well as Tshabalala-Msimang, Mseleku, MCC chairperson Professor Peter Eagles, the Registrar of Medicines, and Uys. Aside from seeking an interdict to stop Rath's 'illegal activities', the TAC asked the court to force the minister and her Director-General to take action against Rath.

The TAC accused the Rath respondents of selling and distributing medicines which were not registered, selling products containing scheduled substances, making false and unauthorised statements that their medicines were effective in treating or preventing AIDS, conducting unauthorised and unethical clinical trials on people with AIDS, and making false statements that antiretrovirals were ineffective in treating AIDS as well as being poisonous. In its affidavit the TAC linked Rath's activities to the deaths of at least twelve people, and warned that by not acting, the government was allowing confusion to take root.

Four and a half years after setting foot in the country, Rath found himself facing the wrath of the law when Judge Dumisani Zondi interdicted Rath, his foundation, Rasnick and Niedzwicki from conducting any further unauthorised clinical trials in South Africa. Brink had by then settled out of court with the TAC and Mhlongo had died in a car accident. Zondi further ordered Tshabalala-Msimang and Mseleku to take reasonable measures to investigate Rath's operations and to take further action depending on the results. At the time of going to press, the Health Department had yet to respond to the ruling.

His tail between his legs, Rath had left South Africa towards the end of 2005 and didn't bother to attend the court hearings. His publications continue to be distributed at various forums where Sanco, the THO or Napwa are involved.

For Zondani Magwebu, left to fend for his children, and like so many others who lost loved ones, the court victory would have meant very little.

Rath's reign in South Africa and Tshabalala-Msimang's inaction opened the door for many similar charlatans to establish themselves in South Africa. It will be up to the next government and the new Health Minister to show whether they have the political will to protect the most vulnerable in our society.

Anso Thom is an award-winning journalist and print editor at Health-e News Service, where she has been a dedicated health writer since 1999. She was part of the investigative team that exposed Rath's activities in South Africa, for which they won the CNN Africa Journalist Award for Excellence in HIV/AIDS Reporting in 2006.

8

Garlic, olive oil, lemons and beetroot

by
Liz McGregor

I first met Tine van der Maas in November 2003 while I was researching a biography on Fana Khaba aka Khabzela, the iconic Gauteng DJ who had earlier that year announced on Yfm that he was HIV-positive. Khabzela had refused to take antiretrovirals and had been rapidly assaulted by a series of calamitous opportunistic infections. He had moved back to his mother's home in Emdeni, Soweto, and the Health Minister, Manto Tshabalala-Msimang, had sent Van der Maas to nurse him.

When Van der Maas arrived, Khabzela was mortally ill. His CD4 count was 2. He was feverish, emaciated and barely conscious. He had peripheral neuropathy of the legs and arms, kidney failure, acute HIV-related colitis, massive bedsores and dementia. He was a difficult patient and his mother and sisters were trying to nurse him themselves. The family was clearly under extreme stress.

They were delighted to see Van der Maas, partly because she had come at the behest of the Health Minister, who had personally phoned Lydia Khaba, Khabzela's mother, to say she was sending her. This showed that someone important and influential was looking after them. Van der Maas's services were free, which was a relief for the Khabas because, although Yfm had been paying Khabzela's medical bills, they were becoming increasingly frustrated and alienated by his suicidal resistance to the only effective medical regimen available to him: antiretroviral treatment. The family themselves had an eclectic approach to health, which embraced traditional healing and the non-interventionist stipulations of Mrs Khaba's Jehovah's Witness faith.

They must also have found Van der Maas's ebullient presence reassuring; she was brisk, energetic and supremely confident. She presented herself as a miracle worker who could cure the sick and the lame alike with her 'Lazarus programme'. This consisted of a liquidised mixture of beetroot, lemon juice, olive oil, ginger, carrots, tomatoes, spinach, yoghurt, ProNutro and various other vegetables. A crucial additional ingredient was a tonic called Africa's Solution. This came in liquid form, and the label on the bottle consisted of a map of Africa in the ANC colours of yellow, green and black and a list of the ingredients it contained. These were African potato extract enriched with plant steroids, vitamins, grapefruit seed extract and olive green leaf extract. Van der Maas said Africa's Solution was made and sold by a company called Bermins, owned by a 'Professor Chris Barnard' from Bloemfontein. 'It works like magic,' she told me.

Van der Maas was the means by which I, a journalist, came to be welcomed to this dying man's bedside. A few weeks before my visit, a picture of her with a dazed-looking Fana had appeared in the *Sunday World* with the caption: 'Godsend: Fana Khaba's new minder, Tine van der Maas, has nursed him back from the brink of death by feeding him her special diet'. She was also clearly eager to promote Africa's Solution although she claimed to be doing so purely because she thought it was the best product of its kind on the market.

Later I met up with Chris Barnard. He was not a professor at all or even a medical doctor. He had a PhD in biochemistry and had started his company, Bermins, in 2001, with the aim of producing a vitamin supplement that would appeal to black people, particularly those with immune deficiencies. The Bermins newsletter of January 2003 claimed:

'Since Africa's Solution has come on the market, we received wonderful and unbelievable [*sic*] stories of people's health improving. What was most interesting was the feedback from Health Educational Services [Tine van der Maas's organisation] who uses Africa's Solution with lemon and olive oil . . . This produce [Africa's Solution with added olive leaf extract] was used in an independent research project at the Technical University of the Free State on severely ill people. The abnormal biochemistry and haematology of these very ill patients was rectified within a month. The viral load decreased significantly in people with HIV infection. The CD4 counts did not decrease further. It was also used in an extensive program for severe HIV/Aids patients in hospitals in South Africa with miraculous improvements in 90 percent of patients (results available from Tine van der Maas).' In facts, these results were not available from Van der Maas and remain elusive. She claims that all her patient records were lost in a burglary.

Much later, after Khabzela had died a miserable and painful death, I met up again with Tine van der Maas and her mother, Nelly, in an attempt to find out more about them. Tine is a large, ruddy-faced, earthy woman of about 50. She chooses her clothes for comfort: loose cotton shirts and pants and flat shoes. She laughs a lot. Both she and her mother are eccentrics who make much of their unconventionality and their disdain for the medical and scientific establishment. They take pride in the meagreness of their formal education. Their remedies are homespun, evolved over the years from their own experience and observations and adjusted where required. A regular refrain from them is: 'You must just use your imagination!'

Nelly, who was trained but has never worked as a social worker, says she first learnt the value of non-traditional remedies from her Jewish grandparents. 'When Tine was 12, she got herpes in her eye. For a year, she was in and out of hospitals.' Then Nelly's father suggested a remedy ostensibly used for generations by Jewish people: turtle doves. Nelly bought a pair, put them in a cage and encouraged Tine to spend time with them. The herpes disappeared. 'So we understood that turtle doves take it over but we don't know how,' said Nelly.

They told me that Tine had been born in Argentina, but her family returned to their native Holland when she was a few months old. In 1966 the family emigrated to South Africa though Tine went back to Holland after some post-matric studies in graphic art at Port Elizabeth Technikon. When she was 29, she returned to South Africa and became a nurse. She got nursing jobs through agencies for a while, and then a friend in Holland discovered she had acquired HIV through her husband, who used to travel frequently to the Philippines. When it surfaced in South Africa, Nelly, who was then still in Holland, sent information on AIDS – then still scarce in South Africa – to Tine. Together they began to work out an educational programme that would resonate in South African culture. Tine said she had finally found her calling. 'When I found AIDS, my CV was about 10 pages long because I had not yet found my passion,' she said. Nelly came out from Holland and together they formed First AIDS Education Service, which set out to sell AIDS awareness programmes to the corporate sector and the state. They were a pair of entrepreneurs with a product to offer an as yet largely untapped market.

In May 2005, Tine explained to Nathan Geffen of the Treatment Action Campaign (TAC): 'Although we have been in the AIDS field since 1989, we started investigating alternative treatment in 1995 as we were not totally impressed with AZT and started treating people on our program in 1997/1998. We noticed two things: people with AIDS had acid bodies and they were lacking in all the essential nutrients. So our thinking was to detoxify the body and restore biochemistry.'

Their prescription for this was various combinations of lemons, olive oil, garlic and ginger. Later, Africa's Solution was added to the mix. In her newsletter, she once explained her commitment to this particular brand. 'One of the most important things I have found that works like magic is Africa's Solution from Bermins and some of his other products.

Over the years working with HIV/AIDS and other immune problems we have tried a lot of different supplements. Before we found Bermins, we taught people how to make a tea from the African potato, which is a tremendous immune booster. Picture the workings of the African potato this way: with it your white blood cells have an AK47, and when an infection enters the body, they shoot it ... *rattattattattattatt*. It makes the white blood cells much stronger. An extract from the African potato is in Bermins.'

At some point in his demented scramble from one potential healer to another, Khabzela consulted – but unfortunately did not listen to – one of the country's most experienced HIV clinicians, Dr David Spencer. I asked Dr Spencer about Van der Maas's programme. This was his response: 'There is growing evidence that so-called natural remedies and even foods taken in excessive quantities can do harm. The consumption of raw garlic cloves has been shown to diminish the absorption of drugs, including antiretrovirals. It is naïve to assume that foodstuffs are without any biological activity. The so-called immune boosters such as the African potato and Sutherlandia impair the metabolic activity of antiretrovirals and the use of the African potato in AIDS patients has been documented to worsen their CD4 cell counts.'

Tine has consistently denied that she received any financial incentive from either the state or Bermins. She harps on her poverty. 'I have only one pair of sandals and one pair of shoes,' she told me at our meeting in 2004. 'And there is only R4000 left to draw on our credit card.' The implication was that they were philanthropists, motivated purely by a desire to help others, regardless of the cost to themselves. She was, however, worldly enough to realise that top-level government co-operation would provide a huge boost to her cause. Barnard told me that Tine had made two dolls with a bottle of Africa's Solution in the stomach of each. She accosted Manto Tshabalala-Msimang at a public meeting in Cape Town and presented her with the two dolls, one for herself and one for the President. A few days later, she had a meeting with the minister.

This seems to have been the spark for the minister's infatuation with the lemon juice, olive oil and African potato diet.

Thereafter Tshabalala-Msimang opened doors for the Van der Maases all over the country. From being a pair of eccentric Dutch women with another wacky Aids cure, they became a force to be reckoned with. Tine explained the process in a media interview in 2005: 'When I contacted the Minister and said this and this works and people can stop dying, she asked me to go and see patients. One of them was Nozipho Bhengu [daughter of an ANC MP] . . . She asked me to go to these different hospitals. So we were in Mokopane [Limpopo], St Barnabas [Eastern Cape], Themba Hospital [Mpumalanga], in Lesotho, which was on TV . . . We told the [Lesotho] Minister of Health to come and look. We only do it if the Ministers of Health or MECs come and look, otherwise it's a waste of time.' This interview not only provided further confirmation that the Minister of Health opened doors for Van der Maas but also threw some light on Van der Maas's motives. She was not averse to treating patients if there was someone important around who could promote her and her programme.

Confirmation that Van der Maas had indeed worked with patients at the hospitals she mentioned – as well as at Bloemfontein Provincial Hospital in the Free State and Kimberley Provincial Hospital in the Northern Cape – came from the Director-General of the South African Department of Health, Thami Mseleku. He noted that Van der Maas had been 'invited by MECs of Health to do voluntary work with AIDS patients' at these hospitals and at 'various clinics in all provinces'. As further proof of Tshabalala-Msimang's support, Dr Cyril Khanyile, a medical adviser in the Health Department's HIV/AIDS directorate at the time, was on hand on several occasions to assist Van der Maas with press interviews and try to explain in scientific terms what she was trying to do.

Van der Maas also commented that Tshabalala-Msimang had referred a number of private patients to her, mostly 'from top families in the ANC and government'. Nozipho Bhengu, daughter of the ANC MP Ruth Bhengu, followed Van der Maas's diet for about two years until her death in 2006. She had been hospitalised with a CD4 count of 55 and adverse reactions to ARVs. She stopped the ARVs, followed the diet, and her CD4 count climbed to 135 over the following three months. 'I have been concentrating on the lemon juice, olive oil, garlic, ginger and Africa's Solution and it has worked. Now I am working. I am normal just like anybody else,' she said. However, Nozipho died of an AIDS-related illness in 2006 and her funeral unfortunately turned into a TAC-bashing event.

Over time Van der Maas became more and more grandiose in her claims. 'When we get them, their viral loads are often extremely high – in the 100 000s,' she told Nathan Geffen of the TAC. 'All of them, their viral loads go to either undetectable or below 8000. Even on Africa's Solution alone, the viral loads went down by almost half in the trial of Dr Elmien van der Heever from in the 400,000s to the 200,000s – and again, this was only on Africa's Solution and people who often only ate every second day and then it was only pap or bread.'

Van der Maas also became increasingly involved with South Africa's AIDS dissident community – and increasingly opposed to ARVs. 'I hate them with a passion,' she told Nathan Geffen. 'If people are taking them and they ask me if they should stop, I always tell them that it is a choice they must make, that they should read about ARVs and read about what we do and then make an informed decision. We also leave them well alone when you can see that the fact this person is taking ARVs is helping them mentally. We do, however, tell people that when their CD4 counts are below 200, and their doctors are advising them to start ARV treatment, to first go on our programme just for three months ... Not once, as far as I know, has anybody gone off our programme and started the ARV programme.' However, as Van der Maas does not follow up people on her diet, it is hard to know what she bases this claim on.

By 2004, Tine was becoming frustrated by what she saw as a lack of recognition for her programme. She and Nelly decided to make a film which could be broadcast on SABC TV and prove once and for all the efficacy of her cure. She seemed to believe that, if she could only persuade the SABC to screen the film, everyone would see the light and her 'programme' would be introduced throughout the country. 'If our programme is implemented in all the clinics, then the clinics will be empty. The hospitals will be empty because if you fix the malnourishment, you will fix all the problems.'

To make the film, they entered into a collaboration with another European AIDS dissident, Kim Cools, a Belgian who had managed to ingratiate himself with Nkosi Bhengu, a chief in the KwaNgolosi district in rural KwaZulu-Natal. The year before, Nkosi Bhengu had allocated a patch of land on the banks of the Inanda Dam to Cools and his South African wife, Delaine. Here they ran a small organic farming project. Nkosi Bhengu also allowed them to use the tribal courthouse to run a 'clinic', from which they conducted an anti-ARV campaign. Cools was a rabid and active AIDS dissident. He announced his stance on his business card, which, alongside his name, contact details and occupation (given as Natural Health Consultant), contained a strident slab of text headed 'SCIENTIFIC FACTS'. The text read: 'People are not dying from HIV; HIV is not the cause of AIDS; AIDS can be reversed 100 percent; ARVs are the cause of AIDS death.' Although neither Cools nor Delaine had had any medical training, they took it upon themselves to urge people living with HIV to throw away their ARVs.

Cools operated under the auspices of an organisation called African Rainbow Circle, describing himself as 'a volunteer committed to bring facts to the people'. 'Propaganda like that of the TAC and the pharma industry are the real reason for the so-called AIDS victims to eventually die. HIV does not cause AIDS and people with AIDS can easily recover if they stop all sugar intake and eat right,' he claimed. This was precisely the same sort of incomprehensible gobbledygook that Van der Maas was spouting.

Like Van der Maas, Cools took advantage of dubious official backing and a poor, under-educated community to establish a base. AIDS in the KwaNgolosi area has been particularly devastating. With unemployment at around 60 per cent, one in three adults was thought to be HIV-positive. The infection rate among women attending the antenatal clinic at the local hospital, St Mary's, was 59 per cent.

In 2003, around the same time as Cools's arrival in the valley, St Mary's Hospital was finally in a position to start offering antiretroviral treatment. Nancy Sias ran an outreach programme, which sent adherence counsellors to the homes of patients on ARVs every month to check on them. Cools's anti-ARV proselytising, she said, was making their jobs particularly difficult. 'They have really presented a challenge to us,' she said. 'Most people there are illiterate and very gullible, especially if it's a white man.'

When I asked Cools how he had managed to persuade the local chief, Nkosi Bhengu, to let him have a prime stretch of land, he said: 'I told the king I would eradicate AIDS and bring health and wealth to the area.'

Tine van der Maas said she initially hooked up with Cools after being interviewed on a 'Special Assignment' TV programme. Cools had phoned her and invited her to visit the 'clinic' he had set up at the KwaNgolosi courthouse. However, his wife told journalist Kerry Cullinan that another AIDS dissident, Anthony Brink, had put them in touch with Van der Maas.

Tine saw Cools as the person who could help translate her dream of a documentary on her programme into reality. 'We thought it's either the soapbox or a documentary,' she said. 'My mother didn't feel like the soapbox. So I phoned Kim and said, How about if we do a documentary?' Kim had a camera and was willing. They persuaded various suppliers to donate the ingredients: 250 litres of olive oil from Kloovenburg Wine Estate in the Cape; Bokomo came up with free ProNutro; and the local Spar supermarket agreed to sell them lemons and garlic at cost. And, of course, Bermins was only too willing to provide all the Africa's

Solution they needed. The Rath Foundation provided R5000 worth of tapes for filming.

Van der Maas mother and daughter hired a trailer, picked up the supplies from the various donors and set off for KwaNgolosi at the beginning of October 2004. They stayed with Cools on the farm and set up shop at the courthouse. 'In the beginning, we had no patients,' said Van der Maas. 'When we left we had 160.' Patients arrived with a wide array of ailments. All of them, no matter what their complaint, were put on the 'programme,' which essentially consisted of various combinations of olive oil, garlic, lemon juice, ProNutro and Africa's Solution. In the four months they were there, Tine and Nelly claimed to have cured cataracts, diabetes, high blood pressure and epilepsy. 'We treated 51 with [sexually transmitted diseases] that were not reacting to antibiotics. They all got better. For gonorrhoea, you fill them up with garlic and Africa's Solution. With herpes, you mix lemon juice, aqueous cream and Disprin. We had a man with herpes on his penis. We gave him our cream – lemon juice is the active ingredient – and some Africa's Solution for its African potato; Disprin opens the pores; aqueous cream makes sure it goes in. You insert a clove of garlic in the vagina and the anus.'

Tine and Nellie ran their bizarre 'clinic' for four months. Cools filmed it all – although Tine insists that only those patients who agreed in writing were included. 'They all signed they could go on TV,' claimed Tine. 'We said, What would you like to say to the people of South Africa?'

But most bizarre of all was the tacit endorsement of this project by the Minister of Health. 'Dr Manto', as Tine called Tshabalala-Msimang, made two visits, the second time bringing an entourage that included Dr Ronald Green-Thompson, the head of Health in KwaZulu-Natal. 'That's why she keeps on saying lemons and garlic because she's seen it work,' claimed Tine. Tshabalala-Msimang also showed the Van der Maas film at a meeting in Pietermaritzburg, ironically to launch ethical guidelines on research.

Early in March 2005, Tine called me and invited me to a screening of the film. It was all a bit cloak and dagger: I had to phone someone else, a man called Winston, to find out where and when the screening was to take place. Their fear, apparently, was that it would be ambushed by the TAC.

At 6.30 pm one Tuesday, I turned up at the designated spot in Florida, in western Johannesburg, to find a motley bunch of AIDS dissidents, traditional healers and white trade unionists whose offices had been used for the occasion. Winston turned out to be Winston Wilken, a pleasant Afrikaans man who was also a salesman for Africa's Solution. Tine and Nelly greeted us, taut with excitement and anticipation. They were clearly hoping this would be the event that would change their lives.

Half an hour later than scheduled, a screen was erected in a corner of the room and the film began to roll. I was appalled. Suppurating ulcers and emaciated limbs were exposed to the close-up gaze of the camera. The illnesses that had give rise to this suffering ranged from AIDS with all its associated opportunistic diseases, to diabetes, arthritis, cataracts and epilepsy. All of these illnesses, the film voice-over informed us, had been successfully treated with olive oil, garlic, lemon juice and lashings of Africa's Solution. During the first half of the film, there was fairly unsubtle placement of product. Bottles of Africa's Solution with its distinctive yellow, green and black label were liberally displayed. In the second half, the marketing was much more overt, with Africa's Solution prescribed for every ailment on view. The refrain of the theme song, performed by a black man who accompanied himself on a drum, was 'Africa's Solution'. There were also several shots of the Health Minister smiling encouragingly as various of Tine and Nelly's patients explained the miraculous cures the pair had wrought on them. Towards the end of the film, Nkosi Bhengu was interviewed, and thanked them for their work. The credits at the end included the National Association of People Living with HIV/Aids (Napwa) and the Traditional Healers' Organisation.

When the last strains of the theme song had dwindled away and the lights had been switched on, there was vigorous clapping from the hundred-strong audience. Then a strange thing happened. Person after person got up to speak, and it became clear that this was a cult-like group, beset with feelings of persecution. The TAC was mentioned repeatedly and bitterly as the enemy, the tool of Big Pharma, the pharmaceutical mafia, well-funded, powerful and ruthless.

Late one night, a couple of weeks after my book on Khabzela came out, I had a call from Tine. She was very angry. She harangued me for a while, ending with a threat to sue me for defamation. What seemed to have upset her in particular was a conversation with Kim Cools which I recorded in the book. Cools told me that one evening, after Tine had had a couple of whiskies, he had wheedled out of her the information that she received R1 for every bottle of Africa's Solution she sold. So much, I thought, for her claim that she derived no material benefit from her promotion of Africa's Solution. Cools said that she had promised to give him a third of the receipts. This, Kim had worked out, could amount to R1.5 million, based on the fact that there were five million people in South Africa with HIV. But then Tine went off to Bloemfontein for a two-week Christmas break and, when she returned, she denied the conversation had ever taken place. The promise of R1.5 million had disappeared, much to Cools's ire.

In any other situation, Tine and Nelly van der Maas would be engaging women. They are hard-working, enterprising, unconventional and adventurous. They are not afraid to get their hands dirty: they personally nursed some very ill patients. But there was a singlemindedness about Tine's treatment of these patients in order to promote her own 'programme'. And, if Cools is to be believed, she was somewhat sparing of the truth in her assertion that there was no material advantage in her relentless promotion of Africa's Solution.

The real scandal of the Tine and Nelly saga, however, is the legitimacy conferred on them by the Minister of Health. The fact that they were allowed to conduct 'trials' on extremely ill and frequently powerless South Africans is quite extraordinary.

Liz McGregor is a journalist who has worked for the Rand Daily Mail, Guardian, Observer *and the* Weekender. *She is author of* Khabzela: The Life and Times of a South African *(Jacana, 2005) and co-editor of* At Risk: Writing on and over the Edge of South Africa *(Jonathan Ball, 2007). She is a writing fellow at the Wits Institute of Social and Economic Research.*

9

Traditional alternatives?

by
Kanya Ndaki

It could have been a great story: the mighty Minister of Health, championing the cause, fighting for traditional medicine to be taken seriously, and, with enough resources for research and regulation, finally clearing the field after centuries of neglect. Traditional medicine certainly needed a champion.

Apart from the much-quoted government estimate that at least 70 per cent of all South Africans consult traditional healers, we still know very little about the industry. Attempts to legislate it have been frustratingly slow, while the World Health Organisation (WHO) has noted with concern that 'the quantity and quality of the safety and efficacy data on traditional medicine are far from sufficient to meet the criteria needed to support its use worldwide'.

Traditional medicine was pretty much left to its own devices until 1994, when the first democratic government took steps to make funds available for the research and development of traditional medicines. This was also the beginning of the long, arduous task of drawing up a regulatory framework for the industry, which eventually culminated in the Traditional Health Practitioners Act.

A great story in the making – and an emotive one, too. Traditional medicine had been one of the casualties after years of apartheid rule, a 'lost' part of our culture which needed to be rescued, and which we needed to feel proud of again. The rediscovery of this long-forgotten system of knowledge and practice was part of the African Renaissance, part of the country's quest to reclaim its heritage.

But this is where the plot, as with most stories involving South Africa's health ministry, took a more convoluted and polemical turn. Much like that hot African potato, nutrition, which was pitted against antiretroviral (ARV) medication in the fight against HIV and AIDS, dodgy traditional remedies began to be promoted as alternatives to ARVs, and the health ministry, the defender of the cause, stood in the forefront of this move.

The Traditional Healers' Organisation (THO) saw Dr Manto Tshabalala-Msimang as a champion, 'the only person in high office to understand the disparities between western and traditional medicine', according to a newspaper interview. Speaking while leading a protest march through Johannesburg in November 2006, Phephsile Maseko, national co-ordinator of the THO, said of the Health Minister: 'She has been trying hard to narrow the gap.' Marchers called for better recognition of traditional medicine. They carried posters showing support for the beleaguered Tshabalala-Msimang, who, a few months earlier, had embarrassed the country when she opened South Africa's exhibition at the Toronto AIDS conference in August. The stand featured garlic, lemon, beetroot and African potatoes, but no antiretroviral drugs – until journalists pointed out the omission.

Two months prior to the Johannesburg protest, traditional healers in Durban marched through the city centre on a Friday in support of the minister. The trademark song of former Deputy President Jacob Zuma, 'Leth' umshini wami' (Bring me my machine gun) was remixed to 'Leth'ikabishi lami, Leth'ubeetroot wami' (Bring me my cabbage. Bring me my beetroot). The crowd of nearly 200 carried posters bearing slogans like 'Viva Dr Rath' and 'Viva Manto'. At the bottom of all printed banners was the notice 'Dr Rath Health Foundation Africa'.

The fact that the THO was in bed with Dr Rath made the protests even more significant and drew the battle lines even more tightly. As Treatment Action Campaign (TAC) leader Nathan Geffen warned in 2006, 'by creating a dichotomy between African solutions and Western interventions, pseudo-scientists like those associated with Rath are able to generate sympathy among many traditional healers and African nationalists and antagonism towards the public health-care system and science'. Somewhere along the line, the poignant notion of restoring traditional medicine to its rightful place and to Africans their dignity collided headlong with orthodox scientific views, creating even more doubt, mistrust and suspicion between Western science and African traditional medicine.

At the time, I was a young health journalist, working for an online HIV/AIDS news service, secretly hoping the furore would pass me by. But naturally it landed on my lap. I was uncomfortable about the controversy because I didn't know where I stood. Did I believe in traditional medicine? In a half-hearted way, I suppose I did. It was part of my culture, something that had always been there, a familiar belief that I had never questioned and was not willing to start questioning now.

For me it was never a mystery why people would spend over R300 on a course of *Ubhejane*, ignoring scientists who warned that the mixture needed to undergo more thorough testing. They believed in the stuff; it was familiar; they could relate to it. Tshabalala-Msimang knew this and, to a certain extent, this informed her zealous support of traditional medicine. 'Apart from its medicinal values, African traditional medicine also defines us as a people. It is this heritage amongst others that we are not simply going to give away purely because of the humiliation we get subjected to for the things we believe in,' she once said.

But belief is not enough to inform policy and practice, especially when it comes to people's lives. Jerry Coovadia, Victor Daitz Professor of HIV/AIDS Research at the University of KwaZulu-Natal, attributes the public patronage of traditional HIV/AIDS 'wonder cures' by top political decision-makers to 'an agenda that has more to do with extreme sensitivity about the legacies of apartheid, discrimination and racism than with rigorous scientific and public utility'. But when leaders tiptoe round potentially harmful traditional remedies and promote them as alternatives to proven treatment, they are playing with the lives of millions of South Africans who believe in traditional medicine. The tragedy is that the discourse made popular by the Health Minister and other public figures in framing traditional medicine in opposition to Western medicine has created an environment ripe for charlatans, quacks and opportunists to exploit a fundamental belief for their own commercial gains.

In 2000, a medical technologist by the name of Siphiwe Hadebe claimed that all it took to eradicate HIV and restore HIV-positive people's immune systems was 30 days of treatment with *umbimbi*, at R2000 for a three-hour session. *Umbimbi*, which was first devised by Hadebe's father as a medicine for chickens and cattle, was made from two traditional herbs and a special salt.

Hadebe was slick: he had a clinic in Johannesburg's northern suburbs and two more in Durban and Cape Town. He handed out business cards at funeral parlours and had a website which went into detail about the *umbimbi* therapy that he administered. According to the website, the treatment consisted of an *umbimbi* drip, oral administration of *umbimbi*, multi-vitamin pills, folic acid as well as an antiretroviral cocktail. A large glass box lined with tin foil was used to give 'radiation therapy'. At one stage Peter Mokaba, outspoken AIDS denialist and ANC leader who described ARVs as 'poison', was treated by Hadebe with *umbimbi*. Another patient was Pinky Tiro, sister of popular television talkshow host Felicia Mabuza-Suttle. She was very ill when a family member told her about Hadebe and his 'magic medicine', so she went to his clinic in Fourways, Johannesburg, where she was admitted and treated for ten days.

Tiro and other patients would undergo 25 pipe-smoking sessions a day for three days, followed by four days of rest, and then another three days of smoking sessions. They also drank a cupful of *umbimbi* mixed with soup once a day for ten days. '*Umbimbi* was so bitter at first; I thought it was olive oil. The pipe sessions, using a long, sophisticated pipe which emitted white smoke, helped to clear my voice but it drained me of all my energy,' Tiro said in a media interview in 2003. After the ten days, Tiro said, patients went back to their homes because they were told they had been healed. 'I'm still HIV-positive, so that means Siphiwe didn't cure me,' the socialite, wife and mother told a journalist during an interview, three years after taking Hadebe's treatment.

Police and inspectors from the Medicines Control Council (MCC) managed to shut down Hadebe's lucrative operation in 2003, after conducting raids on his offices in Durban and Johannesburg. The Asset Forfeiture Unit subsequently seized property worth millions of rands and found files on over 600 patients, This was a major success for the MCC, one they have failed to repeat in recent years. The director of the AIDS and Society Research Unit at the University of Cape Town, Professor Nicoli Nattrass, believes the MCC 'has been starved of the resources it needs to function effectively.' 'Whereas the MCC shut down these sorts of operations in the past, it now appears to be powerless to respond to complaints,' she said in mid-2007, adding that in recent years the MCC appeared to have become 'unable or unwilling' to challenge the Health Minister. Consequently, business has never been better for pedlars of untested AIDS remedies. According to Nathan Geffen, the government's reluctance to crack down on the sale of untested remedies was in line with Health Minister Manto Tshabalala-Msimang's history of endorsing such products. 'All of this sends a signal to people that it's open season to sell untested medicines,' he said. 'There's no enforcement, and even active support of quackery.'

The traditional medicines sector in South Africa is worth about R3 billion a year (or 5.6 per cent of the national health budget) and serves almost 27 million consumers. It is also being forced to change with the times. A proliferation of products has appeared on the streets and the shelves; and not all the purveyors are qualified traditional healers. Aggressive advertising campaigns in the mainstream media are increasingly common, and some suppliers have marketing budgets that range between R10,000 and R25,000 a month, with an average of one newspaper and one radio advert a week, according to research done by *The Star* newspaper in May 2008. The mixtures are also now becoming available at retail pharmacies.

But there are still no checks and balances for this thriving industry. In 2004 the government released draft regulations for the control of complementary and alternative medicines. A second draft of the regulations was finally made available in 2008. Tshabalala–Msimang was quoted as referring to the draft legislation in a 2005 editorial published in *The Star*: 'We cannot transplant models designed for scientific validation of allopathic [conventional] medicine and apply it to other remedies. There is a need for creativity to come up with relevant and pragmatic models to prove safety, quality and efficacy of complementary, alternative and African traditional medicines.'

The Traditional Health Practitioners Act, which provides a framework for regulating the sector, including registering practitioners, was only signed into law by the President in early 2008. Although the Act had been passed five years earlier, the Constitutional Court ruled that it had been improperly processed by the National Council of Provinces and, following public meetings in all provinces, it was only approved in October 2007.

In terms of the Act, an interim Traditional Health Practitioners' Council will be set up to help draw up regulations for the sector. The aim of the Council is to make sure that all practitioners are registered and have a minimum standard of training from an accredited institution. At the same time, the Medicines Control Council has begun the process of registering complementary medicines, including traditional medicine, by means of its Accelerated Registration Programme. By the end of 2007, some 25,000 complementary and traditional medicines had been submitted to the MCC in terms of this programme.

Although the law clearly placed all alleged remedies and cures under the rubric of medicines, the Health Department appeared to act according to a different set of rules for 'traditional' or 'alternative' remedies – even to the point of supporting their distribution through the public health system without their ever having been tested scientifically, according to Professor Nattrass. Case in point? *Ubhejane*, a herbal treatment for AIDS, made by Zeblon Gwala, a former truck driver, who claims that the ingredients for *Ubhejane* came to him in dreams from his healer-grandfather. Gwala says that he personally collects the 89 herbal ingredients from all over Africa and mixes them by hand. The dark brown liquid is sold in old plastic milk bottles – the bottle with the blue lid is for making the viral load undetectable; the bottle with the white lid for boosting the CD4 count (a measure of the strength of the immune system). Patients are advised to stop smoking and drinking while on the treatment, and abstain from sex or else use condoms. No more precise explanation of how the mixture reduces the amount of virus in the body or increases the CD4 count is given. During one visit to Gwala's Nebza AIDS clinic in Pinetown, the customers crammed into the tiny waiting room listening to instructions on how to use the remedy seemed more interested in whether their appetites would increase or if they could stop taking ARVs.

Similarly, the Health Minister and KwaZulu-Natal's Health MEC, Peggy Nkonyeni, did not wait for any scientific evidence of how the remedy worked, before recommending to the mother of Deputy President Phumzile Mlambo-Ngcuka, who runs a Durban hospice, that she should give *Ubhejane* to her patients. EThekwini mayor Obed Mlaba also supported *Ubhejane*, and sponsored its supply to patients at a Catholic hospice in Inchanga. Gwala's main promoter was Professor Herbert Vilakazi, who in 2006 was special adviser to the KwaZulu-Natal premier, and later became the head of the Presidential Task Team on Traditional Medicine.

Despite the scepticism in the national media, on the ground in KwaZulu-Natal there seemed to be far greater willingness to accept the medicine as an effective remedy. When relatives heard that I would be travelling to Durban to write about *Ubhejane*, I was given a long list of orders and requests to courier the liquid to them as soon as I could. And on the day I met Gwala at his Pinetown clinic, I was accompanied by two of my cousins who queued up in the corridors like everyone else to buy the remedy 'for friends of friends'. The cost of *Ubhejane* does not seem to have dented its appeal. Government-supplied ARVs have been free since 2003, but a full course of the herbal remedy retailed at R374 for a month's supply.

But when I visited Gwala, the jury was still out on whether *Ubhejane* was effective in treating HIV, and scientists were understandably cautious about the hype generated by the remedy, and called for more research. Professor Nceba Gqaleni, Deputy Dean of the University of KwaZulu-Natal's Medical School, who is also a member of the WHO's expert committee on traditional medicine for Africa, conducted preliminary laboratory tests on *Ubhejane*, which revealed little more than that the mixture is not toxic to cells grown in test tubes. 'I want to state categorically that I have not performed any studies on humans,' he stated. Gqaleni was angry that Vilakazi had publicised part of an early report he gave to Gwala, as he believed it would confuse those who didn't understand scientific studies. Both Gwala and Vilakazi stated that they had met Tshabalala-Msimang many times since 2003 when they first made a presentation to her on *Ubhejane*. The minister encouraged them to develop a protocol for *Ubhejane* so that it could be studied at the Medical University of Southern Africa (Medunsa, now the University of Limpopo Medical School).

Professor Wim du Plooy confirmed that Medunsa's ethics committee had given permission for an observational study on *Ubhejane*, following an application from Dr Sam Mhlongo, a well-known AIDS denialist, and Dr Patrick Maduna, both of Medunsa's Family Medicine Department.

Dr Maduna's 2004 study of 24 people taking *Ubhejane* over three months found that while not an AIDS cure, it was not toxic, stimulated appetite and enhanced patients' feelings of well-being.

But all this was still not enough scientific evidence for the Health Minister to promote the remedy. When the Democratic Alliance (DA) complained about the manufacture of 'fake cures' such as *Ubhejane* by 'backyard chemists', the Department of Health retaliated with a statement that the DA was 'stagnating in a colonial ideological outlook', and went on to reiterate its support for traditional medicines, declaring in a press release in February 2006 that 'traditional medicine is here to stay'. The DA responded by investigating the matter further and laying charges of fraud and of contravening the Medicines and Related Substances Control Act against Gwala for producing and selling *Ubhejane*. However, the police declined to press charges.

As it happened, Professor Vilakazi was an acquaintance and colleague of my father's; and when I requested help in securing an interview with Gwala, Vilakazi was very helpful. In fact, he gave me a personal tour of the Inchanga hospice and I spent more time with him than I did with Gwala. I was acutely aware that Vilakazi felt obliged to educate me. I was one of the African children he described in a report he assigned me to read before I arrived in Durban, as being as 'culturally alien to principles and patterns of African civilisations as the white or Indian or Coloured children attending school with them'. Over a three-hour interview, Vilakazi went into great detail about the denigration of African knowledge, arguing that the rules for registering medicines were 'pharmaceutical-industry friendly'. In the case of traditional medicine, he wanted to know where the laboratory evidence was meant to come from. According to Vilakazi, African traditional medicine relies on 'walking evidence' and not laboratory evidence, and it was unfair to subject it to the same scrutiny as Western medicine.

Professor Gqaleni of the University of KwaZulu-Natal's Medical School maintained, on the other hand, that traditional medicine has to be comprehensively studied, marketed and licensed properly. 'We have to define what *Ubhejane* is, find out the ingredients, the exact dosages . . . it has to be subjected to proper scientific scrutiny.' He added that there was still not enough information on the effects of traditional medicine on ARVs – which in some cases have proved to be incompatible. Gqaleni stressed that 'nothing prevents Gwala from helping patients' and the dreams telling Gwala which plants to use are 'not just dreams' but Gwala's ancestors guiding him through the process. It's a traditional calling that Gwala has an ethical obligation to carry out. But when you want to put products on shelves and give them to chemists and hospitals, and to people who are taking ARVs, 'you have a duty to do it properly ... you are entering a different terrain altogether,' Gqaleni told me.

To make things even more difficult for scientists wishing to study *Ubhejane*, Gwala has refused to divulge its ingredients. Even Gqaleni, who has signed a confidentiality agreement with Gwala, does not know what is in it and said, 'I don't know whether my ethics committee will give permission to do human trials without this information.'

Unlike Siphiwe Hadebe and his *umbimbi* therapy, Gwala's *Ubhejane* has been subjected to some scientific testing, albeit in a limited way. But still not enough is known about the product, certainly not enough to warrant the support or at least condonation at a high political and official level. For instance, Sibani Mngadi, spokesperson of the Department of Health, said that while the department was working on a regulatory framework for traditional medicine, 'we cannot deny those who find benefit in traditional medicine from continuing to use it. If people are told by a traditional healer that they cannot take traditional medicine and ARVs, they must make their own decisions.'

Gwala's popularity among health officials has not waned despite a statement by the Health Minister in April 2008, which distanced her from the remedy, saying that 'the Minister has never expressed support for *Ubhejane* or any specific traditional medicine product for that matter'. The statement came shortly after a ruling by the Advertising Standards

Authority ordering the immediate withdrawal of an advertisement for *Ubhejane* that appeared in *Ilanga* newspaper. This followed a complaint by the TAC's Nathan Geffen that the *Ubhejane* advertisement contained a number of unsubstantiated claims, e.g. that the product 'increases your CD4 count and reduces the viral load until it disappears in the blood of the person suffering from the disease'.

Thami Mseleku, Director-General of Health, defended Gwala's right to promote *Ubhejane*, and told an American journalist in 2007: 'I am an African, and I will never condemn him.' Gwala himself has not been investigated, and his remedy is sold and marketed extensively. He has addressed Parliament's health portfolio committee; and in May 2008 he was one of the speakers at a bizarre 'HIV information workshop' hosted by KwaZulu-Natal's Health MEC and attended by AIDS denialists and opponents of antiretroviral therapy. The national Health Minister was the keynote speaker.

Having friends in high places must certainly have helped Gwala. And it doesn't get much higher than the Presidential Task Team on African Traditional Medicine. In November 2006, when government announced the members of the task team – a high-level body expected to advise the Health Department on how to regulate the popular field – two names stood out: Professor Herbert Vilakazi and Advocate Christine Qunta. The task team, which will be chaired by Vilakazi, is expected to develop a pharmacopoeia of South African traditional remedies, and help guide policy formulation. The Health Director-General said the task team would also determine whether African traditional medicines should be required to pass the rigour of clinical trials before registration, or be subjected to an alternative screening system.

But according to Durban businessman Caesar Ngcobo, Vilakazi was a partner with himself and Gwala in the company promoting *Ubhejane*, despite claims by Vilakazi that he was merely Gwala's 'adviser' and was not connected to the business. Vilakazi's appointment was greeted with shock and outrage, even among government officials. Nozizwe Madlala-

Routledge, Deputy Minister of Health at the time, was particularly concerned about the mixed signals the appointment would create. 'What brings about that concern for me is that Vilakazi is chairperson of the task team on traditional medicine and . . . Vilakazi . . . is marketing an untested product, *Ubhejane*, so that's a concern because once people see "Oh, Professor Vilakazi has now been appointed by the president to be chairperson of this task team and Professor Vilakazi is saying take *Ubhejane* to cure Aids" – you know what I mean, it's very confusing to ordinary people.' Pressed on whether she was saying it had been a mistake to appoint him, she replied, 'Yes, I think so.'

Christine Qunta is a director of Comforter's Healing Gift, a company that manufactures alternative medication which, according to Qunta's co-director, the Uitenhage 'healer' Freddie Isaacs, can cure AIDS. Isaacs allegedly sold 112 green pills packaged in Comforter's Healing Gift plastic containers to an undercover journalism student, Nompumezo Makinana, who was accompanied by TAC member Emma Baleka, posing as her mother. Makinana said that Isaacs placed his hand on her forehead and told her she was in the dangerous 'third stage' of the virus, but that eight of his tablets (four in the morning, four at night) would cure her. He also gave her a swig from a bottle of black liquid with no label. They paid R210 for the two containers and the liquid and, according to the invoice, a further R200 was owed. Isaacs claimed his capsules had been tested on animals and by the 'MRC Council'. Qunta told Independent Newspapers that Isaacs and his colleagues had been instructed not to make claims for the product until scientific tests were completed. Qunta, a lawyer whose firm defended Matthias Rath, denied personal involvement in the marketing of the products as cures for AIDS. Qunta stated that any comments made by Isaacs on the alleged healing properties of the products reflected Isaacs's own personal views and not those of the company. But in the view of the TAC, Isaacs's sale of substances purporting to be cures for HIV/AIDS to members of the public, substances whose efficacy and safety had not been scientifically verified and whose registration had not been approved by the MCC, constituted a breach of the law. In late 2007 the TAC lodged a complaint against Qunta, Isaacs and Comforter's Healing Gift to the Director of Public Prosecutions, the South African Human Rights Commission and the Cape Law Society.

In February 2008, the Health Minister threw down a challenge to the Presidential Task Team on African Traditional Medicine, asking for 'concrete proposals' on how to deal with the 'daily emergence of charlatans who promise our desperate help-seeking people all sorts of things that are not practically possible to deliver.'

It's difficult to imagine how the task team plans to weed out the charlatans when their members seem dismissive of adopting a scientific approach to their methods. Nicoli Nattrass points out that 'scientific regulation protects the public from abuse by quacks' who sell their treatments to a vulnerable public. But once scientific regulation is 'jettisoned' whether in the name of the African Renaissance or 'New Age' alternative medicine, the door is open to any entrepreneur wishing to enter the lucrative market for 'cures'. The impact is felt in the public health facilities where, despite what the government describes as the largest antiretroviral treatment programme in the world, there are in some areas long waiting lists to begin treatment; in other areas, especially the rural areas, people do not come for treatment because they simply don't know enough about ARVs or just don't trust them. When Dr Mickey Chopra of the Medical Research Council conducted a study into South Africa's ARV roll-out, he found a general lack of excitement about the drugs, and much higher levels of knowledge about alternative remedies. 'Most people knew about the ARVs, but just didn't think they were a big deal.' The respondents tended to view ARV treatment as just one of many alternative therapies for HIV/AIDS, with the added drawback of being more difficult to access and potentially more stigmatising.

Tshabalala-Msimang's promotion of traditional medicine as an alternative to ARVs and the alliance of the THO with Matthias Rath have proved to be counter-productive for traditional medicine. The charlatans continue to thrive, while traditional products that could help people are still unregistered and under-researched. The story could have turned out differently. It could have been a heroic tale of how a government resuscitated the traditional medicine industry, and moved quickly to crush the rampant business of charlatans and quacks who exploit people's belief in traditional medicine simply to make a fast buck.

*Kanya Ndaki is deputy editor of IRIN's HIV/AIDS news service, PlusNews. She has been a journalist for the past eight years, and has spent most of her career writing and reporting on health, with a particular focus on HIV/AIDS. She studied journalism at Rhodes University and is currently doing her postgraduate studies part-time. As IRIN's first specialist HIV/AIDS reporter, she was part of the very small team of two that launched PlusNews almost eight years ago. PlusNews is now the largest provider of HIV/AIDS news in Africa. She has also worked for Health-e, Africa's only specialist health news agency.

10

'Saints and sinners': The Treatment Action Campaign

by
Janine Stephen

Eight years ago, on 5 April 2001, a young woman pushed through the doors of a clinic in Cape Town. She was just 23, healthy, simply curious to find out more about this disease called HIV/Aids that so many people were whispering about. Yet unexpectedly, awfully, she tested positive. She was handed a booklet about 'positive living' – it contained mainly nutritional advice – and was told that the only treatment available was for opportunistic infections. And she'd have to go to Khayelitsha for that.

Devastated by the diagnosis, it was a few months before she visited the Khayelitsha clinic. But once there she encountered a peer educator from the Treatment Action Campaign (TAC) who urged her to visit the organisation – just two minutes away – for support. She was reluctantly propelled to the offices, only to find them virtually empty: everyone was out on a picket. But she was intrigued enough to return. 'I found people who were speaking about science and medicine as if they were doctors,' Vuyiseka Dubula, now current general secretary of TAC, remembers. 'The level of understanding was fascinating. We come from an era where you're not informed as patients. You're just told to take a pink pill.

TAC changed all that. They tell you the name of the pink tablet, who manufactured it, when it came to South Africa, how it works. Just to get that information was empowering.' It was the feeling that she could understand and – if the right medicines became available – control what was happening to her that drew her to join TAC, Dubula says. For that matter, 'it still does'.

By the time Dubula joined TAC, it was already a highly vocal, effective civil society organisation with hundreds of volunteers and thousands of supporters, ranging from middle-class grandmothers to MPs and trade unionists. It was only two and a half years since anti-apartheid and gay rights activist Zackie Achmat had persuaded a handful of like-minded friends to stand outside St George's Cathedral in Cape Town with a petition calling for AZT for pregnant women. The degree to which the voluble, driven, media-savvy Achmat helped put TAC on the map can't be underestimated. Apart from his being politically astute and well-schooled in tactics used during the apartheid struggle, colleagues invariably mention his considerable charisma. And his radicalism: he entered politics in typically flamboyant fashion at 14 by burning down his school in 1976. Soon after that first protest at St George's, Achmat announced that he would not take ARVs until all South Africans could do the same through the public health system – it was 'wrong to be able to buy life'. This stark moral decision caught the world's attention and made him famous. As Stephanie Nolen wrote in the *Globe & Mail* in 2003, 'Mr Achmat has become the face of the fight for drugs in South Africa – a media darling, a bit of a diva.'

While Achmat's powerful personal story grabbed the headlines, TAC's rapid growth was also fuelled by the work of a remarkable collection of community activists. Anneke Meerkotter, one of TAC's initial members, remembers how 'Zackie was the public face' but 'he wasn't the key person to mobilise people on the ground'. In Cape Town, it was a core group of people that included teacher and poet Sipho Mthathi, medical doctor Hermann Reuter and activist Mandla Majola who built TAC's grassroots support. The community activists were fighting terrible stigma. In 1998 Gugu Dlamini was stoned to death by members of her community after she disclosed her positive status on the radio. There was a terrible silence surrounding the disease. 'We could see people who were skinny and dying, but [HIV/AIDS] was just gossip,' Mandla Majola remembers. 'There was so much fear.'

Majola met Mthathi and Reuter, who had begun educating Cape Town communities about the epidemic, in 1999. They'd hold workshops every weekend, transporting participants to meetings and home again in Reuter's old station wagon. At this stage, TAC itself was still 'just a concept, nothing tangible', Majola says. (The first TAC events were actually planned under Napwa, but a fallout over tactics and ideology splintered that relationship.) The community activists worked to build TAC branches, much like the political branches and street committees of the liberation struggle days – structures communities were familiar with. It took leg work: they'd visit clinics, schools, shebeens, funerals and go door-to-door to chat to families, starting off formally with tea and, says Mthathi, branching out into 'extraordinary conversations about sexuality'. Energy was poured into creating an organisation with an identity, a home for people with HIV, not just an organic series of campaigns. 'There were huge issues at stake, and you needed consistency,' Mthathi says. The iconic HIV+ T-shirt helped to draw people in (the first featured Gugu Dlamini and the words 'Never Again'). 'I remember going to a ritual event,' says Majola. 'People were drinking African beer. I took some, and people told me I should be the last to take beer ... because "you're wearing this T-shirt and we don't want you to infect us with AIDS". The T-shirts opened up opportunities for educating people.' What they were fighting was all too real. 'Just as you'd get tired, someone would die,' Meerkotter says. 'And there would be a new sense of how we had to solve the [treatment issue].'

Education was TAC's key focus, and from early on, ordinary people were trained to pass on knowledge. TAC volunteers pledged to 'use my anger, fear, knowledge, emotions and care to win affordable treatment and care for people with HIV/AIDS'. Mthathi drove the creation of treatment literacy: practical information about the science and treatment of HIV, coupled with political and economic information about the epidemic and the continuing battle for treatment. As such, TAC members were (and are) incredibly well informed. Members attending marches would know 'exactly what was going on and what they were fighting for', says Meerkotter – a far cry from rent-a-crowds or 'placard carriers', as some critics tried to paint the ever-growing membership. 'It was an organisation that was building people themselves,' says Dubula. 'As an individual you felt you could contribute. There was a feeling of belonging.'

The solid core of ordinary South Africans that makes up TAC is in many ways the organisation's greatest strength – but keeping them involved and unified its greatest challenge. From early on, there were differences in opinion among TAC leadership about the importance of community work and the demands of national campaigning. But the two elements also complemented each other: branch work meant TAC had an informed support base to support protest action. Another valuable weapon for the growing organisation was legal knowledge. TAC worked with organisations like the Legal Resources Centre and AIDS Law Project. Together with the articulate, targeted campaigns initiated by national leaders, TAC had the voice, the credibility, the moral high ground and the legal know-how to make a difference. By 2001, as Majola put it, TAC was 'fully mobilised'. It was a formidable organisation.

The first salvo in the battle for treatment was prevention of mother-to-child HIV transmission (PMTCT). Once the public understood that AZT could stop tens of thousands of babies a year being born positive, they were behind TAC all the way. Government had back-tracked on pilot sites to provide AZT to pregnant women around the time TAC was formed, and in March 1999 Health Minister Nkosazana Zuma said ARVs were unaffordable – but government and TAC could work together to bring costs down. The way forward was clear: to force drug companies to allow South Africa to import cheap generics, or provide licences that allowed drugs to be made in the country at a fraction of the cost. A key example was Fluconazole, sold in South Africa for R80 a tablet, but available from Thailand in generic form for just R1.78. Essentially, TAC was asking drug companies to relinquish the enormous profits which the patents they held allowed them to make. No company can easily justify profits that cost babies' lives, and TAC's campaigns received considerable international support. In an inspired move, Achmat travelled to Thailand in 2000, bought 5000 capsules of generic Fluconazole and headed back to South Africa with 3000 of them. Pfizer huffed and puffed, Achmat was accused of smuggling, and the medication was confiscated. But TAC applied to the Medicines Control Council to allow the life-saving drug to be distributed, and won. A bit later, TV soap star Morné Visser brought the remaining pills over from Thailand. He received a hero's welcome. 'People were hugging and kissing me. I had done so little but they made me feel like I had done so much.' By March 2001, donated Fluconazole was available at clinics. Soon after, threats of sanctions made by the US in attempts to protect patents were dropped like hot potatoes and legal attempts by pharmaceutical firms to block imports of generics faded. As Stephanie Nolen put it in the *Globe & Mail*, they 'sensed a public relations disaster in what the [international] media presented as a lawsuit against Nelson Mandela and dying babies'.

It was a good example of TAC strategy and would be used again and again: educate people to create demand, march and picket to build public awareness, get the media involved, take your message to the world, and use institutions like the MCC or courts to force the point.

Yet by this point, TAC and the government were seriously locking horns. In what Mark Heywood has called 'a tragic and bizarre coincidence', TAC's call for treatment coincided almost exactly with President Thabo Mbeki's growing concerns with 'toxic' ARVs – concerns his next Health Minister, Manto Tshabalala-Msimang, embraced. Government opposition came as a shock to TAC. As Achmat, a lifelong ANC supporter, told a journalist, 'We never expected to fight the government. I mean, the love we had for them …' Mbeki's dissident views seemed to be linked to a suspicion that, as Heywood has written, HIV might be 'an imaginary epidemic invented by pharmaceutical companies and neo-colonialists to make profits and continue to dent Africa's view of itself'. In a memorial lecture in October 2001, Mbeki resisted what he saw as attempts to paint Africans as 'a diseased and depraved people'. In October 2004 he was still insisting that questions raised in Parliament about HIV and rape were linked to racism: that 'the black people of South Africa, Africa and the world' were facing accusations of being 'lazy, liars, foul-smelling, diseased, corrupt, violent, amoral, sexually depraved, animalistic, savage – and rapist'.

Whatever Mbeki's reasoning, the battle for treatment was punctuated by death. In just over two months in 2003, TAC lost 25 members to AIDS. By January 2000, TAC's lawyers had written to Tshabalala-Msimang to know if – and when – government would treat HIV-positive pregnant women. TAC was now calling for nevirapine, a single dose of which drastically cut the risk of transmission from mother to child. They had to go to court to get it. Using the courts to force government's hand was soon a TAC staple, although taking on government was not done lightly. Former TAC national organiser Linda Mafu remembers how the organisation faced hostility in communities who thought TAC members were 'hooligans' fighting 'our black government' – this was in 2002, well before the relationship with government was at its worst. But legal action won TAC some of its most important victories. The protracted battle for nevirapine was eventually won in 2002 when the Constitutional Court upheld court orders for government to roll out treatment. Government had delayed and appealed at every possible point in the process. Even after this final judgment, it was reluctant to comply: Tshabalala-Msimang sourly told media at a 2002 AIDS conference in Barcelona that the court had 'decided the Constitution says … I must poison my people'.

TAC wanted treatment for more than just pregnant mothers. Like Achmat, thousands needed ARVs. In a PR coup, Nelson Mandela had visited Achmat at his Muizenberg home in July 2002 and called him a role model. According to the *New Yorker*, the two spoke regularly on the phone afterwards – conversations between what Achmat called 'the sinner and the saint'. While concerted pressure and a complaint to the Competition Commission had seen the prices of ARVs drop dramatically, government was still prevaricating. The battle came to a head towards the end of 2002 when TAC and the Congress of South African Trade Unions (Cosatu) managed to get a Framework Agreement for a National Treatment Plan agreed to by the National Economic Development and Labour Council (Nedlac), but government refused to endorse the plan. On 14 February 2003, up to 15,000 people marched on Parliament in protest. And in March, TAC embarked on a non-violent civil disobedience campaign – a hugely controversial move, only undertaken after considerable consultation. Mthathi remembers how Cosatu wanted TAC to call the campaign something else – they felt the words 'civil disobedience' were 'associated with an illegitimate state'. TAC members staged demonstrations and sit-ins, some at places irrevocably linked with the struggle against apartheid, like Sharpeville. They disrupted speeches, pasted up 'Wanted' posters of the Health Minister, and charged Tshabalala-Msimang and Minister of Trade and Industry Alec Erwin with culpable homicide for failing to provide life-saving ARVs. There were farcical moments (such as when a shoe was thrown at the Health Minister's car), but the protests were deadly serious. Activists were arrested; in Durban some were taken to hospital after police retaliated with violence. TAC leaders insisted they were not interested in 'seats in Parliament', but in saving lives. The political fallout for Mbeki's government was huge.

And then it happened: Cabinet announced plans for a National Treatment Plan on 8 August 2003 and by 19 November the Operational Plan for Comprehensive Treatment and Care for HIV and AIDS was adopted. There would be many, many more battles to ensure government delivered on its promises, but there can be no doubt that TAC was largely responsible for this decisive victory.

It was time to sit back, breathe and take stock. But as former TAC general secretary Sipho Mthathi says, TAC is 'about doing, doing, doing': she feels the organisation was never particularly good at taking time to assess strategy. Current general secretary Vuyiseka Dubula agrees that TAC culture often doesn't 'look back and reflect. There's no time.' Yet TAC was changing dramatically. By February 2004, it had 150 branches across the country and over 8000 members. By 2006, this had doubled to 16,000 members. Today, there are about 250 branches. This is no lean and mean organisation – especially as consultation and education remain key. 'TAC today is complex,' says Majola. 'You need to submit plans, you need to submit budgets, you need approval … [Before] we could react so quickly.' And different members have very different needs: TAC caters for people living with HIV, rural and urban dwellers, men and women, those who want to build communities, and also individuals who want access to resources or opportunities. 'TAC is a difficult organisation to hold together at the best of times,' TAC co-founder Mark Heywood says. 'It often represents different things to different people; it's not like a trade union where there's cohesion due to the fact that people go to the same workplace everyday.'

TAC prides itself on giving its membership a voice. It tries to encourage bottom-up decision-making and local solutions to local problems – impossible unless people are empowered to lead at branch and district level. Local campaigns are encouraged, but the secretariat unapologetically drives day-to-day political and strategic decision-making. TAC's goals guide this process. As Dubula puts it, 'among ourselves we don't always agree, but we still work together. What we try to find is the underlying principle. If the principle is justice for all, human rights for all, health care for all – that's our focus. That's what draws us together.' Yet bringing diverse constituencies together can be tough.

Post-2003, it was the broader TAC membership that was pushed to the forefront of the battle for treatment. More and more, TAC needed to build strength at a local level: locals had to ensure clinics were accredited and had the drugs and resources they needed. By March 2005, the Health Department reported that 42,000 people were on ARVs; TAC estimated 500,000 needed the drugs to stay alive. The Health Department was not accrediting sites for treatment fast enough, refused to provide targets, and Tshabalala-Msimang was using delaying tactics like waiting for a tender process to be completed, rather than buying drugs to stop deaths immediately (she had to be taken to court before agreeing to shop for medication). In this transition period, treatment literacy needed to be stepped up, and TAC trained over 1200 activists in the year 2004 alone. All these concerns had to be juggled with fighting pseudo-science, ongoing denialism and the deadly feet-dragging on treatment roll-out.

TAC also took on gender issues, as women's status has vital implications for prevention and treatment efforts. Sexual violence is a serious factor in the spread of HIV and takes place on a huge scale in South Africa. Between April 2004 and March 2005, 55,114 rapes were reported to police – and only one in nine cases is thought to be reported. South Africa is one of the most dangerous places in the world to be female: an excessively patriarchal country where one in four women experiences domestic violence. As with any organisation, TAC's members reflect the society they live in; the organisation is not immune to sexism. Changing attitudes towards women and promoting equality have become a vital focus. But changing mindsets is not something that happens overnight. Just as in the wider South African society, putting non-sexism into practice meant challenging existing power structures and entrenched beliefs – a considerable challenge.

In May 2007, TAC efforts to build women's leadership experienced a heavy blow. Their general secretary Mthathi, the organisation's strongest woman leader, resigned quietly but quickly. This was followed by a further four resignations including national organiser Linda Mafu (who'd been with TAC since 2002). There was no official TAC press release to explain the resignations. For an organisation that prides itself on openness to the degree that salary scales are posted on its website, the silence was unusual, especially considering Mthathi occupied the most senior position in the organisation. Rumours started doing the rounds, one being that the resignations were linked to a lack of commitment to women's issues.

It must be said upfront that while in Heywood's view there were very different reasons for different people leaving, he feels the resignations were not due to a lack of commitment to gender issues (concerns about performance within the national management team were evidently a factor for some). But there were complex reasons for Mthathi's resignation. Suggestions that she left in part because of concerns about the extent of TAC's commitment to gender transformation continue to circulate. While Mthathi had made it clear to TAC that she did not intend to stand for a second term as general secretary, there is little doubt that underlying ideological tensions and questions about leadership style and approach also contributed to her early resignation.

TAC had been aware that the majority of its members were women from early on (estimates put the figure at about 70 per cent). There had been talk about tackling gender issues since about 2002, and more formal moves to address these began in about 2005. Some remember early calls for women's voices to be heard in the organisation – such as an incident in a national executive committee (NEC) meeting in about 2002 or 2003, when a woman suggested that if PMTCT was being portrayed as a campaign for women's rights, then women should speak at press conferences and be heard in the media. She was shouted down by Achmat, and left the meeting in tears. The incident, cited as an early example of tensions around gender in the organisation, also points to Achmat's sometimes confrontational leadership style.

At TAC's 2005 national congress, firm resolutions were taken. The organisation had to reflect that the South African epidemic affected more women than men. At this point men occupied more leadership positions in TAC, such as provincial organisers and co-ordinators, while treatment literacy was seen as TAC's 'nursing school' and largely staffed by women. Mafu tells of getting flak from feminist groups at an international conference, where she was asked why the leaders of TAC were men when more women lived with HIV in South Africa. At the 2005 congress, people called for equality in leadership positions, for women's voices to be heard, and, says Mthathi, for recognition that 'women want to stop doing the secretarial and catering and caring jobs and become leaders'.

TAC's national leaders supported the stance. All agreed that building women leaders (as well as leaders living with HIV/AIDS) was imperative. Attempts to build equality are well documented. A quota system was introduced which pushed for a minimum of 50 per cent women's leadership in provinces and districts as well as at national level, and an empowering Women in Leadership programme was launched. A women's reference group began to look at key health issues faced by HIV-positive women – such as the need for regular Pap smears (cervical cancer is a greater threat for HIV-positive women). Programmes to educate men about women's rights were also implemented. Speaking to a young TAC volunteer in Khayelitsha drove home the complexity of the task: '[I used to think] a woman was someone you need at a certain time for sexual pleasure,' the 25-year-old said. 'Now I know women must be treated with respect and be loved and supported ...' TAC also began to campaign around specific cases of gender violence, like the rape and murder of TAC activist Lorna Mlofana in 2003. This focus has remained key. Dubula says TAC is now working towards a national case that will tackle the justice system's failure to deal adequately with gender-based violence.

So although it would be unfair to say that TAC wasn't trying to tackle gender divides, it would be false to pretend they didn't exist. Mafu notes that the shift to equal representation was 'painful' for some. Individuals grumbled about the leadership quotas, saying women 'weren't ready'. To help break down divides, Mafu insisted that all organisers attend treatment literacy courses. There was resistance: some men argued that it wasted time; 'people are dying while we are sitting here'. According to Mthathi and Mafu, in some areas branches would put in requests for gender work in their budgets, but on occasion these requests were dropped, presumably at provincial level. Mafu thinks it was difficult for women to challenge male leadership in some provinces or districts – women were afraid that if they did so, they would be pushed out and lose access to resources. Cracks in unity also appeared over sexual violence cases – in particular, Jacob Zuma's 2006 rape trial. Mthathi and Mafu recall a 'huge fight' in one branch over whether or not to show support for Zuma's accuser, 'Khwezi', as a woman speaking out (she was vilified by Zuma supporters long before he was acquitted).

Trying to change the way the public saw TAC also contributed to tension. For years, TAC had been criticised by government and others for being run by 'white men'. A 2003 article by Christine Qunta is a good example: she criticised 'white male rage' as embodied by 'current media darlings' Heywood and Nathan Geffen. Mthathi came to their defence, criticising Qunta in turn for blindly joining 'the boys' club which labels human rights activists as unpatriotic' in order to deflect attention from hard questions government had to answer on HIV. Majola says claims that TAC is led by white men are 'an insult to the rest of us ... as Africans we have led TAC.' Still, like any organisation, TAC has had to grapple with issues of race, class and gender.

The criticisms did illustrate how the public needed to recognise TAC's new leaders – black women – as well as the vocal founders. When Mthathi became general secretary, the organisation asked leaders like Achmat, Geffen and Heywood to try to withdraw from speaking to the media so as to allow other voices to get through, but attempts to up the public profile of new leaders were not particularly successful. Vuyiseka Dubula says that although she and chairperson Nonkosi Khumalo are now official TAC spokespeople, nationally the most dominant voices in TAC are still 'mainly Zackie, Nathan and Mark', because the media is used to dealing with them (this is despite Zackie stepping down as chair in March 2008; Geffen resigned as policy coordinator in August 2008). Journalists evidently remain reluctant to speak to lesser-known leaders – as was the case when Mthathi was elected. Just as problematically, government and its allies are sometimes dismissive of the new leadership. A number of individuals spoke of how key members of the ANC and Cosatu prefer to talk to Achmat or Heywood rather than Dubula or Khumalo. As one person put it, 'They don't want to speak to a woman "child".' Dubula and Khumalo are both 30 years old; Dubula says that for them to be validated, the male leaders need to 'allow space for the new leadership'.

Heywood maintains that gender issues in TAC have not been divisive, although they have been 'difficult'. 'Gender issues are not an optional add-on to the work TAC does,' he says. '[They're] absolutely central to whether people get on to treatment or not, to whether people stay on treatment, to participation and leadership at a local level.' And there does seem to be room at the top for strong women – TAC representatives voted Dubula and Khumalo into the organisation's top two positions at the 2008 congress. But in the words of a former TAC staff member who asked not to be named, although the two were strong leaders, they would have to take care not to appear to be 'puppets'. 'We don't want them to be told what to do by Zackie,' she says. 'They must be absolute leaders.'

Majola questions 'why people are always saying that TAC doesn't take gender issues seriously and why men in TAC do not care about gender issues' and points to early work done around PMTCT and the TAC campaign for a rape centre in Khayelitsha. His comments acknowledge that gender issues are contested terrain. Mthathi says there was criticism from the highest level that the gender emphasis was excluding men and dividing the organisation. She believes that many men were involved in gender work and supported it and that she had sought and received a mandate to prioritise the work. But how the women's reference group addressed gender appears to have led to disagreement. Heywood felt that at one point the women's reference group had become 'detached' from TAC's ordinary campaigns, leading to some 'misunderstandings'. As a September 2007 synthesis report of the TAC provincial and district organisational review process to the NEC notes: 'While there is a general acceptance of the need [in TAC] to have a focus on women, and gender relations, this meets with some resistance from male members, and care must be taken to ensure that activities designed to strengthen women's roles and abilities are done so in ways that do not alienate supportive men.' It noted that the women's reference group should be formalised and 'has a responsibility to report back and engage other elements of TAC'.

Despite the different views, TAC has continued to make progress. Dubula feels the drive to build women's leadership 'is 60 per cent there'. Provinces on the whole are complying with the quotas (and are challenged by the national TAC if they fail to elect women). The Women in Leadership programme is continuing, and there is now a national women's rights coordinator. The 2007 synthesis report recognises that 'TAC members clearly see the on-going development of leadership – especially women and [People Living with AIDS] – as a key, but neglected, process of the organisation'. Contradictions remain. 'There's no disagreement or tension when it has to be agreed that [gender work] is core business, but practically it's another story,' Dubula says. Leadership continually struggles with issues like funding for gender work, who should speak on behalf of the organisation, and why the women's leadership programmes are important. She thinks that because the struggle is continuing, some individuals inside and outside TAC may feel the stated commitment is just lip-service.

Mthathi's resignation has also been attributed in part to fatigue. It's true that TAC demands a lot from its staff. People work exceptionally hard, giving '110 per cent', as a TAC evaluation report noted. Mafu admits asking a staff member who told her that she needed a break: 'What have you done for your country this year that you deserve time off?' And the work can be emotionally and physically draining. Post-2003, work grew in intensity, owing to the need to beef up branches. (It was largely because of endless pressure from TAC to accredit sites and make drugs available – and on-the-ground education work – that South Africa's ARV roll-out grew to be the largest programme in the world. Over 370,000 people were on ARVs through the public health system by the end of 2007.) Mthathi says exhaustion was an issue, but there was more to it. She remains unsure 'how much willingness there is to fully engage with the gendered dynamics of the epidemic' – and internal gender issues. In addition, she questions TAC's organisational culture and leadership style. 'The aggression we displayed to government became the kind of aggression we displayed to each other and part of the culture. Particularly in the leadership ... who shouted the loudest; whose voice got heard ... there was a culture of having to win the argument,' she says. TAC, while working so hard to save lives, didn't always take time to cultivate a culture of care and respect. She mentions Mandela's term 'the RDP of the soul' – something she thinks the organisation has neglected. The painful, sometimes alienating nature of the work and its effect on staff were seldom acknowledged.

It must be said that strong personalities were involved. Mthathi stood up strongly for decisions she believed in. And Achmat is known for being direct, even aggressive in his views. The general secretary position is the most senior position in the organisation. But in 2005 it was new, with some unclear boundaries, and came at the time when TAC was changing direction. It was a time for cohesive leadership, yet Achmat was having health problems and battling depression; he was not as involved as before. Mthathi began working closely with people in management, to the extent that there was talk of a 'clique' or group that excluded others. Heywood feels that some of these individuals didn't understand the politics of TAC, and 'began to respond to the challenges of TAC in a much more bureaucratic and organisational fashion'. Some of the people involved were among those who later resigned.

There was, then, a lot of tension simmering in the organisation by 2007. This manifested in different situations. When women decided to campaign around a member's rape case in KwaZulu-Natal, criticism was later levelled at them for taking up a case that couldn't be won – and for supposedly not involving men, although men from the province took part. It appears to have been an incident that crystallised some of the key differences in TAC's approach in Mthathi's mind. Also destructive to internal harmony was a damaging allegation made against a district co-ordinator. It turned out to be false, simply gossip, but led to considerable conflict between some national leaders.

Another crisis occurred at a volatile meeting, unusually called by TAC national management with the secretariat, in which Achmat lost his temper and confronted management about lack of participation in a campaign. Mafu found the meeting so upsetting that she packed her bags that same day, finalised some work in the Eastern Cape, then left. While noting it was the secretariat's responsibility to step in and deal with problems, Heywood acknowledges that conflicts were not always handled too well. The intensity of the disagreements does raise the question whether Achmat's temperament and aggressive leadership style contributed to conflict, or whether there may be a wider desire for a change in leadership (a 2005 evaluation report identified the dominance of the founding members as a possible future issue).

Criticisms levelled at Achmat include favouring big, media-attracting events. That national strategy is his key focus is not in question – criticisms centred more on approach and attitude, which set the tone for the entire organisation. Some felt national campaigns could put strain on local community programmes with limited resources. As was noted in the 2007 synthesis report, members had concerns that 'national priorities do not always reflect the needs and priorities of branches'. Achmat's combative approach (to issues as well as personal disagreements) also drew some criticism, and there are some who feel a change of leadership is due. One former staff member felt that while Heywood has good leadership skills, Achmat didn't always listen to others.

Interviews with current TAC leaders don't reflect a desire for Achmat or Heywood to go. Achmat remains a high-profile newsmaker – generally a huge advantage for TAC. Yet when Achmat co-founded another organisation called the Progressive ANC Voters Party in 2007, staff had to explain to some branches that TAC was not becoming a political party. 'I'd explain that this is Zackie's thing, not TAC's,' says Mafu. 'But for many people, Zackie is TAC.' Majola, who agrees that the face of the organisation must be a woman, feels the founders still offer a lot. 'Zackie is very popular and has charisma,' he says. 'Instead of seeing that as a disability, it should be an ability, something that takes us forward.' Majola and Dubula believe TAC is slowly building a new tier of leaders. That said, the influence the founding members still wield means that the degree to which new leaders are seen to stand confidently on their own feet remains an issue.

Dubula points out that Achmat himself is tired. 'He has been in the struggle forever,' she says. ' There will come a point where we will have to realise that people will have to move on.' TAC will survive the change, she says. 'Even if the perceived leadership of Zackie, Mark and Nathan left, nothing would change drastically.'

Once again, the climate in which TAC operates is changing. TAC's relationship with government has lurched from bad to terrible over the years (there was the 2006 campaign to have Manto fired), but in 2007 government genuinely included civil society groups, including TAC, when drafting the country's latest National Strategic Plan on HIV. This has placed the authorities on slightly less shaky moral ground, despite lacklustre leadership on the epidemic. And now that South Africa can claim the world's largest treatment project, government is that little bit less easy to criticise – even as reports of a health system failing its people continue to flood in. As one person noted, the public is asking, since there is treatment, why there is still so much confrontation. Dubula says that TAC now makes sure it always gives those it disagrees with a chance to act before taking confrontational steps. 'For example, Zackie said we have to draft our strategy for litigation on TB and I said no, we first have to [explain the issues] to the Deputy President and meet with her ... we have to give her time to react.' More creative strategies than marching and protests may also need to be found in the future – and this applies not only to TAC, but to all civil society groups.

As Heywood says, 'the early years [of TAC], 1998 to 2004, were often easier because we were mobilising people around some clear goals like access to treatment. That held people together, it created a movement around which people marched.' Taking on broader issues – like gender equality or food security or xenophobia – inevitably makes unity more difficult. Internal organisational choices – like finding ways to accommodate different voices, opinions and leadership styles – are arguably as important at this juncture as the organisation's choice of public campaigns. The 2007 organisational review synthesis report reflects that TAC's attempts to build new leaders and confront gender issues are continuing. But for TAC to continue to be one of South Africa's most successful civil society organisations, there has to be a way to continue that 'pink pill' effect that so effectively drew Vuyiseka to TAC at the beginning: the feeling that TAC was offering something very real, very tangible – knowledge about how to make a difference, hope, and the feeling that ordinary people could contribute meaningfully to change.

*Janine Stephen is a freelance journalist based in Cape Town. She has worked as deputy editor of Benetton's Colors *magazine, based in Italy; as a parliamentary reporter in South Africa for* ThisDay *and Independent Newspapers; and has contributed to publications such as the* Mail & Guardian, Sunday Times, Weekender, Marie Claire SA *and* Business Day Art.

11

Deadly cells: The struggle of HIV-positive prisoners

by

Khopotso Bodibe

It was September 2005. AIDS activists were busy focusing their energy on countering the rampant AIDS denialism and trying to get an intransigent government to speed up access to antiretroviral medication for the millions of desperate South Africans living with HIV. At Durban's Westville Prison, a massive and soulless correctional facility in the bustling port city at the epicentre of South Africa's raging AIDS epidemic, another sad chapter in the country's AIDS history was starting to play itself out. Fifteen HIV-positive male inmates were fighting for their lives. While outside its walls the country was trying to put structures in place to make access to antiretrovirals easier for the general population, prison authorities were denying these men access to lifesaving treatment. Court papers would identify them only by their initials: EN, BM, DM, EJM, LM1, MAZ, MSM, ND, SEM, TJX, TS, VPM, ZPM and LM2.

Medical records revealed that these prisoners were at a critical stage of their HIV infection by 2005. In stark clinical terms they had AIDS. All 15 of them had critically compromised immune systems. Their CD4 counts had plummeted to levels well below 200, the point at which an infected person needs to start taking ARV treatment or face death. In fact, eight had CD4 counts below 100 and a further five had counts below 50. By the time the men's plight became known, none of them were on ARVs despite the fact that the Department of Correctional Services had known for many months that some were in urgent need of the medication.

HIV and AIDS in Westville Prison, as in the rest of South Africa, is a common reality. Since the beginning of 2005 an estimated 110 AIDS-related deaths had occurred at the prison and there were about 50 offenders with a CD4 count of less than 200. Yet many of those who urgently needed antiretroviral treatment were not getting it, despite Cabinet's approval in late 2003 of a comprehensive plan for the treatment of HIV and AIDS that included prisons as well.

In the general population, many people living with HIV became critically ill and others died while waiting for the effective roll-out of the plan to take root. Prisoners were not spared this fate, either. In fact they were easier to ignore – not only were they convicted criminals, but they also faced the stigma of being men who were having sex with men, a taboo subject in an already highly stigmatised environment.

The Department of Correctional Services responded by saying that two things stood in the way of Westville inmates receiving ARV treatment. One was the ludicrous explanation that the national Department of Health required individuals, including prison inmates, to have a valid South African identity document (ID) in order to enrol for treatment. This was a massive hurdle as most of the prisoners were not in possession of the document nor could they afford the R35 required to get one. At Westville Prison, this policy saw more than 200 enraged HIV-positive prisoners embarking on a three-day hunger strike in March 2007 to draw attention to their demand for treatment, after months of negotiations with the prison authorities to resolve the bureaucratic obstacles. The Treatment Action Campaign (TAC) revealed at the time that in the three months preceding this desperate action, more than 20 inmates had died in the prison from AIDS-related infections.

The second obstacle, according to Westville officials, was that the prison had difficulty in gaining access to public health facilities where inmates could begin treatment with ARVs. An arrangement had been made with the nearby King Edward VIII Hospital to counsel and treat prisoners but only one prisoner per day could be seen – Mondays to Thursdays – or four a week. What is more, each would have to return a week later after reflecting and deciding on the implications of starting treatment. If this ludicrous arrangement was followed, it would take approximately a year before all 50 inmates with dangerously low CD4 cell counts could be put on treatment.

Westville is surrounded by six other hospitals, excluding King Edward VIII, which had received accreditation from the Department of Health to provide a fully fledged AIDS service, including the provision of ARVs. Why Westville did not try to use the services at these hospitals, the prison failed to explain.

The AIDS Law Project (ALP), a non-profit human rights-based law firm, was first alerted to the 15 Westville inmates in September 2005 by TAC volunteers who were running education and care programmes in the prison. ALP lawyers led by Jonathan Berger visited the prisoners in October to establish the facts. The ALP immediately wrote a letter to the Department of Correctional Services and the authorities of Westville Prison to notify them of the prisoners' complaints and asked that those inmates who qualified for treatment be given access to it. At a subsequent meeting held between Correctional Services and the ALP in December 2005, the Department undertook to fast-track the provision of ARV treatment to those prisoners who qualified. This did not happen and only a few inmates received treatment, some when it was too late.

After vigorous and unsuccessful engagement of the Department in an effort to resolve the matter, the ALP eventually filed an urgent application with the Durban High Court on 12 April 2006 on behalf of the inmates at Westville. As a result, the departments of Correctional Services and Health requested a meeting with the TAC (also an applicant in the case) and the ALP on 25 April 2006. At the end of the meeting, both departments made various commitments which would have gone a long way in solving some of the problems and ensuring that no further lives were lost. The ALP agreed not to proceed with the case if the respondents noted the agreement in writing by Friday, 28 April 2008. But they failed to deliver, and after giving them a two-day extension, the ALP proceeded with litigation. An urgent application was brought before the Durban High Court on behalf of the prisoners on 3 May 2006. The case was postponed because government was unprepared and failed to file any papers.

Describing in graphic detail what AIDS can do to a human body in the absence of appropriate treatment, Berger and the TAC's Nathan Geffen and Cynthia Golombeski wrote to the *Mail & Guardian* during the Westville trial: 'Coughing blood, wasting away from diarrhoea, uncontrolled bowel movements, a strange white fungus growing on your tongue and throat that prevents you from eating: this is what tens – if not hundreds – of thousands of people in South Africa experience daily, as they watch their once healthy bodies deteriorate. Dying from AIDS is usually painful, slow and undignified. But it is also avoidable. For the vast majority of people whose HIV infection has brought on AIDS, antiretroviral treatment can restore health and dignity.'

The article was written to argue the right of prisoners with AIDS to be treated for their illness. Prisoners' rights are enshrined in the country's Constitution, which states: 'Everyone who is detained, including every sentenced prisoner, has the right to conditions of detention that are consistent with human dignity, including at least exercise and the provision, at state expense, of adequate accommodation, nutrition, reading material and medical treatment.' Section 27 of the Constitution goes a step further and binds government to ensure that everyone, including prisoners, has access to medical care, where needed: 'Everyone has the right to have access to health care services ... The State must take reasonable legislative and other measures, within its available resources, to achieve the progressive realisation of each of these rights. No one may be refused emergency medical treatment.'

Dr Juno Thomas, a physician specialising in the management of AIDS at the largest hospital in the southern hemisphere, Chris Hani Baragwanath Hospital, explains: 'Prisoners, once incarcerated, lose their liberty and their volition. They are not able to access health care themselves. They are dependent on the prison system to identify that they are in need of health care and then to make sure that the system is in place that they get the adequate care.' Every week, Thomas sees several prisoners at the hospital's AIDS clinic. Her experience and services were later enlisted by the Southern African HIV Clinicians' Society as part of an expert panel to formulate guidelines aimed at assisting governments in the southern African region to prevent further prison infections as well as to treat inmates already infected with HIV. The guidelines were released in mid-2008. They sought to recognise prisoners' rights to life and dignity, irrespective of the wrongs they may have committed against society.

On 22 June 2006, Judge Thumba Pillay granted the relief sought by the ALP and TAC on behalf of the 13 inmates at Westville. Not surprisingly, this did not go down well with the government, and on 25 July the Department of Correctional Services was granted leave to appeal against the order. But Judge Pillay made an interim execution order that compelled the government to provide ARV treatment to prisoners in line with the earlier order, pending the outcome of the appeal.

On 28 August 2006, Judge Chris Nicholson upheld the execution order. He criticised the government for still not having made any attempt to improve its ARV roll-out programme at Westville, saying the failure to comply was in contempt of Judge Pillay's order and posed a grave constitutional crisis for the country. Following the damning court ruling, Correctional Services slowly started a process to accredit correctional centres to provide antiretroviral therapy from the beginning of 2006.

Although the court's decision was specific to the 13 men and other inmates who needed ARVs at Westville, it had far-reaching spin-offs for all prisons. By the end of September 2006, health facilities at four correctional centres had been accredited to provide ARV treatment. The first to receive accreditation was Grootvlei Prison in the Free State, followed by three prisons in KwaZulu-Natal – Qalakabusha (Empangeni), Pietermaritzburg and Westville. Since then, other prisons have been accredited. Correctional centres that don't have the capacity to provide a service now routinely send inmates to accredited health facilities nearby to get treatment. It's a not uncommon sight on any given day to see chained prisoners in their bright orange uniforms at civilian hospitals escorted by warders.

To roll out antiretroviral medication to prisons is logical because the number of deaths occurring among prisoners in recent years is astounding. Retired Judge Johannes Fagan brought this to the government's attention in 2003 in a report to Parliament on behalf of the Judicial Inspectorate of Prisons when he cautioned: 'There has been a rapid escalation in the number of natural deaths in prison.' His figures revealed that, whereas during 1995, the natural death rate among prisoners was 1.65 deaths per 1000 prisoners, in 2002 the figure had risen to 7.75 deaths per 1000. There was general agreement that this dramatic increase in the mortality of prisoners was largely the result of HIV infection.

According to figures released in December 2007 by the Department of Correctional Services, South Africa's prison population had a 20 per cent HIV prevalence rate, which translates into over 20,000 inmates being infected. However, there is a strong belief that this is an underestimation as the study was only carried out among convicted prisoners, and excluded awaiting-trial prisoners and children residing in prison. Another study released by the Institute for Security Studies (ISS) in 2003 showed that about 41 per cent of inmates in South Africa's overburdened prison system were HIV-positive. Since 1995, reported cases of HIV/AIDS in South African prisons have risen by an astounding 750 per cent and the number of natural deaths by about 600 per cent over the same period. Between 90 and 95 per cent of the natural deaths were believed to have been AIDS-related. Most of the HIV-positive inmates came from communities which had limited access to public health services, and these were the same communities to which they returned.

Studies have shown that there is a much higher prevalence rate of infectious disease among prison populations around the world than populations on the outside. UNAIDS revealed in its 2006 directory of *Prisons in Africa* that HIV prevalence among prisoners was between 6 and 50 times higher than that of the general adult population. HIV prevalence was highest in South Africa (45 per cent). While HIV prevalence in prisons is usually higher than in the population at large, many HIV-positive prisoners are already infected by the time they reach jail. A report by the Judicial Inspectorate of Prisons shows that the vast majority of deaths in prisons occur in the first twelve months of people being incarcerated. This again suggests that people are not being infected within prisons, but are coming in sick. According to the Civil Society Prison Reform Initiative (CSPRI), prisoners are not screened properly when they enter the system. 'When prisoners arrive, they are asked if they have any medical conditions or if they are on medication. This is the extent of their medical screening,' says Lukas Muntingh of CSPRI.

After admission, the progression of the HIV disease is exacerbated by the harsh conditions associated with imprisonment, including extreme overcrowding (which may lead to poor infection control), poor nutrition, rape and unprotected consensual sex, stigmatisation, discrimination and poor access to health care. Inmates stand an enormous risk of contracting a range of infectious diseases such as tuberculosis and sexually transmitted infections, including HIV. Overcrowding also creates a fertile environment for all kinds of problems. South African prisons have the capacity to accommodate 114,559 prisoners, but there are currently over 165, 000 prisoners incarcerated.

High-risk sex is commonplace in South African prisons, usually in the form of unprotected anal sex, as well as rape and sexual assault.

Gang violence is common and sex is intertwined with gang life. Two of the most powerful prison gangs are the 26s and 28s; the latter's power structure is reputed to be based on homosexual partnerships and the prostitution of certain male inmates. The institutionalised victimisation of younger, weaker prisoners appears to be a direct result of the relatively unobstructed power of gangs, facilitated by corruption among the warders.

Dr Anthony Minnaar of the Institute for Human Rights and Criminal Justice Network said in a media interview in 2005 that there are extremely strong gang cultures in South African prisons and that rape was used for control and as punishment of non-members. 'Gangs catch up with so-called enemies and one of the forms of punishment is a so-called "slow puncture".' This is the rape of an inmate by an HIV-positive prisoner, thereby inflicting a death sentence.

The ISS study points out that the extent of sexual activity in prisons is difficult to determine because studies have to rely on self-reporting, which is distorted by embarrassment or fear of reprisal. Sex is prohibited in most prison systems, and inmates consequently deny their involvement in sexual activity. The Centre for the Study of Violence and Reconciliation (CSVR) found that there is a lot of stigma attached to male rape. 'For example, you are viewed as having lost your manhood and often the victim carries that sense very profoundly. We know that that's what keeps a lot of people who have been raped sort of suffering in silence.'

There are no reliable statistics on prison rapes because, according to the Department of Correctional Services, sexual assault is generally classified under one category of 'assaults'. The CSVR claims that prison staff members are often aware of the rapes but are bribed into keeping quiet. This means that the perpetrator is free to repeat these horrific acts. Other staff simply choose to turn a blind eye.

Gustav Wilson, HIV/AIDS Programme Director for the Department of Correctional Services, admits that when new offenders are admitted, they are informed that sexual assaults do take place. According to Wilson, prisoners are given information on HIV and AIDS. If they report that they have been raped, Correctional Services provides them with post-exposure prophylaxis within 72 hours. This is to minimise the risks of getting HIV infection. However, according to a CSVR survey, only 12 per cent of young offenders at the Boksburg Youth Centre said they had received such information.

It is also generally acknowledged that prisoners partake in consensual sex, whether they are gay or not. 'Although prison authorities and prisoners themselves won't admit to it, there is a substantial amount of consensual sex between prisoners, and informing them beforehand of the risks of sexual transmission and, importantly, providing them with condoms and appropriate lubrication will definitely decrease risks of transmission in that setting,' a CSVR research paper noted. Rather than accepting the reality of sexual activity and its attendant risks, most prison authorities do not make condoms easily available, believing it will encourage homosexuality or sodomy. UNAIDS is clear that prison authorities have no option: 'Recognising the fact that sexual contact does occur and cannot be stopped in prison settings, and given the high risk of disease transmission that it carries, UNAIDS believes that it is vital that condoms, together with lubricant, should be readily available to prisoners.' However, in a number of South African prisons, inmates have to approach a medical officer to ask for condoms. This is despite a policy directive that condoms be available in dispensers throughout the prisons.

The reason for the denial by the authorities is not clear. The only logical conclusion is that policy-makers and administrators are uncomfortable with the idea of being seen to formulate programmes linked to homosexuality, a taboo in our highly stigmatised society, where we struggle to discuss issues of sex between men and women, let alone men having sex with men. This is despite the fact that the Constitution explicitly outlaws discrimination based on sexual orientations and that South African law recognises same-sex marriage. The continuing failure of prison authorities to acknowledge and act against rape could be interpreted as state-sanctioned homophobia.

As long as rape and consensual sex between men in prisons are ignored, these will remain unacknowledged, silent factors driving South Africa's HIV epidemic. Some men who are introduced to sex with other men in prison may continue to seek similar sexual relations once they leave; it is important that they are properly educated on how to protect themselves. Currently this is not happening in prisons. Moreover, the prison population is not static. About 360,000 people move through the prison system in one year. Of these, around 240,000 are awaiting trial, get sent to court and are eventually released once their cases are thrown out. This means that if the prisons don't deal appropriately with HIV and other diseases such as TB, they are undermining public health.

There is also much anecdotal evidence of awaiting-trial prisoners who enter the prison system HIV-negative, are gang-raped within prison, fail to gain access to post-exposure prophylaxis, contract HIV and are suddenly released after the charges are dropped.

'You may well go out and don't know you have HIV, don't test or don't get access to testing services, and then have unsafe sex once you're released. You never have been convicted of a crime and suddenly you're now HIV-positive,' argues ALP's Jonathan Berger.

The government has been praised for finally trying to roll out ARV treatment for prisoners, as ordered by Judge Thumba Pillay in 2006. But unless the prison authorities also address HIV prevention, the numbers of HIV-positive prisoners will continue to grow. To address HIV prevention, Correctional Services will have to accept that men do have sex with men in prison. In addition, they need to make it possible for rape survivors to feel safe in reporting rape and get access to ARVs as post-exposure prophylaxis. By ignoring its responsibilities to prisoners, the government is at the same time failing in its responsibility to protect the wider society.

*Khopotso Bodibe is Health-e News Service's multi-award winning radio editor based in Johannesburg. He was part of the investigative team that exposed Dr Matthias Rath's activities in South Africa, for which they won the CNN Africa Journalist Award for Excellence in HIV/AIDS Reporting in 2006.

12

'Speaking truth to power'

by
Claire Keeton

Imagine for a moment being appointed in a senior government job with the potential to save people's lives and improve the lives of millions. But from your first weeks in office your boss makes it clear that she resents you, and is reluctant to delegate responsibilities to you. In fact, she never bothers to meet with you. She pulls rank when you take the initiative and obstructs your plans. You are sidelined and senior staff quickly learn that it is taboo even to talk to you. You do not have a team to support your work, or a functional budget. You are isolated and frowned on when you make critical contributions to your ministry or department. Undaunted, you try to overcome all the hurdles and provide unequivocal leadership to your country on HIV/AIDS. As a result, your days are numbered and you are fired on a technicality after speaking your mind about failures made by your department.

That's the invidious situation in which former Deputy Health Minister Nozizwe Madlala-Routledge found herself, almost from the time she was appointed in April 2004 through to her controversial dismissal in August 2007.

When reportedly asked why, in his opinion, Madlala-Routledge had been handed the job of trying to work with a health minister with a history of disdain for strong personalities in her department, ANC president Jacob Zuma shared the belief that if you put two bulls in a kraal, only one will survive. He laughed and declined to answer when asked which 'bull' he thought would survive.

Reflecting on her trajectory in the health ministry, Madlala-Routledge feels that the odds were stacked against her, from the top down – and a source who was close to the ministry suggests that from day one Minister Manto Tshabalala-Msimang wanted her out and would do anything in her power to make it happen. Madlala-Routledge said publicly after her dismissal that the Minister had warned her two years before her final dismissal that she was on borrowed time. The minister said: 'I will fix you,' a frank Madlala-Routledge told journalists. According to sources from both 'camps', the minister was a territorial and defensive politician with a retributive streak, though her deputy was 'no softy' and could be stubborn herself.

Madlala-Routledge said she started off positively in her post but found she was systematically undermined in the ministry. She recalled: 'When I was appointed I had a lot of energy and enthusiasm, thinking that my role would be to support my minister.' On taking up her position she immediately wrote to the minister listing her strengths 'and saying I wanted to support her. She called [by telephone] at the start to welcome me. She said that the morale was very low and there was going to be a workshop for staff and she wanted them to speak openly. But at that workshop, only a few weeks into my job, staff members were already uncomfortable relating to me or talking to me. It was a serious situation.' Low morale in the critically understaffed department and ministry – which cascaded right down to overworked health professionals in the public sector – worsened markedly during Tshabalala-Msimang's term as Health Minister and there was an accelerated exit of doctors and nurses from state hospitals.

Madlala-Routledge said she requested a one-on-one meeting with her boss several times, but the minister never once met her face to face. She said at that time: 'I was still waiting for delegations from the minister. It was as if she didn't want me there.' The minister viewed her deputy as a potential usurper and was unwilling to give her the resources to fulfil her role, even if this reflected negatively on the ministry. For example, Madlala-Routledge says she had no staff allocated to assist with the preparation of her first health budget speech in May 2004. She did, however, have prior experience of the awkward role of deputy ministers from her time in the defence ministry (where she advanced HIV awareness and care) and she turned to the department for back-up. 'In my own experience as Deputy Defence Minister, I had very few staff and made good use of the department to support me. Then suddenly in the Health Department, I was not allowed access to staff and had to go via the minister. The Director-General [Thami Mseleku] issued an order.' According to a source who was close to the minister, this may have had less to do with the existing ministerial structure – which did make a provision for a deputy in the loop – and more with a deliberate move by the minister to exclude Madlala-Routledge.

After a delay stretching over several months, Madlala-Routledge was finally allocated her 'delegations', which turned out to be on the margins of the health agenda: chronic illnesses, geriatrics and disability; health technology; mental health; oral health; and forensic pathology. When she approached key staff members in these areas to brief her, she found that they were jittery *even* about doing this.

Sources close to the minister, as well as her admirers in the health sector, have said that Madlala-Routledge did not make much impact on the few areas of responsibility accorded to her. But the former deputy has remarked that she found she would be blocked or frozen out when she tried to implement her own 'strategic plan' in these areas. 'When I took the initiative, then I was told the minister would want to take over the programme,' she said, describing how the minister had intervened when she started making progress on the transfer of mortuaries from the Police to the Health Department.

This erosion of her role took place in every forum. At meetings of the

National Health Council (where the minister and Health MECs of the nine provinces conferred), Tshabalala-Msimang would routinely ignore her deputy. If the minister stepped out of the meeting to take a call, she refused to acknowledge her deputy as the acting chairperson. One time when Madlala-Routledge did pick up the role as chair, the minister returned and simply ignored this, resuming the meeting from the point where she had left. MECs who were initially warm towards the deputy became increasingly nervous to engage with her as they feared the wrath of the minister.

The former ANC national health secretary, Dr Saadiq Kariem, who now runs Groote Schuur Hospital, one of the country's largest tertiary hospitals, has positive memories of his interaction with Madlala-Routledge. 'One of her first tasks was to start looking at policies and strategic plans. She grabbed the bull by the horns and brought a lot of energy and insight to this.' But it wasn't long before Madlala-Routledge was reined in even further. She was increasingly provoking the minister's ire by questioning the wisdom of emphasising nutrition for people with AIDS – the minister's mantra – to the detriment of antiretroviral treatment. The minister, who had cut her political teeth in the traditions of Soviet-style loyalty while in exile, could not abide being challenged.

Madlala-Routledge's staff received subtle warnings to be careful, that 'they' were after their boss, and it became a clear political risk to be associated with her. Thami Mseleku, appointed to his post as Director-General in January 2005, also showed signs of being wary of dealing with the deputy minister even though he was her former comrade from the United Democratic Front in KwaZulu-Natal. Before long the politically ambitious DG had aligned himself with the minister's camp and, by the time of the third South African AIDS conference in June 2006, he was echoing the minister's rhetoric in promoting vegetables, garlic and olive oil as alternatives to antiretrovirals.

Despite consistently being pushed to the periphery, Madlala-Routledge refused to give in. As one of her former colleagues noted,

Madlala-Routledge – who spent a year in solitary confinement under apartheid – has a 'fighter pedigree'. One source close to the minister said that appointing such a strong-willed deputy to a hard-headed minister was clearly a mistake. He claimed that the former deputy could also be tough and would on occasion reduce her staff to tears. But a former colleague, who operated independently from both the minister and her deputy, said that Madlala-Routledge was sensitive to people and tended to side with the underdog. By the time Madlala-Routledge arrived, 'Staff had grown fearful and cowed by the minister. The culture was that you were not able to challenge the minister.' This undercurrent of deference was even visible: staff would always stand up for the minister when she entered a room with bodyguards while staff members were often seen walking meekly behind her carrying her handbag and files.

On one rare occasion when Madlala-Routledge got to address a senior executive management meeting in the minister's absence, to the surprise of her audience the crux of her speech was that she operated differently from the minister and cared about delivery more than appearances.

Despite the hostile environment, Madlala-Routledge soon identified as an urgent priority the struggle against HIV/AIDS. She legitimised her involvement by saying that, as HIV could now be managed as a chronic illness, it fell under her 'chronic illnesses' delegation. She also openly celebrated the contribution of HIV organisations and activists, and demonstrated her willingness to partner with them. Madlala-Routledge's approach to HIV provided a striking contrast to the obstructive and feet-dragging attitude of the minister. As she says: 'What I saw inside the department was a clear agenda from the minister that was different to what the rest of the country was doing on the 2003 comprehensive plan [which first approved the antiretroviral rollout in state hospitals]. There was a reluctance to move fast and putting obstacles in the way . . . HIV was a matter of life and death and people's lives were being lost. That is what galvanised me into action. Also this was violating party policy.' Certainly, Tshabalala-Msimang did not want to accelerate HIV/AIDS delivery and even swiped at provinces like the Western Cape and Gauteng which moved faster than the national department in implementing HIV policy.

During her first year in office, Madlala-Routledge spent time and energy reaching out to those active in the HIV arena, including groundbreaking meetings with civil society organisations. Zackie Achmat, head of the Treatment Action Campaign (TAC) and a thorn in the side of the minister, described their initial meetings as very good. 'The deputy minister clearly understands the issues. We are speaking on the same page.' Madlala-Routledge echoed this sentiment in an interview in March 2005: 'We are on the same side. We need them as much as they need us.' Mark Heywood, also a TAC leader, believes that she played a brave, personal leadership role when the country needed it.

Madlala-Routledge's commitment to advancing HIV/AIDS delivery and awareness in defiance of the minister's orders gained momentum from 2005 into 2006. Even though the minister ordered that nobody but herself speak publicly on the epidemic, her deputy nevertheless became an outspoken political leader on HIV/AIDS. Madlala-Routledge ignored the blackout on HIV/AIDS communications with bold, unequivocal statements about the value of antiretroviral treatment in marked contrast to the minister's unscientific and confusing messages on the matter.

While she was not on the Inter-Ministerial Committee on HIV/AIDS, the former deputy nevertheless found she had silent allies within the health ministry and department, as well as in the ANC, something which buoyed her to continue along the path she had chosen.

Another positive development was that, by May 2006, Deputy President Phumzile Mlambo-Ngcuka had taken charge as head of the South African National AIDS Council (SANAC) and demonstrated her willingness to provide high-level leadership. Of her own increasing involvement around HIV, Madlala-Routledge declared: 'I could not continue to pretend nothing was wrong [inside the ministry]. It became more and more difficult to defend the indefensible.'

The watershed 16th International AIDS Conference in Toronto in August 2006 marked the moment when Madlala-Routledge realised she could no longer keep silent about the minister's approach to HIV. While Cabinet and many in government were committed to rolling out antiretroviral treatment, the South African stand at the eminent conference was decorated with beetroot, garlic, African potato and lemons, all ingredients the Health Minister proclaimed to be excellent immune boosters for people living with HIV/AIDS. It was only after probing questions from journalists, who had arrived early at the stand in anticipation of the minister's arrival, that antiretrovirals used by one of the South African government delegates were placed on a shelf. But it was too late and South Africa became the laughing stock of the world. Madlala-Routledge reacted by stating publicly that South Africa's stance was an international embarrassment.

Not surprisingly, this exacerbated existing tensions with the minister. But Madlala-Routledge refused to retreat. In October 2006, she attended an HIV/AIDS summit held by the TAC, Cosatu and the South African Communist Party (SACP) and made further statements about the need to scale up the prevention of mother-to-child-transmission of HIV. She chose also to take a personal stand as an HIV champion and on 26 November 2006 she became the most senior member in the ANC government to take a public HIV test with her husband and son. (She had to hastily deny British press reports that she had also called on Mbeki to take an HIV test.)

Shortly before the HIV test, Tshabalala-Msimang was admitted to hospital with an undisclosed illness, giving her deputy a short-term reprieve from her heavy-handed control. After repeated bouts of sick leave and ill health, the minister had a liver transplant in February 2007. Many hoped that she would use this opportunity to retire gracefully and allow her deputy to run the show. But it was not to be.

In her absence, Transport Minister Jeff Radebe was appointed Acting Health Minister. He sent the right signals in support of Madlala-

Routledge's role and mission, in what proved to be a 'Prague Spring'. Madlala-Routledge credits Radebe, her former commander in the SACP underground in the 1980s, as the person who gave her the authority she needed to do her job: 'He realised [my] delegations were meaningless without authority, and he signed.' At the same time, Deputy President Mlambo-Ngcuka played a vital role in restructuring SANAC into a more representative and powerful body, with Heywood elected as her deputy chairperson. Madlala-Routledge was present at a couple of the meetings about the restructuring as well as at its first meeting. Heywood says of her: 'Her real importance came after Toronto in the [minister's] absence on sick leave. She was stepping into her shoes and using the space to push forward the process started by the Deputy President.' SANAC members contributed to the development of a new five-year national HIV/AIDS strategic plan. According to Heywood, Madlala-Routledge 'created an environment where it was possible to pay attention to the nitty-gritty of change though she was not involved in the detail'.

Many observed that Tshabalala-Msimang's return to office in June 2007 led, however, to a marked drop in productivity and momentum. The Health Minister came back with guns blazing, her sights fixed on her deputy. With an apparently compliant President Mbeki behind her, it took her barely two months to get rid of her deputy. The final straw for the minister and the President was Madlala-Routledge's visit on 13 July 2007 to Frere Hospital in East London. Responding to repeated pleas about a crisis in Frere Hospital's maternity ward, she wanted to see for herself, and informed the MEC for Health, Nomsa Jajula, of her concerns and of her intention to pay an official visit. What she saw and heard shocked her: 2000 infants had been stillborn in the hospital's maternity ward in the past 14 years and hundreds of newborns were dying every year. Accompanied by a journalist on the trip, Madlala-Routledge described the situation as a 'national emergency'. A day later her comments were all over the front pages. She later said of her condemnation over the situation at Frere: 'My comments were informed by the shocking realisation that some of the deaths were avoidable and that the situation I had observed was not unique to Frere Hospital.'

Madlala-Routledge had acknowledged a festering problem in the Health Department – the rapidly deteriorating state of its hospitals and services – and her frank observations infuriated not only the minister but also the President, not least since she spoke out in the press and not just behind closed doors. In the ANC newsletter, Mbeki branded the newspaper reports about the crisis as false while Parliament's health portfolio committee chairman, James Ngculu, a Mbeki loyalist, accused her publicly of creating hype. 'I never aimed to embarrass or defy [the government] or to be a rebel but I grew up in an ANC of mutual respect,' Madlala-Routledge said at the time. She also firmly believed that she was acting in defence of the constitutionally enshrined right of all South Africans to health care, not as a lone ranger, as Mbeki's subsequent letter of dismissal implied.

On 5 August Mbeki summoned her to the Union Buildings to discuss 'complaints' about her and asked her to resign. Madlala-Routledge responded that she needed to consult her comrades and went to Luthuli House, the ANC's headquarters in Johannesburg, seeking advice. From Luthuli House, reportedly under the guidance of then ANC Secretary-General Kgalema Motlanthe, she faxed Mbeki to say that she refused to resign, an unprecedented move. Mbeki asserted his authority, and on the eve of National Women's Day on 9 August 2007, he fired one of the country's most outspoken and formidable female leaders during his term of office. In his letter of dismissal, he wrote: 'I have, during the period you served as Deputy Minister of Defence, consistently drawn your attention to the concerns raised by your colleagues about your inability to work as part of the collective, as the Constitution enjoins us to … This leaves me no choice but to relieve you of your duties.'

Mbeki also pounced on a procedural (and expensive) error by Madlala-Routledge to justify his decision. In June she had attended an International AIDS Vaccine Initiative meeting in Madrid, seemingly without the President's approval. When she left for the trip, accompanied by her adviser and son, she had been made to believe that the President had authorised the trip. As soon as she was informed he had declined her request to travel, she turned around and came back to South Africa, at the cost of R160,000.

Mbeki's move was highly unusual. Authorisation was usually merely a procedural matter. Members of Mbeki's own Cabinet, including Deputy President Mlambo-Ngcuka, had committed much more expensive travel transgressions at the taxpayers' expense and never faced punitive action from their chief. The most likely reason for sacking Madlala-Routledge was that the minister wanted her deputy gone, and this was a convenient justification.

Once her sacking was official, Madlala-Routledge returned to Cape Town, now an ordinary MP. At Cape Town International Airport she chose to enter through the public arrivals hall, where she was met by ululating activists and ordinary South Africans. Before diving into a waiting car, she stood still for a moment, clenched her fist and flashed a broad smile. Forty-eight hours later, Madlala-Routledge again broke with ANC custom – and, loyal members say, party ranks – by holding a press conference to explain her actions. The atmosphere at this unprecedented press conference was charged, with TAC supporters and members of the public demonstrating in Madlala-Routledge's support at the entrance to the Cape Town radio station where she was due to speak. The large conference room at the back was overflowing with flowers from well-wishers. When the axed deputy stood up to speak, she was remarkably forthcoming and honest about her difficulties in the ministry and said that a person 'must never be afraid to speak truth to power'. Responding to criticisms that she was out of order, she said: 'I did try to raise issues internally and had no sense they were appreciated, or that my concerns were given a chance. What was I supposed to do in that situation?' When asked if she was fired for doing her job, she replied: 'I agree I was doing my job.'

The government response following the press conference was unusually harsh and some say spiteful, with the dismissed deputy being ordered to repay the cost of the overseas trip. The AIDS Law Project and TAC leapt her defence, creating a fund to raise contributions for this payment, and within days they raised R40,000.

International commentators sided with Madlala-Routledge, who gave interviews to the foreign and local press. The *New York Times* accused Mbeki of sacking 'one of the few effective Aids fighters in his administration ... [who] had provided a brief interlude of sanity and seriousness after the Health Minister ... fell ill,' while *The Economist* observed that Mbeki had 'fired the wrong minister'.

A month later Mbeki again hit out at Madlala-Routledge at an ANC National Working Committee meeting, asking for her to be disciplined on the grounds that she was anti-ANC and had attacked his integrity. The committee members were apparently divided, and in the end the principle that a person should not be punished twice for the same offence prevailed. After that meeting Kgalema Motlanthe (elected as South African President in September 2008 after the ANC sacked Mbeki) told reporters that the ANC could only discipline members in breach of its constitution. 'She might have breached Cabinet protocol and the President has dealt with that in government,' he said, confirming that no action would be taken against her and apparently keeping his assurance to give her a 'safe landing as an ordinary MP'. Madlala-Routledge said of the ANC's threatened disciplinary action: 'Everything was hanging in the balance. I did not mind so much losing my job but I would mind being disciplined by my party.'

Since that bleak time, Madlala-Routledge has played an increasingly prominent role in the ANC and seems to be in the ascendant. She was elected to its National Executive Committee in December 2007 with more votes than the Health Minister and was appointed chairperson of the ANC caucus in Parliament in February 2008. Six months later, when Motlanthe was sworn in as South Africa's new President, Madlala-Routledge was elected unopposed as Deputy Speaker in Parliament. On the other hand, her nemesis, Tshabalala-Msimang, has had to face the embarrassment of being stripped of the Health portfolio and being redeployed as Minister in the Office of the President.

One of the minister's former staff has cynically commented that Madlala-Routledge deliberately pursued her path on HIV/AIDS with the intention of developing a public profile and building a mass support base. But if you talk to Madlala-Routledge, it is clear that it's where her heart was, and is. And as her one-time comrade in the ANC health committee, Dr Saadiq Kariem, observed: 'One of her strengths, which also led to her downfall, was to listen to what people were saying and try to implement it.' Though her appointment as deputy was controversial and her tenure – under a tough and territorial minister – was difficult, she offered a white flag to civil society and delivered a clear message at a time when it was urgently needed.

Claire Keeton is a senior HIV/health reporter at the Sunday Times *newspaper. She has won awards and was chosen as a southern African Rosalynn Carter Mental Health Fellow for 2005–6, choosing to focus on HIV/AIDS. Keeton has worked for Agence-France Presse, the* Sowetan *newspaper and the Eastern Cape News Agency. She has a Master's in Journalism from Columbia University in New York.*

13

Remembering a decade of the Treatment Action Campaign

by
Zackie Achmat

This is a short reflection of personal memories, people, ideas, evidence, campaigns, science and struggles but above all the pain of lives lost and the work of lives saved during the past decade. A personal memory is subjective because it invokes the 'I' of personhood and through the eye of the writer evokes her or his past. Emotion is the lens of memory and the past its life. Therefore, this note will contain mistakes and omissions.

This is my tribute to all Treatment Action Campaign (TAC) members, staff and leaders: an expression of gratitude to allies, comrades, friends and supporters locally and globally. (Apologies to Denis Hirson, whose simple evocative style is copied with respect and probably mistakes.)

I remember:
• ANC, gay and HIV/AIDS activist Simon Nkoli in a coma in Johannesburg Hospital where I visited him with Edwin Cameron.
• Edwin speaking to Simon in a coma about their friendship, its highs and lows, speaking to himself.
• But also fearing for my own future, the future of many of my friends, and vowing never to go to the sick bed of a person living with HIV again.

- The speech of Enea Motaung, the AIDS Gogo of Soweto, at Simon's memorial: 'Parents, love all your children equally including your gay and lesbian children.'
- The face of 'Terror' Lekota, comrade of Simon and co-treason trialist in Delmas in 1987, then the chairperson of the ANC, as I appealed in St Mary's Cathedral for the formation of a Treatment Action Campaign. This call was made after discussions with many comrades.
- The tears of Roderick, Simon's partner, all his former lovers, comrades and family.
- The pain of Peter Busse, who started the Township AIDS Project with Simon.

I remember:
- Launching the TAC on the steps of St George's Cathedral on 10 December 1998 with Anneke, Deena, Anne, Queenie, Sue, Josie, Midi, Laddie, Jenny, Theresa, Jack, Mrs B, Jenny, Colwyn, Mikey, Rick, Rhoda and comrades who joined during the day. Also Phumi, Mazibuko, Edwin, Mark, Sharon, Jonathan, Morna, Prudence and Paul in Johannesburg; Ronald and Mercy in Durban.
- Mostly comrades from the anti-apartheid struggle, the human rights struggle in democratic South Africa and people living with HIV/AIDS gathered because we remembered St George's Cathedral as hallowed non-racial ground during apartheid – the People's Parliament next door to apartheid prime ministers Vorster, Botha and De Klerk – and St George's Cathedral after apartheid – a neighbour to Mandela and a refuge from Mbeki.
- 10 December 1998 was the 50th anniversary of the Universal Declaration of Human Rights, and our struggle for HIV treatment required global mobilisation to hold drug companies accountable. Our struggle was simultaneously local and global.
- The *Cape Times* article by Judith Soal the next day.

I remember that December:
- Gugu Dlamini's murder in Umlazi for openly living with HIV. The shock and horror.
- The reason for the HIV-positive T-shirt, which was to allow every person to be open to showing solidarity.
- The debates on the consequences of wearing a T-shirt that says 'HIV-positive'.
- The apocryphal story of the King of Denmark who asked all Danish people to wear the sign of David in solidarity with Jewish people when Hitler invaded that country.
- The beautiful daring of Act Up in its media.
- The defiance of the United Democratic Front (UDF) in our T-shirts. All these were our tradition in TAC and as activists everywhere.
- The venomous spit of stigma from taxi-drivers.
- The fear of openness.

That December, I also remember:
- My own oesophageal thrush and the cost of Fluconazole (R3000 for a week's treatment).
- The love of Jack, Thellie, Johann, Midi and Theresa. And the big party of my closest comrades held just in case I died.
- The decision not to take ARV medicines until they were affordable and available.
- The support of friends, lovers and comrades through my chronic depression, which was more debilitating than HIV. Their enduring my depression as a painful burden of dysfunctionality less explicable than HIV and more hidden.
- Their fortitude in the face of my life-long hypochondria.

I remember:
- The opening of Parliament in 1999 with our 'HIV-positive' T-shirts.
- The fast for life on 21 March 1999 at the gates of Chris Hani

Baragwanath where I was born. Glenda Gray's slogan 'No AZT, No Vote' and Florence Ngobeni's and Prudence Mabele's speeches.
- The support of the AIDS Consortium and the AIDS Law Project.
- Queenie Qiza and Colwyn Poole tirelessly working for a shared TAC income of R500 per month.

I remember:
- Mbeki's election and my campaigning for the ANC. The hope that our country would go to work, and singing *Vulindlela* with Brenda Fassie to make Thabo one of us.
- My ANC branch election rally where Nkosazana Zuma came to address us and agreed to meet TAC.
- Her farewell at Parliament where she sent for us to come and meet with her. Adeline Mangcu, Busi Maqungo, Villas Tyegu, Midi and other comrades came to the meeting. Midi said she supported all her health policies to make medicines affordable but not her smoking and tobacco controls! Nkosazana laughed.
- I remember the friend who worked in President Mbeki's office until the end and who warned me of Mbeki's HIV denialism and helped throughout Mbeki's reign in times of crisis.
- Edwin Cameron's disbelief and insistent warning of the impending catastrophe if I was correct when I told him of Mbeki's denialism.
- I remember Hermann Reuter, an old comrade from the Marxist Workers' Tendency of the ANC, joining TAC and bringing his partner, Sipho Mthathi – two of the best activists in TAC's history, and Sipho one of the best leaders of TAC. They built our treatment literacy programme from scratch with the support of Gay Men's Health Crisis, Treatment Action Group and Project Inform in the United States.
- The work of Jack Lewis on the television series 'Beat It!' Ten years of an archive – countless lives touched. The first episode showed more than thirty people living with HIV/AIDS wearing the 'HIV-positive' T-shirt.

- Mandla Majola, whom I initially feared as a Pan Africanist Congress (PAC) influence, while he was deeply suspicious of TAC's ANC and white members. And his mum, who gave us supper of black tea and dry toast.
- Eric Goemaere, a leader, doctor, humanitarian and internationalist from Médecins Sans Frontières (MSF). His family, our family.
- Ayanda Ntsaluba, our Director-General of Health, and other government leaders and politicians including Dr Abe Nkomo, Dr Essop Jassat, Fareed Abdullah, Saadiq Kariem and others, who helped. Also the head of HIV/AIDS in the Health Department, Dr Nono Simelela, who struggled and suffered under the terror of HIV denial.
- The MSF meeting in Holland on access to medicines. Learning about compulsory licences and parallel importation.
- Studying the science of antiretroviral medicine.
- Studying the Patent Act and World Trade Organisation rules, including the Agreement on Trade-Related Aspects of Intellectual Property Rights (TRIPs).
- The support of Jamie Love, Act Up New York.
- Meeting the tireless and remarkable US activist Asia Russell from Health Gap and Act Up Philadelphia.
- Bill Clinton's sanctions threat against South Africa in support of multinational drug companies and their patented drugs.
- Our demonstrations, songs and actions outside offices of GlaxoSmithKline and the Pharmaceutical Manufacturers Association (PMA). The support of the International Gay and Lesbian Human Rights Commission outside the PMA.
- I remember the ANC leader who demanded royal treatment from the day of her arrival from exile. The trepidation I felt when she became Health Minister in 1999 and the attempts to work with her. Her loyalty to Mbeki always stronger than the Hippocratic oath.

I remember:

- In December 1999, a teenage-looking computer scientist at UCT, Nathan Geffen, who came for a discussion about TAC and promised to volunteer for four hours' work a week on our website. He became a stalwart of our policy development and a critical voice in our national leadership.
- Our songs and our choir 'The Generics'.

The first year of TAC, now a distant memory, steeled us in knowledge of law, medicine and international trade. Many new friends and comrades were made locally and globally. The battle was engaged. Mbeki's denial became open and world disbelief, later coupled with anger, became the norm.

The ground of struggle for health, life and dignity would shift over the decade with battles won but always return to the old forms of government neglect and denial, coupled with profiteering by drug companies and private health services at the expense of individuals, families and countries, thereby creating continents of suffering.

There are nine more years that I remember: years of love, years of pain, years of anger, years of intensity, years of leadership, years of responsibility, years of failure and mistakes, years of learning and celebration. Sometimes years and decades of suffering and celebration in a day.

Today, TAC is going through its saddest and its most exciting period. Saddest because, after years of lack of management capacity and growing too fast, the organisation must refocus and this will lead to the loss of some of our key workers. The change is based on the available human, management and financial resources to serve properly all people living with HIV/AIDS in South Africa and our members. The loss of staff is hard for us and much harder for them. It is also sad because the lack of capacity in the Department of Health undermined the TAC's grant application to the Global Fund to Fight AIDS, TB and Malaria, affecting our frontline volunteers the hardest. This is part of the cruel legacy of Manto Tshabalala-Msimang.

Our country and most TAC members are also sad because of the politics of intolerance and smears that mask our real problems. These include a global financial crisis, the worst inequalities in education and health for many generations, mass unemployment and, above all, the viciousness towards the vulnerable – 'curative' rape of black lesbians, gender-based violence on an unprecedented scale, and hate crimes against refugees and immigrants.

But there is also optimism and excitement. Our politics are real and alive with possibility for the first time. TAC has a leadership committed to ensuring that health and HIV remain at the top of the agenda. Our general secretary, Vuyiseka Dubula, is the first black woman living with HIV to lead TAC and its most courageous and far-sighted leader since our first day. Nonkosi Khumalo is the first black woman chairperson. She is supported by Lihle Dlamini, Nathan Geffen, Mark Heywood and the Rev. Teboho Klaas, who lead a National Council that works and remains committed to the TAC ideals of the first day. The commitment of our staff in difficult times shines through, in our provincial coordinators and managers, as well as the many leaders and members in branches and townships and campuses across the country.

We have contributed significantly to the transformation of HIV treatment in our country and on our continent. More than 500,000 people now have ARV treatment and live healthy lives. The leadership of Minister Barbara Hogan and Deputy Minister Dr Molefi Sefularo is strong but they will need the help of every person and institution to rescue our health system – a task that is possible, but not without a citizens' movement such as TAC.

I will always remain a TAC member. I am serving my last term as a member of the TAC secretariat and will give this organisation some but not all of the blood and sweat necessary to build its leaders for the next fifty years. I described it to Jacqui Boulle as both a home and a prison. Our members are ready to take on the challenges of education, organisation and leadership. The lessons I have learnt in TAC, the friends and comrades I have made, will live on in my heart always. It is a journey that has saved my life.

* Zackie Achmat is the co-founder of TAC and its second chairperson after Mazibuko Jara. An internationally renowned activist, he has won numerous awards including the inaugural Desmond Tutu Leadership Award in 2002 and the Jonathan Mann Award for Global Health and Human Rights in 2003. He has also directed documentaries on children's rights, language, the history of the lesbian and gay movement, and the Constitutional Court. Aside from holding a BA Honours (cum laude) from the University of the Western Cape in South Africa, he has been awarded honorary degrees from the universities of Cape Town, Western Cape, KwaZulu-Natal and Rhodes. He has also worked for the Bellville Community Health Project, the AIDS Law Project, Community Health Media Trust, the National Coalition for Gay and Lesbian Equality, and the Southern African Clothing and Textile Workers' Union. Since November 2004, Achmat has served on the World Health Organisation's HIV Strategic and Technical Committee. He is also a member of the Technical Task Team on Treatment, Care and Support of the South African National AIDS Council and co-chairperson of Equal Education, a community-based activist movement, and a member of the Social Justice Coalition.

Postscript

Post-Mbeki hope or hype?

by
Sipho Mthathi

Within the first year of his presidency, Thabo Mbeki turned HIV/AIDS into a matter for public contestation and political wrangling instead of a national crisis that deserved decisive leadership. During his term of office, a political culture of intolerance became entrenched. ANC spokesman Smuts Ngonyama referred to people living with HIV/AIDS who were calling for treatment as 'agents of pharmaceutical companies'. ANC Youth League leaders compared AIDS activists to the Afrikaner Broederbrond and the vigilante-style group People against Gangsterism and Drugs (PAGAD). Yet these citizens were not vandalising property or threatening to overthrow the government with guns. They used the armour provided by the new democratic dispensation – the courts, the Constitution.

Some have argued that TAC was too aggressive towards the government and that this was counterproductive, as 'we need the government to achieve our goals'. The National Association of People Living with AIDS (Napwa) even claimed that TAC's tactics showed that it did not recognise the legitimacy of the democratically elected government. Indeed, TAC made its fair share of tactical blunders and was sometimes too angry to articulate its message properly. For instance, while it correctly identified the failure of political leadership as an impediment to the development of a proper socio-political response to match the scale of the epidemic, it developed a fixation with the personalities of Mbeki and Manto Tshabalala-Msimang. While these two invited public anger by pushing denialism to extreme levels, targeting them absolved every other government minister and the ANC leadership of responsibility for acting urgently against HIV/AIDS. Today it is easy for those who now hold the strings of power in the ANC to scapegoat departed leaders. True, Mbeki has a lot to answer for, but the ANC cannot conveniently disclaim responsibility for past failures with regard to its AIDS policies.

Before being fired as Deputy President, Jacob Zuma held several positions of influence in the ANC, including as chairperson of the South African National AIDS Council (SANAC). As ANC president, he now stands tall on political podiums proclaiming himself the saviour of our country. But the deep chauvinism and lack of judgement he displayed during his rape trial are only becoming magnified in his campaign for election as the country's next President. With his silence in the face of his supporters' actions, he endorses a culture of violence in a country where violence has tragically become a way of life and where those of us without guns will be the only casualties of 'the war' they threaten. At the same time the resurgent version of traditionalism that he embodies threatens to subvert the core values of our Constitution.

What, then, is the basis for people's belief that the new ANC leadership will offer viable alternatives and opportunities for change, with regard to HIV and AIDS and everything else?

After the conference that endorsed the new national HIV/AIDS strategic plan for South Africa (NSP) in March 2007, I could feel my body sinking into the ground. For a while I could not feel my limbs. It was as if my body had left the rest of me, retreating into a lighter place. The futility of the bitter contest between government and civil society on AIDS had been soul-destroying. But now – relief! There was no turning back. The NSP marked a decisive shift from eight years of denialism to a new era of acknowledgement and action. It intends by 2011 to halve new HIV infections, provide care and support to 80 per cent of those affected, and widen access to treatment for those with AIDS. Importantly, it recognises the need to address the social, cultural and economic landscape in which infection thrives: 'The HIV epidemic and AIDS [in South Africa] is clearly feminised, pointing to gender vulnerability that demands urgent attention ... In view of the high prevalence and incidence of HIV amongst women, it is critical that their strong involvement in and benefiting from the HIV and AIDS response becomes a priority.'

But the difficulties on the road ahead are enormous. Figuring out how to change behaviours in a deeply patriarchal society is a challenge as well as an opportunity. It requires more than the social marketing of generic, pre-packaged advertisements or billboards that sweep from villages to towns to cities. Then again, the momentum generated by the NSP cannot be sustained without champions in civil society and government as well as high levels of coordination within and between sectors. SANAC intends to perform this role, but the challenges are vast. SANAC can only be effective if supported by vibrant, well-resourced local AIDS councils. After all, it is at the local level where implementation happens, not in Pretoria. This is not yet the case and there is a real danger that SANAC may calcify into another bulging national structure with no real accountability and material relevance to communities.

While it seems that, for once, government is now speaking with one voice on AIDS, it is doubtful that all levels of government are methodically implementing what the new plan requires. Given the medicalisation of HIV/AIDS over the years, most government departments have tended to regard AIDS as the primary concern of the Health Department. While this is changing, the real nature of the work that each government department needs to do is less clear. The local tier of government faces particularly huge challenges, ranging from finances to infrastructure and human resource capacity. As the country's political dynamics evolve, there is the risk that the momentum will be reversed as officials become preoccupied with their own careers. An equally dangerous possibility is that civil society becomes complacent, relaxing its watchdog role because 'the government now agrees with us'. The organising adage that one guards one's victories might sound like a cliché, but in South Africa we have learnt the hard way that, without consistent public pressure, the gap between policy and implementation is hard to bridge.

Although the removal of the intransigent Health Minister has been hailed as 'a new window of opportunity', it will take unequivocal leadership to transform the South African health system. It is a life-and-death question for the millions who rely on the public health system for care. Putting the next 500,000 people on antiretroviral treatment will be no small undertaking. Drastic and bold decisions – medical and political – need to be taken on a range of fronts to ensure that the health system has the capacity to sustain that number of people on lifelong treatment. This year, more than 300,000 people living with HIV will progress to AIDS, and the pattern will repeat itself the following year, regardless of what is done to delay the progression. The new leadership needs to turn up the pace of its response. The work required to rid society of the epidemic is the work of every day. While priorities have to be set, it is essential that the priorities are assessed, redefined and modified to match the pace and nature of the epidemic's progress. The UNAIDS mantra 'know your epidemic' is true and bears huge research, operational and political leadership implications. It is a clarion call for vigilance.

When the Cabinet approved an HIV/AIDS treatment plan in November 2003, the TAC gathered more than 3000 people at a march in Qunu village in the Eastern Cape. The 'long walk to a people's health service, treatment and life' honoured both those who had died while struggling for access to health care and also leaders like Mandela who, after his term as President, had dedicated himself to defending the rights of people living with HIV/AIDS. During that march, Nopasika, a 75-year-old woman, said philosophically: 'Ningoyiki bantwana bam. Iphupha lethu lenkululeko. Wonk'umntu balulekile, singaze siphinde siyekele nabani asisengele phantsi. [You must never be afraid. Nothing must ever be bigger than our dreams. No leader, party, organisation, political ideology, identity, idea, value, God, version of truth or promise must ever be bigger than our dream to be free. Each human being matters profoundly and nothing and no one must ever substitute for our worth in society.]'

The AIDS struggle has been bitter and debilitating. Recent policy shifts provide space for building anew, and much work has to be done to prevent a retraction of the gains. Focused leadership by government and civic advocacy remain important. But both have to step out of old, entrenched modes of framing and engaging with the issue.

In the past year and a half, I have spent time with women, men and youths in different provinces who provide care to the sick, primarily those sick with AIDS, and the elderly. They feed, care for and support orphaned children. They relieve grandmothers whose daughters and sons have died from AIDS and have left them the legacy of young children in need of energetic, attentive care. Unpaid, they walk from house to house, seeking the sick so they may wash and feed them and keep them company. They are heroes of the nation and examples of *ubuntu* because they keep society going, plug the holes, substitute for the state. But this work masks the fact that the burden of care has shifted, and has locked black working–class, rural women, in particular, into unrecognised, unpaid roles.

But AIDS will not be addressed by poor volunteers or by the enthusiastic activism of groups who have thus far worked incredibly hard. No HIV/AIDS plan will succeed unless it is matched by a set of comprehensive social and economic programmes to eradicate inequality and poverty, provide basic services, put jobs, resources and social power in the hands of the majority, including women, and build people's sense of individual and social agency.

The economic and other crises currently sweeping the world, and the political uncertainties proliferating in South Africa, are a harsh reminder that it is time to go back to the trenches of radical, visionary organising – where new alternatives and visions of the social change we want can start to be built. We have done enough compromising of our dreams.

* Siphokazi (Sipho) Mthathi is a feminist activist, writer, poet and educator. She has organised on HIV/AIDS since 1999, working first as a volunteer, then programme co-ordinator and subsequently General Secretary of the Treatment Action Campaign. As a member of the working group set up by South African National AIDS Council, she was involved in drafting South Africa's new strategic plan for HIV/AIDS. Among other things, Sipho is now focusing her energies on setting up a Women's Writing Institute to ensure that women's voices are heard and influence social, economic, political and cultural production spheres. Sipho is currently completing her first novel and poetry anthology.

Other titles by Jacana

Khabzela: The Life and Times of a South African
by Liz McGregor

Love and Courage: A Story of Insubordination
by Pregs Govender

Sugar Girls and Seamen: A Journey into the World
of Dockside Prostitution in South Africa
by Henry Trotter

The Extraordinary Khotso: Millionaire Medicine
Man from Lusikisiki
by Felicity Wood with Michael Lewis

Take Two Veg and Call Me in the Morning by Zapiro
Pirates of Polokwane
by Zapiro

New South African Keywords edited
by Nick Shepherd and Steven Robins

The Politics of Prevention: A Global Crisis
in AIDS and Education
by Tania Boler and David Archer

At the Heart of Healing: Groote Schuur Hospital 1938-2008
by Anne Digby and Howard Phillips